VOLVO 1800
1960-1973

Compiled by
R.M. Clarke

ISBN 0 907073 15 8

Distributed by
Brooklands Book Distribution,
'Holmerise', Seven Hills Road,
Cobham, Surrey, England.

BROOKLANDS ROAD & TRACK SERIES

Road & Track on Alfa Romeo 1949-1963
Road & Track on Alfa Romeo 1964-1970
Road & Track on Alfa Romeo 1971-1976
Road & Track on Alfa Romeo 1 77-1984
Road & Track on Aston Martin 1962-1984
Road & Track on Austin Healey 1953-1970
Road & Track on BMW Cars 1975-1978
Road & Track on BMW Cars 1979-1983
Road & Track on Cobra, Shelby & Ford
    Ford GT40 1962-1983
Road & Track on Datsun Z 1970-1983
Road & Track on Corvette 1953-1967
Road & Track on Corvette 1968-1982
Road & Track on Ferrari 1950-1968
Road & Track on Ferrari 1968-1974
Road & Track on Ferrari 1975-1981
Road & Track on Fiat Sports Cars 1968-1981
Road & Track on Jaguar 1950-1960
Road & Track on Jaguar 1961-1968
Road & Track on Jaguar 1968-1974
Road & Track on Jaguar 1974-1982
Road & Track on Lamborghini 1964-1982
Road & Track on Lotus 1972-1981
Road & Track on Maserati 1952-1974
Road & Track on Maserati 1975-1983
Road & Track on Mercedes Sports & GT Cars
    1970-1980
Road & Track on MG Sports Cars 1949-1961
Road & Track on MG Sports Cars 1962-1980
Road & Track on Pontiac 1960-1983
Road & Track on Porsche 1951-1967
Road & Track on Porsche 1968-1971
Road & Track on Porsche 1972-1975
Road & Track on Porsche 1975-1978
Road & Track on Porsche 1979-1982
Road & Track on Rolls Royce & Bentley
    1950-1965
Road & Track on Rolls Royce & Bentley
    1966-1984
Road & Track on Saab 1955-1984
Road & Track on Triumph Sports Cars
    1953-1967
Road & Track on Triumph Sports Cars
    1967-1974
Road & Track on Triumph Sports Cars
    1974-1982

BROOKLANDS CAR AND DRIVER SERIES

Car and Driver on Corvette 1956-1967
Car and Driver on Corvette 1968-1977
Car and Driver on Corvette 1978-1982
Car and Driver on Ferrari 1955-1962
Car and Driver on Ferrari 1963-1975
Car and Driver on Ferrari 1976-1983

BROOKLANDS MOTOR & THOROUGHBRED & CLASSIC CAR SERIES

Motor & Thoroughbred & Classic Car
    on Ferrari 1966-1976
Motor & Thoroughbred & Classic Car
    on Ferrari 1976-1984
Motor & Thoroughbred & Classic Car
    on Lotus 1979-1983
Motor & Thoroughbred & Classic Car
    on Morris Minor 1948-1983

BROOKLANDS PRACTICAL CLASSICS SERIES

Practical Classics on MGB Restoration
Practical Classic on Mini Cooper Restoration
Practical Classic on Morris Minor Restoration

BROOKLANDS MILITARY VEHICLES SERIES

Allied Military Vehicles Collection No. 1
Allied Military Vehicles Collection No. 2
Dodge Military Vehicles Collection No. 1
Jeep Collection No. 1
Military Jeep 1941-1945
Off Road Jeeps 1944-1971

BROOKLANDS BOOKS SERIES

AC Ace & Aceca 1953-1983
AC Cobra 1962-1969
Alfa Romeo Giulia Coupés 1963-1976
Alfa Romeo Spider 1966-1981
Austin Seven 1922-1982
Austin 10 1932-1939
Austin A30 & A35 195-1962
Austin Healey 100 1952-1959
Austin Healey 3000 1959-1967
Austin Healey 100 & 3000 Collection No. 1
Austin Healey 'Frogeye' Sprite
    Collection No. 1
Austin Healey Sprite 1958-1971
Avanti 1962-1983
BMW Six Cylinder Coupés 1969-1975
BMW 1600 Collection No. 1
BMW 2002 Collection No. 1
Buick Cars 1929-1939
Buick Riviera 1963-1978
Cadillac in the Sixties No. 1
Camaro 1966-1970
Chrysler 300 1955-1970
Citroen Traction Avant 1934-1957
Citroen 2CV 1949-1982
Cobras & Replicas 1962-1983
Cortina 1600E & GT 1967-1970
Corvair 1959-1968
Daimler Dart & V-8 250 1959-1969
Datsun 240z & 260z 1970-1977
De Tomaso Collection No. 1
Excalibur 1952-1981
Ferrari Cars 1946-1956
Ferrari Cars 1962-1966
Ferrari Cars 1966-1969
Ferrari Cars 1969-1972
Ferrari Cars 1973-1977
Ferrari Cars 1977-1981
Ferrari Collection No. 1
Fiat X1/9 1972-1980
Ford GT40 1964-1978
Ford Mustang 1964-1967
Ford Mustang 1967-1973
Ford RS Escort 1968-1980
High Performance Escorts MkI 1968-1974
High Performance Escorts MkII 1975-1980
Hudson & Railton Cars 1936-1940
Jaguar (& S.S) Cars 1931-1937
Jaguar Cars 1948-1951
Jaguar Cars 1951-1953
Jaguar Cars 1957-1961
Jaguar Cars 1961-1964
Jaguar Cars 1964-1968
Jaguar E-Type 1961-1966
Jaguar E-Type 1966-1971
Jaguar E-Type 1971-1975
Jaguar XKE Collection No. 1
Jaguar XJ6 1968-1972
Jaguar XJ6 Series II 1973-1979
Jaguar XJ6 & XJ12 Series III 1979-1985
Jaguar XJ12 1972-1980
Jaguar XJS 1975-1980
Jensen Cars 1946-1967
Jensen Cars 1967-1979
Jensen Interceptor 1966-1976
Jensen-Healey 1972-1976
Lamborghini Cars 1964-1970
Lamborghini Cars 1970-1975
Lamborghini Countach Collection No. 1
Land Rover 1948-1973
Land Rover 1958-1983
Lotus Cortina 1963-1970
Lotus Elan 1962-1973
Lotus Elan Collection No. 1
Lotus Elan Collection No. 2
Lotus Elite 1957-1964
Lotus Elite & Eclat 1975-1981
Lotus Esprit 1974-1981
Lotus Europa 1966-1975
Lotus Europa Collection No. 1
Lotus Seven 1957-1980
Lotus Seven Collection No. 1
Maserati 1965-1970
Maserati 1970-1975
Mazda RX-7 Collection No. 1
Mercedes 230/250/280SL 1963-1971
Mercedes 350/450SL & SLC 1971-1980
Mercedes Benz Cars 1949-1954
Mercedes Benz Cars 1954-1957
Mercedes Benz Cars 1957-1961
Mercedes Benz Competition Cars
    1950-1957
Metropolitan 1954-1962

MG Cars in the Thirties
MG Cars 1929-1934
MG Cars 1935-1940
MG TC 1945-1949
MG TD 1949-1953
MG TF 1953-1955
MG Cars 1952-1954
MG Cars 1955-1957
MG Cars 1957-1959
MG Cars 1959-1962
MG Midget 1961-1980
MG MGA 1955-1962
MGA Collection No. 1
MG MGB 1962-1970
MG MGB 1970-1980
MGB GT 1965-1980
Mini Cooper 1961-1971
Morgan Cars 1960-1970
Morgan Cars 1969-1979
Morris Minor 1949-1970
Morris Minor Collection No. 1
Oldsmobile Toronado 1966-1978
Opel GT 1968-1973
Pantera 1970-1973
Pantera & Mangusta 1969-1974
Pontiac GTO 1964-1970
Pontiac Firebird 1967-1973
Porsche Cars 1960-1964
Porsche Cars 1964-1968
Porsche Cars 1968-1972
Porsche Cars in the Sixties
Porsche Cars 1972-1975
Porsche 356 1952-1965
Porsche 911 Collection No. 1
Porsche 911 Collection No. 2
Porsche 914 1969-1975
Porsche 924 1975-1981
Porsche 928 Collection No. 1
Porsche Turbo Collection No. 1
Reliant Scimitar 1964-1982
Rolls Royce Cars 1930-1935
Rolls Royce Cars 1940-1950
Rolls Royce Silver Cloud 1955-1965
Rolls Royce Silver Shadow 1965-1980
Range Rover 1970-1981
Rover 3 & 3.5 Litre 1958-1973
Rover P4 1949-1959
Rover P4 1955-1964
Rover 2000 + 2200 1963-1977
Saab Sonett Collection No. 1
Saab Turbo 1976-1983
Singer Sports 1933-1934
Studebaker Hawks & Larks 1956-1963
Sunbeam Alpine & Tiger 1959-1967
Thunderbird 1955-1957
Triumph 2000·2.5·2500 1963-1967
Triumph Spitfire 1962-1980
Triumph Spitfire Collection No. 1
Triumph Stag 1970-1980
Triumph Stag Collection No. 1
    1970-1984
Triumph TR2 & TR3 1952-1960
Triumph TR6 1969-1976
Triumph TR6 Collection No. 1
Triumph TR7 & TR8 1975-1981
Triumph GT6 1966-1974
Triumph Vitesse & Herald 1959-1971
TVR 1960-1980
Volkswagen Cars 1936-1956
VW Beetle 1956-1977
VW Beetle Collection No.1
VW Karmann Ghia Collection No. 1
VW Scirocco 1974-1981
Volvo 1800 1960-1973
Volvo 120 Series 1956-1970

BROOKLANDS MUSCLE CARS SERIES

American Motor Muscle Cars 1966-1970
Buick Muscle Cars 1965-1970
Camaro Muscle Cars 1966-1972
Capri Muscle Cars 1969-1983
Chevrolet Muscle Cars 1966-1971
Dodge muscle Cars 1967-1979
Mercury Muscle Cars 1966-1971
Mini Muscle Cars 1961-1979
Mopar Muscle Cars 1964-1967
Mopar Muscle Cars 1968-1971
Mustang Muscle Cars 1967-1974
Shelby Mustang Muscle Cars 1965-1970
Oldsmobile Muscle Cars 1964-1970
Plymouth Muscle Cars 1966-1971
Muscle Cars Compared 1966-1971
Muscle Cars Compared Book 2 1965-1971

CONTENTS

ACKNOWLEDGEMENTS

There are cars which due to circumstances, we are destined never to own, the Volvo P1800 unfortunately falls into this category in my case. When it made its debut in 1960 my wife and I had a bouncing baby girl and when it exited in the early seventies we were blessed with two robust school-children which ruled out even the elegant ES versions.

The first 6,000 cars were assembled in Britain by Jensen Motors Ltd. who even before the war had gained an enviable reputation for fine coachwork. In 1963 however it became possible to build this model in Sweden due to increased capacity at the Gothenberg factory and subsequently these vehicles became known as the 1800S.

The most famous 1800 owner was undoubtedly The Saint alias Simon Templar who each week thrilled us on the television screen by speeding the heroine to safety in what must have been the fastest 1800 in captivity.

The 1800 power unit was always a sports version of the standard Volvo engine as used in both the 120 and 140 series cars. Initially the power output was a modest 100 h.p. from the B18 engine and this progressed in steps up to 135 h.p. in the final B20 powered 1800E version in 1972. In total 39,414 units were built the majority of which can be seen on the roads of the free world today.

This is the first of two Brooklands Books covering Volvo models, the second will deal with the 120 Amazon series. Brooklands Books are compiled to assist current owners of interesting cars, and it is hoped that by making these out-of-print articles available once again that it will help to keep in this instance Volvo 1800s on the road for future generations to enjoy.

I am sure that Volvo enthusiasts will wish to join with me in thanking the publishers of the following magazines for their generosity in allowing their copyright articles to be included in this historical reference series.

Autocar, Autosport, Cars & Car Conversions (previously Cars Illustrated), Car & Driver, Modern Motor, Motor, Motor Sport, Road & Track, Road Test, Track & Traffic, and Wheels.

My thanks are also due to the Volvo Owners Club for their practical assistance and encouragement and to Rob Nicholson who on a cold winter's day made available his beautifully preserved 1800S which can be seen on the front cover.

R.M. Clarke

VOLVO
P-1800

THE VOLVO P-1800 coupe made its first public appearance at the Brussels Auto Salon in January, and its first U.S. appearance at the New York International Auto Show in April.

A very pretty car, it uses many of the standard components from existing Volvo models, but a new engine has been designed specifically for the coupe. This engine is an inline ohv 4-cyl unit displacing 1.78 liters (84.1 x 80 mm bore and stroke) and producing 100 SAE horsepower at 5500 rpm.

The gearbox is based on the 4-speed unit installed in the 122-S and PV-544, but it has been redesigned for the coupe. An electrically operated overdrive is listed as an optional extra.

The brakes are servo-assisted hydraulic, with discs on the front wheels and drums at the rear; a practice that may be applied to U.S. cars in the near future.

Principal dimensions of the coupe are: wheelbase 96.5 in.; tread, both front and rear, 52; overall length 173; width 67; height 51 and ground clearance 6.3 in.

Although the body was designed in Italy, it will be produced in England by Pressed Steel, Ltd. The car will also be assembled in England, as all the available assembly capacity at Volvo, in Sweden, is being utilized by existing Volvo production.

Series production is not scheduled until September, and sometime early in 1961 production is expected to be in the neighborhood of 100 cars per week. Delivery in the U.S. has been tentatively promised for late fall of this year and no actual price has been quoted.

ASSEMBLY of Volvo P1800 coupés is now in full swing, in a new factory built specially for the purpose in the Midlands. Body shells arrive from Scotland, engines and gearboxes with other parts from Sweden, and there are also American and German components incorporated. Production targets are 3,000 cars in 1961 and 7,500 a year in the future.

1961 Cars

The VOLVO

A Sturdy, Sa
Coupé Built Und

P LANNED in Sweden whence its power unit comes, styled in Italy, built in England around a Scottish-made body shell, and incorporating components from Germany and the U.S.A., the Volvo P1800 must be the world's most international car. What sort of a model is it which, now coming off the assembly lines at West Bromwich in left hand drive form, will be offered to British customers as a right hand drive car in the autumn?

As a first essential the Volvo P1800 is meant to be a tough car, just right for Sweden where the summer can be very hot, the winter is very cold, and the roads can be very fast or very rough. Gunnar Engellau who is President of Volvo believes that Sweden's place in world car markets is as a builder of strong, safe and durable cars. In accordance with that philosophy, the new Volvo weighs about 22 cwt. although it is only a very occasional four seater of 1.8-litre engine size. It is built on thoroughly modern lines, above-average weight being claimed to go with above-average strength and durability, and a completely

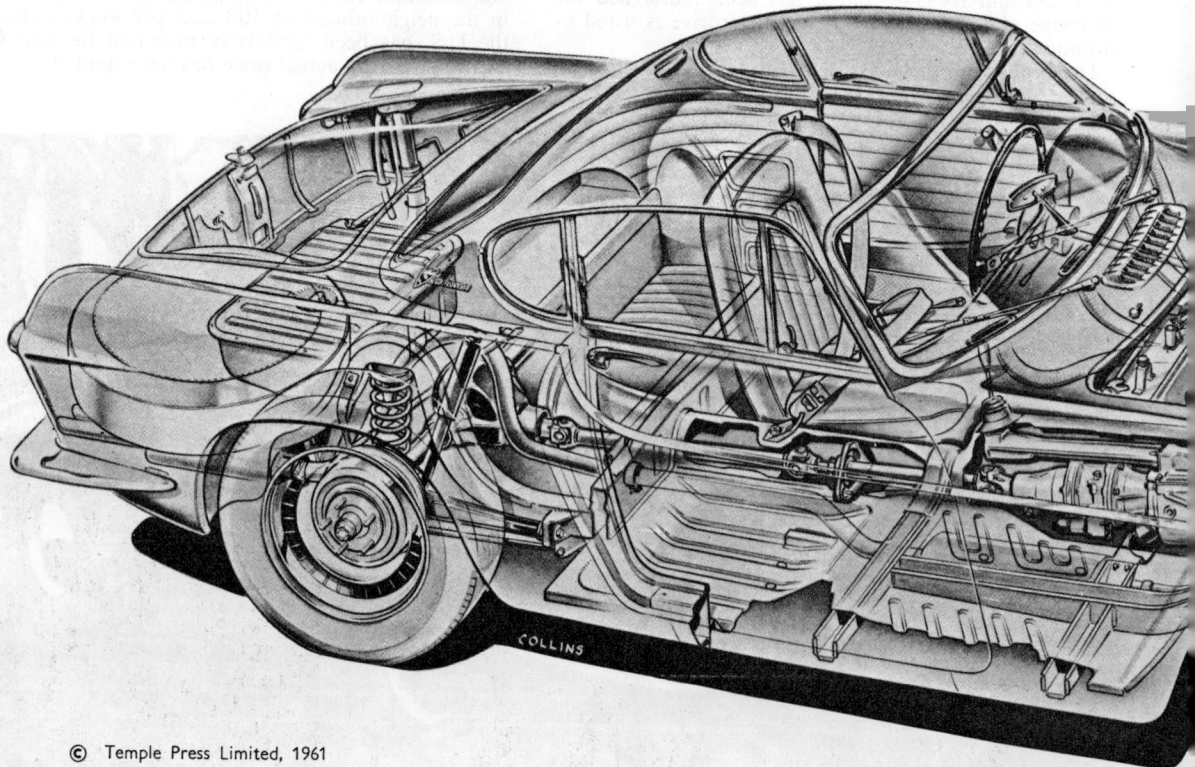

COLLINS

new engine (which represents a lineal descendant of preceding Volvo designs but is not merely an existing engine enlarged), is potent enough to provide excellent acceleration to speeds in excess of 100 m.p.h.

Styled by Frua, the P1800 is not especially in the fashion, but the shape chosen gives modest wind resistance and the designers hope that it will be able to continue in production for many years without looking dated. Manufactured in the Linwood factory of the Pressed Steel Co. Ltd., who did a great deal of development work on details of its design, the body shell serves also as frame for the car.

Volvo attach much importance to safety in accidents, and every car is equipped with harness for the front seats. A double strap, extending over one shoulder from the central body pillar and over the lap from a strong point on the body floor, clips firmly to a bracket on the propeller shaft tunnel to hold the driver or front-seat passenger securely in place; when not in use, the harness clips quite neatly on to an additional mounting on the body pillar. Elimination of hard and sharp projections inside the body, and sheer structural strength, are other safety features.

Conventional coil-spring independent front-wheel suspension is used, with ball joints on the outer ends of the wishbones serving as steering swivels—these four ball joints and a splined coupling on the propeller shaft are the only points requiring greasing, and then only at 3,000-mile intervals. Less orthodox, although substantially akin to what has been used on the Volvo 122S, is the linkage associated with a coil-sprung rigid rear axle; one rubber-cushioned radius rod on each side of the car to give fore-and-aft axle location, and secondary radius rods below the main ones to take torque reaction through rubber buffers. The telescopic dampers used to control four coil springs, like the rear axle, come from the U.S.A., and are of the type which compresses Freon gas in a flexible nylon bag to allow for piston-rod displacement, instead of using free air which could mix with the working fluid to form froth.

Girling disc brakes have been chosen for the front wheels of this model, with pads applied by one cylinder on the inner side of each disc and two cylinders on the outer side. Drum brakes with leading and trailing shoes are used at the rear, and the hydraulic system has a vacuum servo (with reservoir) to augment the driver's pedal effort.

(Continued overleaf)

d Elegant 100 m.p.h.
nglo-Swedish Co-operation

FEATURES of the P1800 Volvo are shown in this drawing by *The Motor* artist. A pressed steel hull is supported on four coil springs, radius arms with rubber noise insulation locate the rear axle, the propeller shaft is in two sections, and the optional overdrive is shown fitted behind the four-speed gearbox.

DISCREET use of fins on the body tail is a feature of Frua's styling which, it is hoped, will not date quickly. Some floor area in the luggage locker is occupied by a covered spare wheel lying flat.

The VOLVO P1800

RESPONSIBLE for maintaining the impetus of Volvo expansion plans is Gunnar Engellau, now president of the company founded by Assar Gabrielsen and Gustaf Larsen which made its first car in 1927.

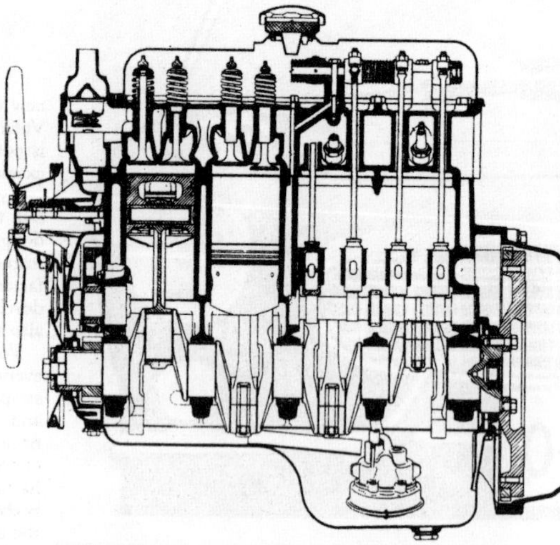

FIVE BEARINGS support the crankshaft in the 1.8-litre Volvo engine, which despite greater size and such extras as an oil cooler weighs only 4-5 lb. more than the existing 1.6-litre units.

The power which makes such a sturdily built car run fast and economically comes from a new Volvo engine, rather similar in its straightforward appearance to recent 1.4- and 1.6-litre units of the same make, but with larger-bore cylinders spaced farther apart, a five-bearing counterbalanced crankshaft, and other inconspicuous refinements. By using aluminium castings for lightly stressed parts, the weight of this new engine has been kept within 4-5 lb. of earlier Volvo engines.

The overhead valves are in a single line above the cylinders, but each valve of the new engine has its own individual port, and a lot of careful work has been done to secure good mixture flow from the two 1¾-inch bore S.U. carburetters. Fully machined combustion chambers in the cast-iron cylinder head give smooth running on 97-octane fuel with a 9½ : 1 compression ratio, and the engine is said to be unfussy about sparking plug grades. Much store is set by the layout of the cooling system, which directs cool water from the radiator to potential hot-spots inside the cylinder head casting before circulating it around the cylinders.

Developing its 100 b.h.p. (this is a "gross" rating taken without accessories, but Volvo engineers imply that it is a figure which most production models can better) at 5,500 r.p.m., the engine has hardened crankpins, and its bearing shells are lined with indium-plated lead-bronze. There is a full-flow oil filter, and an oil-to-water heat exchanger will reduce oil temperature by 20°-30° C. during fast driving or conversely will accelerate warming-up of the oil in winter conditions. In unit with the engine, a Volvo gearbox has synchromesh on all its four forward gears, and is operated from a central remote-control lever; a switch-controlled Laycock-de Normanville overdrive, operating only in conjunction with top gear, is an optional extra, cars thus equipped having a low-ratio rear axle.

We look forward to publishing a Road Test Report on this model when it becomes available in Britain; our first impressions of its behaviour on Swedish roads were of firm but comfortable springing, sensitive steering with plenty of castor action, and effortless fast cruising. Factory performance claims for an overdrive-equipped car carrying two people include rest to 60 m.p.h. acceleration in 12.5 sec., a top speed of 106 m.p.h. in overdrive, and a touring fuel consumption of 32½ m.p.g.

Britain's Contribution to the Volvo P1800

We are informed by AB Volvo that British suppliers of material for the Volvo P1800 include the following:—

Clifford Covering Co. Ltd.; Dunlop Rubber Co. Ltd.; Girling Ltd.; Imperial Chemical Industries Ltd.; Jensen Motors Ltd.; Joseph Fray Ltd.; Joseph Lucas (Electrical) Ltd.; Pianoforte Supplies Ltd.; Pirelli Ltd.; Pressed Steel Co. Ltd.; Joseph Sankey & Co. Ltd.; Silent Channel Co. Ltd.; Smiths Motor Accessories Ltd.; The S.U. Carburetter Co. Ltd.; Triplex Ltd.; Wilmot Breeden Ltd.; Worcester Windshields Ltd.

VOLVO P1800 SPECIFICATION

Engine	
Cylinders	4 in line with 5-bearing crankshaft.
Bore and stroke ...	84.14 mm. × 80 mm. (3.312 in. × 3.15 in.).
Cubic capacity ...	1,780 c.c. (108.6 cu. in.).
Piston area	34.5 sq. in.
Compression ratio ...	9.5/1.
Valvegear	In-line vertical overhead valves, operated by pushrods and rockers from gear-driven camshaft.
Carburation	Two 1¾ in. S.U. Type HS6 inclined carburetters, fed by rear-mounted electrical pump, from 10-gallon tank.
Ignition	12-volt coil, centrifugal and vacuum timing control, 14 mm. Bosch W.225.T.1 sparking plugs.
Lubrication	Submerged oil pump, full-flow filter, oil-to-water heat exchanger and 5¾-pint sump.
Cooling	Water cooling with pump, fan and thermostat; water passes from cylinder head to block; 14-pint water capacity.
Electrical system ...	12-volt 58 amp/hr. battery charged by 360-watt generator.
Maximum power ...	100 b.h.p. at 5,500 r.p.m., equivalent to 133 lb./sq. in. b.m.e.p. at 2,880 ft./min. piston speed and 2.90 b.h.p. per sq. in. of piston area.
Maximum torque ...	108 lb. ft. at 4,000 r.p.m., equivalent to 150 lb./sq. in. b.m.e.p. at 2,100 ft./min. piston speed.
Transmission	
Clutch	8½ in. single dry plate, hydraulically actuated.
Gearbox	4-speed and reverse with direct top gear; synchromesh on all forward ratios. Laycock-de Normanville overdrive optional, in conjunction with lower axle ratio.
Overall ratios ...	4.10, 5.58, 8.16 and 12.83; rev. 13.32.
Propeller shaft ...	Divided open shaft with flexibly mounted centre bearing.
Final drive	Spicer hypoid bevel gearing. 10/41 gearing without overdrive or 9/41 gearing with overdrive.
Brakes	Hydraulic with vacuum servo assistance, Girling disc type at front and drum type at rear.
Brake dimensions ...	Front discs 10⅞ in. dia.; rear drums 9 in. dia. × 2 in. wide.
Brake areas	94 sq. in. of lining (29 sq. in. front plus 65 sq. in. rear) working on 345 sq. in. rubbed area of discs and drums.
Front suspension ...	Independent by unequal-length transverse wishbones (outer ball joints), coil springs enclosing telescopic dampers, and anti-roll torsion bar.
Rear suspension ...	Rigid axle located by twin rubber-cushioned trailing radius arms at each side, with transverse Panhard rod; vertical coil springs controlled by splayed telescopic dampers.
Wheels and tyres ...	5-stud steel disc wheels with 4½J rims, and Pirelli Cintura 165-15 tyres.
Steering	Cam-and-roller gear with three-piece track rod.
Dimensions	
Length	Overall 14 ft. 5¼ in.; wheelbase 8 ft. 0½ in.
Width	Overall 5 ft. 7 in.; track 4 ft. 3¾ in. at front and rear.
Height unladen ...	4 ft. 2½ in.; ground clearance 6 in.
Turning circle ...	31 ft.
Kerb weight	22 cwt. (without fuel but with oil, water, tools, spare wheel, etc.).
Effective Gearing (without overdrive)	
Top gear ratio ...	17.5 m.p.h. at 1,000 r.p.m. and 33.4 m.p.h. at 1,000 ft./min. piston speed.
Maximum torque ...	4,000 r.p.m. corresponds to approx. 70 m.p.h. in top gear.
Maximum power ...	5,500 r.p.m. corresponds to approx. 97 m.p.h. in top gear.
Probable top gear pulling power... ...	250 lb./ton approx. (computed by *The Motor* from manufacturer's figures for torque, gear ratio and kerb weight, with allowances for 3½ cwt. load, 10% losses and 60 lb./ton drag).
Overdrive Transmission	
Overall ratios ...	3.46 (o/d), 4.56 (direct top), 6.20, 9.07 and 14.26; rev., 14.80.
M.p.h. at 1,000 r.p.m.	15.7 in top and 20.8 in overdrive.
Speeds at max. torque	63 m.p.h. in top and 83 m.p.h. in overdrive.
Speeds at max. power	87 m.p.h. in top and 114 m.p.h. in overdrive.
Probable top gear pulling power	285 lb./ton in top and 200 lb./ton in overdrive.

THE AUTOCAR, 9 JUNE 1961

• • • • • • • • • ▶ INTERNATIONAL COUPÉ

VOLVO P.1800 NOW BEING PRODUCED IN BIRMINGHAM

Integral overriders and bumpers are a distinctive feature of Frua styling

A FAMILIAR exhibit in its prototype form at international motor shows during the last year, the Volvo P.1800 sports coupé is at last being delivered to agents in Sweden and the United States. By now more than 300 left-hand drive cars have been assembled at Jensen's factory in West Bromwich and some 200 of them have arrived in Gothenburg, Sweden, where the parent factory is situated. The plan is to check and try-out the early production cars in Sweden, before delivering others to the several markets in Europe and elsewhere for which this model is also intended.

Right-hand drive versions for the British market—there is one prototype at present—may be ready by the end of the year, by which time a final price between £1,800 and £2,000 will have been settled. In Sweden the car · costs 16,950 Kr and the Laycock-de Normanville overdrive is 900 Kr extra (£1 = 14.48 Kr.S.). The American price will be $3,800; West coast buyers will probably be the first after Swedish ones to get deliveries.

Production is now building up to 150 cars a week, and 3,000 should be turned out this year. After this the rate is expected to be 7,000 per annum.

The P.1800 is a truly international product; more than 50 per cent is British in construction. To give some examples, the U.K. engineered and provided the body shell (Pressed Steel Scottish factory), Jensen assemble and finish all the cars. Many electrical components are Lucas; Girling make the disc (front) and drum (rear) brakes; Vandervell supply the engine bearings, Sankey the wheels and Laycock-de Normanville the overdrive; carburettors, as on the Volvo 122S model are made by S.U. From Germany comes the steering and the engine electrics—dynamo, starter and distributor. America contributes Spicer back axles and Delco dampers, and Italy the Frua body design and Pirelli Cinturata tyres. Volvo designed and developed the mechanical side of the car and makes the engine, gearbox and suspension components other than the coil springs which are British. The Swedish-produced components are shipped to the Jensen factory for final assembly.

Volvo's B.16 engine, as fitted to the 122S, has demonstrated its performance and reliability on many competition occasions. Closely related engines are used in commercial vehicles and for stationary and marine installations. The B.18 unit for the P.1800 is similar in many respects and grew from a bored-out B.16 (84.1 mm compared with 79.4 mm); both have an 80 mm stroke. However, with its five (in place of three) main bearings and different head it can be regarded as a new engine. The compression ratio is 9.5 to 1 and it develops 100 b.h.p. (gross) at 5,500 r.p.m. from its 1,780 c.c. capacity; this relatively high compression motor requires the use of super-premium fuel. The wide use of light alloys for components not highly stressed, such as casings and housings, has enabled the weight of the 1,780 c.c. engine to be kept within a kilo or two of that of the earlier 1,600 c.c. unit. The cylinder block is again of cast iron.

In character, the P.1800 coupe is like the 122S, a car of above-average refinement and finish in its class. Although it is obviously of a sporting nature, comfort has not been subordinated to all-out performance. Saloon car trim and equipment are included, and the engine and exhaust noise have been held down to saloon car levels. It is introduced as a two-seater with a good deal of luggage space; in fact, there is room for two children on the rear seats or one adult diagonally. Headroom is the main limiting factor here.

Last week the Editor drove a production P.1800 in Sweden (which, of course, has a left-hand rule of the road but usually favours also left-hand drive cars). Since we expect to be able to offer a complete road test report a few weeks hence, we do not propose to anticipate it now, except in terms of some general comments.

Engine Extremely Flexible

Immediate impressions are that the P.1800 is both substantial and refined. It feels a car of more than 2 litres capacity and its brisk performance is given readily and without fuss. In spite of the 9.5 to 1 compression and relatively high gear ratios, the engine pulls evenly in top gear down to 12-15 m.p.h. and under 1,000 r.p.m. This exceptional flexibility is also reflected in the whole of the car's traffic and open road cruising performances. Noise is well below sports car level and the suspension, though quite firm, gives

Safety features include generous padding at danger points and Volvo three-point harness as standard

Continued on page 19

VOLVO P-1800

Sports car enthusiasts look closely, there may be a Fjord in your future

AB VOLVO, which manufactures a line of quality, low-priced automobiles in Gothenburg, Sweden, has been exporting cars to the U.S. for only a short time but has already established quite a good reputation with its relatively high performance economy sedans. These sedans have provided a sort of bridge between the true sports car and the utility car for many enthusiasts with growing families and for that, and other reasons, the sale of Volvo automobiles in this country has been brisk. And brisk they should be, for there are no other cars available that reach into exactly that segment of the market.

Now, Volvo is preparing to enter another specialized market—that of the medium-priced, fast Grand Touring class sports car. This is, at least for the present, an area in which not many cars are available—at least not for the under-$4000 price of the new P-1800 Volvo GT coupe. (Porsche, Alfa Giulietta, and Facellia will be the P-1800's most obvious competition in this market.)

Volvo's P-1800 is a sports car of a type we can expect to become extremely popular. It is nothing like the traditional wind-in-the-face sports car of years past, which was good sport and all that, but had a tendency to wear on one at times. The 1800 is, rather, a very civilized touring car for people who want to travel rapidly in style, a Gran Turismo car of the type already much in the news these days—but at a price that many people who cannot afford a Ferrari or Aston Martin will be able to pay.

In order to test this new car we flew to Sweden where we were given the final-stage prototype of the P-1800 to drive, anywhere, at any speed, and in just about any fashion that should happen to strike our fancy. So, in addition to the usual banging about on the public roads—and in Sweden there are no speed limits—we were also given permission to try the car on Volvo's proving ground, where there is a huge skid-pad along with the usual turns and straight stretches. The weather was quite bad—and that was good, because it gave us an opportunity to try the car under conditions that were likely to reveal any bad handling traits. As it turned out, the car never gave us a bad moment, even though the roads were very wet through most of the time that we were driving the car.

From the driver's seat it is a bit hard to tell, except for the comprehensive instrumentation, that you are not sitting in an American car, for the interior is roomy and done in the rather futuristic fashion that characterizes the U.S.-built car. The seat is comfortable and is placed so that one has a good view through the various windows and out over the steering wheel and instrument cluster. The pedals are widely enough separated to allow us big-footed Americans to drive the car without difficulty and all of the various controls are conveniently located.

When driving the car, one is immediately impressed with the fact that it has been designed mostly for tractability, rather than racing, for it is possible to plug along in top gear at just about any speed. The engine has a long, flat torque curve and there is no thudding or thumping; even if one bangs the throttle wide open at anything over idle speed the accelerating characteristics of the car have a sort of electric-motor feeling. Just apply the accelerator and the car pulls smoothly, if not too vigorously, up toward its top speed of just over 100 mph. We might mention that Volvo's development engineers have gotten several runs with this pre-production prototype that average out to about 105 mph, with a best run of 107. They expressed the opinion that after the kinks are smoothed out, the version that reaches the market will be capable of about 110—enough to satisfy most people. Actually, this car is not designed for short bursts of speed of over 100 mph, but rather for the long stretches at about 95-100. It will, in the overdrive version, run almost indefinitely at its top speed, but not too many people will want to drive that fast for any distance.

A part of the charm of this machine can be attributed to the inclusion of the 5th gear—actually a Laycock de Normanville overdrive with a ratio of 0.756. This unit adds $145 and 33 lb, both items included in our data panel. Acceleration is good even in overdrive (3.44:1), particularly from 60 mph and up where the Tapley meter hit 150 lb/ton. However, for those who do not want overdrive, the P-1800 will be supplied with a 4.1 rear axle ratio. This will reduce the acceleration ability slightly,

but the transmission ratios are well chosen—and if properly used the deficiency will be very hard to detect.

Since the calculated data in the panel summary are based on an overdrive-equipped car, it may be pertinent to point out what happens when each of the three alternative ratios is used.

	TEST CAR		OPTIONAL
Axle (effective)	4.56	3.44 (o/d)	4.10
Engine revs/mile	3600	2720	3240
Mph at 6000 rpm	100	132.5	111
Cu ft/ton mile	80.7	61.0	72.7
Wear Index	68.0	38.9	55.0

As the engine develops its peak horsepower at 5500 rpm, it seems likely that a car without overdrive (i.e., the 4.10 axle ratio) will be the fastest of the three choices shown because the 132.5 mph figure (for overdrive) is purely theoretical and would require at least 50 more bhp than is available.

Of all the components of the P-1800, easily the most interesting is the engine, which embodies nothing new or exciting except that it has been designed and is being built with remarkable care. The single item that attracts the most attention is the fact that the crankshaft is carried in 5 main bearings, 2 more than the usual number. And is this important? That question can be answered much better after a couple of years or so have passed and the private owner, always the person most likely to discover design flaws, has had his chance at the engine. We personally consider this engine to be quite unbreakable—at least so long as it has plenty of water and oil—because we were given almost complete access to the development records (as many as we requested) and we know that the reliability test consisted of 500 continuous hours on the engine dyno pulling full-throttle and full load . . . in other words, 5500 rpm for 500 hours non-stop, and pumping out 100 bhp all the while. As one Volvo engineer put it, "The driver will tire long before the engine does." The crankshaft is a great, stout-looking thing with a goodly amount of overlap between journals, and the journals themselves are induction hardened and run in fatigue-resistant copper-lead bearings. Needless to say, the bottom end appears to be capable of withstanding far more than the present 100 bhp. The main bearing caps are a sort of *piece de resistance,* as they are also uncommonly large and have the distinction of being supported from the sides as well as being just pulled up into place by bolts. The

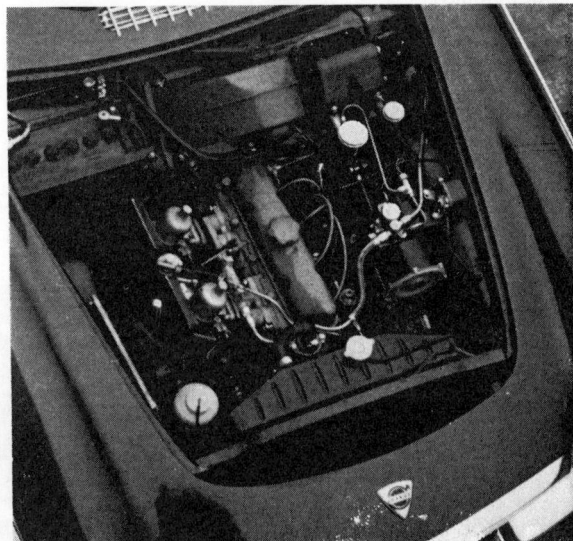

FEBRUARY 1961

main bearing cap slips into a 3-sided groove in the crankcase and, as it is a tight slip-fit on each side, it looks like a rather expensive system to us, but the people at Volvo didn't seem to think that it was at all out of the ordinary.

The complete engine is a really amazing thing that has potentialities far beyond what is now being used. Once, during the driving part of the test, we expressed some concern that we might get over-exuberant and get well beyond the recommended 6000 rpm. This brought on a most unusual demonstration; Volvo's test driver took the wheel, blasted off down the road in first gear and just wound the engine until the valves began to float, then he feathered the throttle and held the engine at the valve float point. We proceeded for some distance with this ghastly clattering ringing in our ears until it had been properly demonstrated that an occasional accidental over-revving of the engine was not going to break anything. Later, we were also informed that if you persevere it is possible to get past the point of valve-float (a phenomenon caused by a resonating of the valve springs) and then the engine will turn right on up until a piston breaks, or some other type of mechanical disaster occurs. Naturally, Volvo does not recommend that the private owner try any of this unless, as Mr. Larborn, who is chief engineer in Volvo's test laboratory, says, "The private owner is prepared to underwrite the possible costs of the experiment."

The transmission, like the engine, is not particularly unusual in concept, but does its job in a most satisfactory manner. It is constructed in a proper, straightforward fashion and feels as though it would be nearly impossible to break. The synchromesh is unbeatable, no matter how fast one moves the lever, and the ratios are perfectly spaced. All four gears are synchromesh.

Brakes are probably as important as any other factor on any car, but in the case of the GT car, which is intended for high speed use on public roads, the braking system is of much more than average importance. Of course, many of the individual states in America have speed laws that severely limit the vigor with which one may drive, but in others the laws are less restrictive and one may proceed at any velocity that falls within the vague limits of "reasonable and proper." Moreover, in at least one state, and in much of the rest of the world, there are hardly any limits beyond those imposed by the nature of the vehicle in question and it is in such areas that the GT car is at its best. Under such conditions the ability to stop without any weaving or wheel locking is a prerequisite for fast cruising, and the P-1800 was designed with this in mind.

Disc brakes are used at the front and drum brakes at

the rear, which is an odd mixture on the surface of things, but quite logical if one considers all of the facts. Actually, the best reason for the mixing of drums and discs is somewhat negative but true nonetheless; there is simply no point in going to the expense of disc brakes at the rear since only about a third of the braking effort is carried there. Even the least inspired of drum-type brakes will carry the effort of stopping the rear wheels without the slightest difficulty. Further, it is much easier to provide an effective emergency brake if drums are used and, last, the drum-type brakes are lighter than available disc-type units. Volvo engineers picked the Girling calipers for their car's front brakes and use these British-made units in conjunction with a disc of their own design and manufacture. One point that we noted with some interest was the shield used on the side of the disc that faces inboard. We asked about this and were told that without the shield, the pad on the inboard side of the disc was subject to vastly greater rates of wear than the pad on the outboard side, which is shrouded by the deeply dished wheel. This wheel uses a rim 4.5 in. wide to conform to the particular requirements of the tires. The tires are "low-profile" Pirelli Cinturatos, which have a special reinforced tread and are especially well suited to sustained high-speed operation. These tires really do give an outstanding grip on the road under all conditions and, we feel, contribute materially to the car's stability.

The suspension is taken directly from the parts bins that supply Volvo's 122-S, but springs of a slightly altered rate are used in the P-1800 and the Panhard rod at the rear has a revised location which provides an altered roll center. All of the front suspension and steering are carried on the front suspension member, which bolts into place rather than being an integral part of the frame.

The rear suspension is a study in refined orthodoxy, with a conventional solid rear axle. The springing medium, like the front, is coil and the axle is positioned by a pair of non-parallel rubber-bushed links on each side. Lateral movement is restricted by a Panhard rod. Because the rear axle is so firmly positioned, no rear-end "steering" is evident and the car felt secure under all conditions.

Little can be said about the body that is not apparent in pictures of the car—except that it looks somewhat larger "in the flesh." As a structure it benefits considerably from Volvo's long experience with unitized construction and from a most rigorous testing program. It is a design that typifies unit-structure practice, having a stressed floorpan and inner paneling to which the roof and outer panels add strength. And, of course, there are the usual small frame-like extensions of box-section structure that carry the suspension links and sub-frames.

The car, in its final production form, will not be a fire-breathing racing machine, but it will be absolutely dry and warm, and an altogether civilized and comfortable conveyance in which to travel about. More important, it remains comfortable right up to its top speed of just over 100 mph with very little wind or engine noise. The P-1800 is one sports car in which a good quality radio will not be wasted. Further, for the driver with sporting propensities, the handling of the car adds even more allure to the overall package. Our experiences with it, on both wet and dry surfaces, demonstrated that the P-1800 has stability, adhesion and agility, and can be drifted with *brio* without causing the driver any anxious moments.

On top of all its other virtues, the P-1800 offers the advantage of adequate luggage space, which, as many enthusiasts know, is sadly lacking in some cars they would like to own. The fact that the P-1800 is *new* is also an advantage sometimes overlooked; there are still those who want the first of anything.

ROAD TEST
VOLVO P-1800

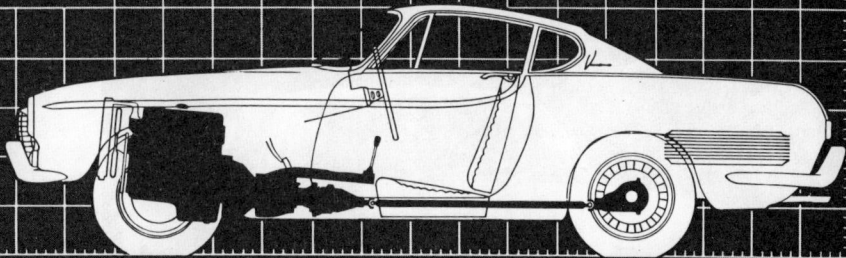

SCALE: 10" DIVISIONS

DIMENSIONS

Wheelbase, in	96.5
Tread, f and r	52.0
Over-all length, in	173
width	67.0
height	51.0
equivalent vol, cu ft	342
Frontal area, sq ft	19.0
Ground clearance, in	5.3
Steering ratio, o/a	15.5
turns, lock to lock	3.2
turning circle, ft	30
Hip room, front	53.5
Hip room, rear	50.5
Pedal to seat back	39.0
Floor to ground	10.8

CALCULATED DATA

Lb/hp (test wt)	28.0
Cu ft/ton mile	61.0
Mph/1000 rpm (o/d)	22.1
Engine revs/mile	2720
Piston travel, ft/mile	1430
Rpm @ 2500 ft/min	4760
equivalent mph	105
R&T wear index	38.9

SPECIFICATIONS

List price	$3940
Curb weight, lb	2500
Test weight	2800
distribution, %	51/49
Tire size	5.90–15
Brake lining area	97.7
Engine type	4 cyl, ohv
Bore & stroke	3.31 x 3.15
Displacement, cc	1780
cu in	108.5
Compression ratio	9.5
Bhp @ rpm	100 @ 5500
equivalent mph	121.5
Torque, lb-ft	108 @ 4000
equivalent mph	88.3

GEAR RATIOS

O/d (.756)	3.44
4th (1.00)	4.56
3rd (1.36)	6.20
2nd (1.99)	9.09

SPEEDOMETER ERROR

30 mph	actual, 29.5
60 mph	58.2

PERFORMANCE

Top speed (o/d), mph	105
4th (6000)	100
3rd (5950)	73
2nd (6000)	50
1st (6000)	32

FUEL CONSUMPTION

Normal range, mpg 22/26

ACCELERATION

0-30 mph, sec	3.6
0-40	5.6
0-50	9.0
0-60	12.4
0-70	16.9
0-80	23.5
0-100	
Standing ¼ mile (est)	18.0
speed at end	72

TAPLEY DATA

4th, lb/ton @ mph	200 @ 65
3rd	280 @ 48
2nd	400 @ 35
Total drag at 60 mph, lb	147

ENGINE SPEED IN GEARS
ACCELERATION & COASTING

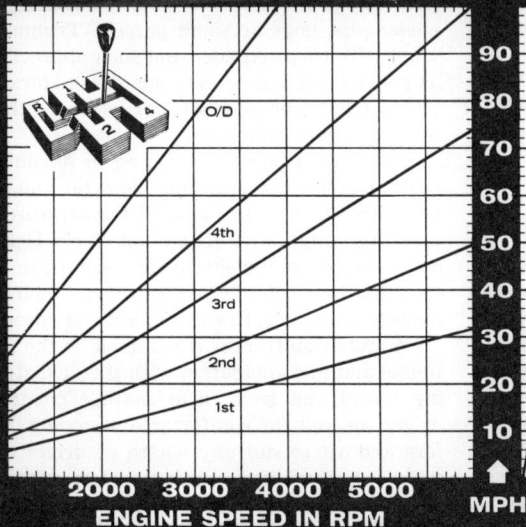

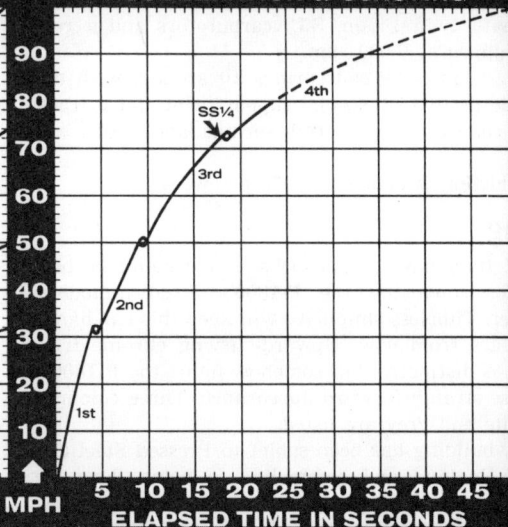

CT&T ROAD TEST

VOLVO P-1800

Long-Awaited Sports Coupe From Sweden

The Car

Swedish designed, Italian styled, British built, the P-1800 is Aktiebolaget Volvo's caviar addition to its bread-and-butter line of utility-first cars and trucks.

Orthodox in design, the P-1800 uses proven mechanical components from existing Volvo cars — thus cutting costs and adding reliability — with exception of the all-new B 18 B engine. Designed for high-speed running and representing 20,000 man-hours of development, this ultra-sturdy 4-cylinder unit carries light alloy pistons and other parts, a five-main-bearing crankshaft, twin $1\frac{3}{4}$-in. S.U. carburetors and a rev-limit redlined at 6,000 rpm.

Suspension is by coil springs all around, with the rear axle located by special support arm and a track bar in connection with coil springs and shock absorbers.

Production is planned at 150 per week.

Styling

Frua of Italy has created looks that couldn't be bettered for conveying the P-1800's Swedish-modern character. Timeless simplicity will keep this car handsome years from now. Upward-curving chrome trim on sides is distinctive but somehow fights the P-1800's otherwise straightforward appearance. Three colours: red, white and grey are listed.

Body-building has been sublet to Pressed Steel Co. Ltd. of England and assembling is being done by Jensen, but traditional Volvo standards are maintained. Despite its carriage-trade intentions the P-1800 isn't fussy or frilly; it's neat and functional. Work-

manship follows suit. Bumpers, a good case in point, are not only integrated with the car's styling but actually serve their protective purpose well. Doors clunk and controls click on and off; the ash tray (big enough to hold more than butts) slides easily out and back; panels fit snugly. One sour note: the wheel covers seem a little tinny.

Interior

Follows current GT coupe practice of two seats with room in back on small bench for occasional passengers, dogs or small parcels. Trimmed in bright vinyl with carpeted floor and such appreciated touches as padded sun visors and under-dash storage compartments for driver or passenger use — with map lights for rallying or rummaging.

Instrument panel is sporting in flavour with large speedometer (incorporating odometer and trip mileage recorder), tach, water and oil temperature gauges, oil pressure gauge, fuel gauge and clock. Deluxe touches as standard equipment include cigarette lighter and twin horns. Visibility par excellence and large dash-mounted mirror refuses to vibrate at speed.

A stubby shift lever is mounted on the transmission tunnel and in combination with the drilled-spoke steering wheel and snug, firm seating position sets the driver up well for comfortable motoring. Seats adjust fore and aft to suit any length of driver and there is more leg-room than a car this low usually delivers, though headroom in our test car was minimal. We understand seats on future models are to be lowered two inches to overcome head-bumping.

Driving

Key-started ignition brings the 4-cylinder, 100-hp engine alive quickly but noise is barely perceptible. Accelerator pedal requires firm pressure. With a rear axle ratio of 4.56:1 and overdrive, the all-synchro M-40 gearbox (same as used on other Volvo models except for forward gears being carried in needle bearings) is undiluted pleasure to use and pushes the P-1800 through its well-spaced paces flawlessly. Electrically operated (Laycock de Normanville) overdrive is flicked on via a dash-mounted toggle switch and a small blue light beams when it's in operation. Steering seems to become progressively lighter with higher speeds but is tight and accurate in any range. Standard Pirelli Cinturato tires assist the P-1800's road-holding which, with its low centre of gravity and hefty anti-roll bar is absolutely the best we have yet encountered in a car of this type. Suspension is not independent at the rear but this car doesn't miss it; rough roads and twisty driving can be undertaken with as much verve as the driver has nerve to use. Noise is unobtrusive at cruising speeds.

Servo-assisted disc brakes in front with V-type drums at rear must be used hard and often to be fully appreciated. They are virtually fade-free and allow leaving the anchors to the last split second during vigorous driving. Special shields in front ward off water's effects. Pressure is medium, making it hard to induce sudden crash-stops unless you want to.

Rough riding reminded us that whatever Volvo builds stays built; the P-1800 is no exception and a tribute to its construction is the fact that passengers are considerably more shook-up over bad surfaces than the car is. A few slight squeaks could be detected somewhere in the interior panelling but that was it. This should be a winning rally car, if only because the navigator is unlikely to become carsick.

Economy

Average consumption (premium fuel) over combined city and highway driving was 32 mpg with overdrive. Cruising at 60-70 mph steadily in o/d could appreciably hike this figure, while 30 mpg with the nonoverdrive model is easily attained.

Storage space

Aside from passenger-compartment space for trifles there is a wide, deep trunk capable of carrying luggage for two on an extended trip with little crowding. The spare tire (covered) rests on the trunk floor in the right lower corner, rather marring the rectangular layout. In spite of this, the P-1800 still has more room behind than almost any GT-type coupe and as much as some compacts.

Heater and Ventilation

Sweden has few palm trees, and the P-1800 has been realistically planned for a variety of climates. Thus the heater is big and efficient and there are fresh air intakes on each side of the passenger compartment, beneath the dash.

Options

Considering the items listed as standard equipment on the P-1800, options are superfluous except for a radio (mounted on the instrument panel), and such goodies as a power-operated radio antenna. Overdrive is a worthwhile extra for long-range cruising. The standard-equipment list includes: servo-assisted disc brakes in front; oil cooler; electric windshield washer; Pirelli Cinturato tires; electric clock; cigarette lighter; shoulder safety belts; double horns; overdrive warning light, anti-theft coil device and Abarth exhaust.

Last word

At $6,000 this car would be a bargain. At $3,995 we feel it's a steal and Volvo will be hard-pressed to fill the orders. Carefully advertised as a sports coupe and not a sports car, the P-1800 has as much to offer as most sports cars we have encountered plus a degree of creature comfort and sheer liveability unmatched by anything near its price class. With Volvo's reputation for ruggedness, reliability and low maintenance behind it, it can't lose.

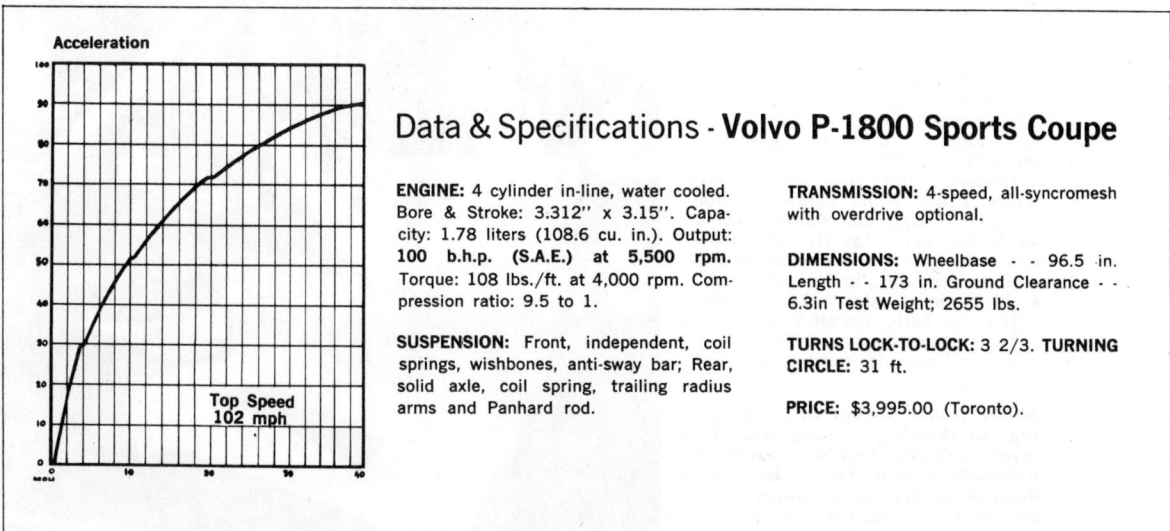

Data & Specifications - Volvo P-1800 Sports Coupe

ENGINE: 4 cylinder in-line, water cooled. Bore & Stroke: 3.312" x 3.15". Capacity: 1.78 liters (108.6 cu. in.). Output: 100 b.h.p. (S.A.E.) at 5,500 rpm. Torque: 108 lbs./ft. at 4,000 rpm. Compression ratio: 9.5 to 1.

SUSPENSION: Front, independent, coil springs, wishbones, anti-sway bar; Rear, solid axle, coil spring, trailing radius arms and Panhard rod.

TRANSMISSION: 4-speed, all-syncromesh with overdrive optional.

DIMENSIONS: Wheelbase - - 96.5 in. Length - - 173 in. Ground Clearance - - 6.3in Test Weight; 2655 lbs.

TURNS LOCK-TO-LOCK: 3 2/3. **TURNING CIRCLE:** 31 ft.

PRICE: $3,995.00 (Toronto).

Acceleration — Top Speed 102 mph

Exclusive 700-mile test of first Volvo coupe to reach Australia — by David McKay

modern MOTOR ROAD TEST

SPEEDY

IF you sight a sleek red coupe bearing foreign plates and a left-hand-drive warning, don't rush your guess — it is NOT a Ferrari, an Alfa Sprint Veloce or a Zagato Aston.

It is Sweden's Volvo P1800. Such is the design that it invites wild guesses — and its road performance, when enterprisingly driven, adds to the recognition problem.

One interesting feature of the coupe — as you may recall reading in Douglas Armstrong's overseas report last September — is that it is actually the result of collaboration between several countries.

The basic engineering design — including engine, suspension and most other mechanical components — is Swedish; but the body was styled in Italy by Frua and is produced in England by Jensen Motors, who also do the final assembling. In addition, the rear axle is American, and the ignition equipment comes from Germany — as do some of the lighting units.

The car looks much better in the metal than in pictures, which tend to make it appear very high-sided. The Frua body is styled on the classic G.T. lines — rather like a scaled-down Ferrari 250.

However, unlike most Ferraris, the Volvo P1800 is no lightweight for its size. Though 2in. shorter and a whole 8in. lower (at 4ft. 3in.) than the Volvo 122S saloon from which it is derived, it's also 3in. wider and a bit heavier than the latter—22½cwt. at kerb, against 21½.

This implies sturdy construction — and the Volvo IS sturdy. Our test

ROOF is low — but so is the seating, so there's fair headroom. Full array of instruments is recessed into well-padded dash. This is latest production model, with longer, freer gearshift than used on our test car.

car was an obviously hard-worked factory demonstrator that had clocked up almost 20,000 km. (12,000 miles) in Europe before being brought out to Australia — but its body structure and major mechanical components showed few signs of abuse.

Nor does the weight impair the coupe's performance — it's a genuine 100 m.p.h. car that can be cruised at very nearly its maximum.

Such performance is remarkable, considering that the four-cylinder, o.h.v. engine has a capacity of only 1780c.c. This is 200c.c. more than the Volvo saloon's power unit, the increase being obtained by a 5mm. larger bore.

A five-bearing crankshaft ensur[es] extremely smooth running — a[nd] 9.5-to-1 compression, plus a pair [of] 1¾in. carbies, help extract an ou[t]put of 100 b.h.p. (SAE) at 5500 rev[s] against the saloon's 85 b.h.p. An [oil] radiator is fitted as standard, and o[ur] test car had the optional Layco[ck] electric overdrive.

The well-planned interior h[as] fully adjustable twin seats up fro[nt] and a well-cushioned "occasiona[l]" bench in the back, suitable for tw[o] children or one transversely-seat[ed] adult. A pair of lap-and-sash safe[ty] belts are fitted as standard.

The front-seat squabs are almo[st] flat; instead of relying on backre[st]

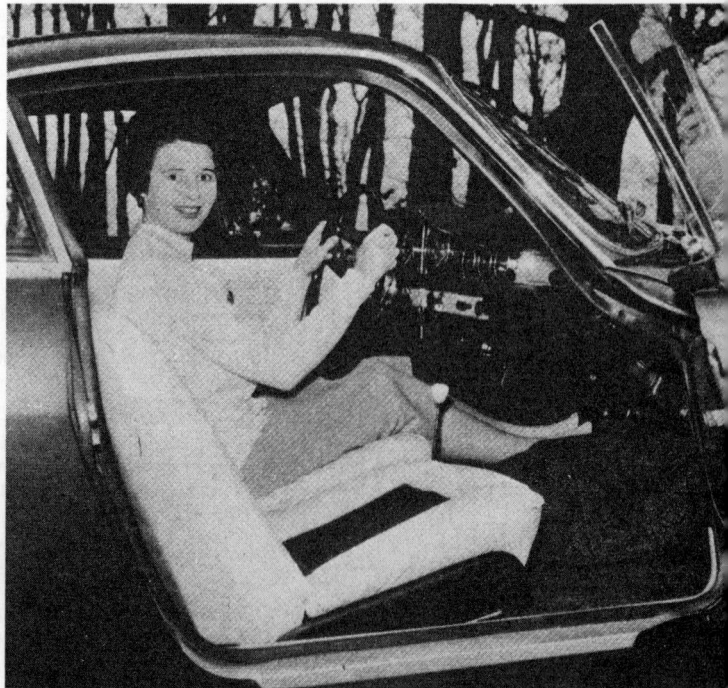

ing circle, and disc brakes are fitted on the front wheels. Boot space is generous for a sporty coupe, and the horizontally-housed spare has a neat plastic cover to protect the luggage.

Getting Acquainted

That's the general picture. Now for the road test, which was a good deal longer than usual — close to 700 miles, including a trip from Sydney to Melbourne via Canberra.

I got the car late at night before leaving for Melbourne from Peter Antill, Volvo's N.S.W. concessionaire, who had been pounding it around the outback to test its suitability for local conditions.

Before the Volvo could draw

(rev-counter and all) — particularly the vertical thermometer-type water- and oil-temperature gauges (in degrees centigrade) and the oil-pressure gauge (registering in kilograms per centimetre).

As the car had had no oil-change since leaving Sweden and the relatively small sump was a shade low on oil, I was glad of these instruments.

The lights were good in the Continental fashion, and I noted that a flasher unit was provided for rapid overtaking, in cases where a horn is not always heard. The Volvo's horn note was a little disappointing: Italian air horns would be more in keeping with this type of car.

SWEDE

P1800 looks fast, IS fast — a genuine 100 m.p.h. car. Warwick Farm provides a fitting background.

shaping to hold you on corners, the Swedes provide a rubber-padded block for the driver's left foot, which I found a very handy "steadying influence."

Trim is first-class, and there's plenty of crash-padding around the cockpit. The dash especially is well protected, and the generous array of individually hooded instruments is recessed deeply between two padded rolls.

There's a four-speed, all-synchro gearbox, cam-and-roller steering with 3¼ turns lock-to-lock and 31ft. turn-

breath, I had it out on the road again, headed for my "private" mountain test course.

The left-hand drive didn't bother me; in fact, it helps you to "clip" those left-handers and use every available bit of bitumen — so it's an aid rather than a hindrance, except when overtaking big transports.

The coupes that will be sold here, of course, will have right-hand drive; this has just been put into production in England.

Behind the wheel, I enjoyed the very comprehensive instrumentation

The driving position is almost intimate — rather in the style of a G.P. racer's cockpit. Everything is near at hand, and there's a profusion of knobs and stalks, all carefully labelled in Swedish, to the left of the wheel.

The coupe seems to have been designed more for the Swedish female than for her mate, who is usually a burly 6ft.-plus. Personally, it suited me fine — but then, I wouldn't even be as large as, say, Miss Ekberg.

The gracefully low roof line does limit headroom; but as you sit well

ENGINE extracts 100 horses from 1780c.c. with help of two big-throated carbies.

Handling, Performance

On clearing the suburbs, I soon found that the P1800 is no ordinary coupe when it comes to handling. It's highly sensitive to any heavy-handedness; but once the technique is mastered, you can flick the car through the corners at quite awe-inspiring speeds with confidence.

It was a great pity the throttle linkage collapsed on the test run, for the coupe was well ahead of schedule when this happened and still managed to get home in remarkably good time, with only one carby working.

The P1800 proves how good the conventional "chassis" layout can be if properly designed in the first place. The car is coil-sprung and uses a stabiliser bar up front, with torque arms and Panhard rod at the rear.

For a live-axle layout, adhesion and acceleration out of bends are outstanding. And I have no doubt that the rare Pirelli "Cinturatos" contribute greatly to the car's agility.

(Cinturato braced-tread tyres are used by such "race rally" experts as Gendebien and Mairesse on their Ferrari Berlinettas for all but the high-speed "special sections" on circuits, when they switch to Dunlop RS racing tyres.)

Equally amazing is what the Swedish engineers have been able to extract from the thoroughly conventional engine. The four-cylinder, 1.8-litre unit looks almost placid in its MG-like coat of red paint — but its **forte** is its ability to keep up high

down in the P1800, this doesn't worry you. The rather high doors, however, make looking out to the rear a little difficult for parking — it's better to sight back through the sloping rear window.

Steering wheel and pedals are perfectly placed, and I particularly appreciated the resting block for the clutch foot — hope it isn't omitted from the right-hand-drive version when the clutch pedal is moved next to the transmission hump.

A strange thing, however, is the angle of the throttle pedal. To get full throttle I had to extend the toe like a ballet dancer — a tiring business. Peter Antill had the same complaint — so it isn't just a question of driver size, since Peter could be taken for a Swede in stature.

It could be that the full-throttle position was out of adjustment, for the linkage came adrift that night on my test run. Luckily, mechanic Bob Atkin was then burning the midnight oil, preparing our Studebaker Lark for the Armstrong 500; he fixed the throttle in a jiffy, and we were able to leave for Melbourne on schedule.

Gearshift action of the coupe's all-synchro box wasn't quite in keeping with the rest of the car. It suffered from the usual sports-car type of lever — too short and consequently heavy in movement. This is in direct contrast to the Volvo saloon, which has a long lever with very easy action.

But "our" coupe was an early model, and it seems that the lever has since been lengthened a little and given a larger knob (the new type

is shown in the picture of the interior, which we obtained from Sweden).

Apart from first gear, which balks a little in the Porsche and VW manner, the ratios and synchros are first-class and they invite quick, precise changes.

MAIN SPECIFICATIONS

ENGINE: 4-cylinder, o.h.v.; bore 84mm., stroke 80mm., capacity 1780c.c.; compression ratio 9.5 to 1; maximum b.h.p. 100 (SAE) at 5500 r.p.m.; maximum torque 108ft./lb. at 4000 r.p.m.; twin S.U. carburettors, electric fuel pump; 12v. ignition.

TRANSMISSION: Single dry-plate hydraulically operated clutch; 4-speed fully synchromeshed gearbox with (optional) Laycock electric overdrive; ratios, 1st, 3.13; 2nd, 1.99; 3rd, 1.36; top, 1 to 1; overdrive ratio, 0.756 to 1.

SUSPENSION: Front independent, by coil springs and rubber-bushed, ball-jointed control arms and stabiliser bar; coil springs over axle, with torque arm and Panhard rod at rear; telescopic hydraulic shock-absorbers all round.

STEERING: Cam-and-roller; 3 2-3rd turns lock-to-lock, 31ft. turning circle.

WHEELS: Pressed-steel discs with 15in. diameter, 4½in. rims; Italian 165cm. tyres.

BRAKES: Servo-assisted, self-adjusting; discs at front, drums at rear.

CONSTRUCTION: Unitary.

DIMENSIONS: Wheelbase, 8ft. 0½in.; track (front and rear) 4ft. 4in.; length 14ft. 5in., width 5ft. 7in., height 4ft. 3in.; ground clearance 6in.

KERB WEIGHT: 22¼cwt.

FUEL TANK: 10 gallons.

PERFORMANCE ON TEST

CONDITIONS: Fine, cool; no wind; two occupants; Methyl-benzine and premium-grade petrol fuel mixture.

BEST SPEED: 105 m.p.h.

FLYING quarter-mile: 100 m.p.h.

STANDING quarter-mile: 19s.

MAXIMUM in indirect gears: 1st, 30 m.p.h.; 2nd, 50; 3rd, 75.

ACCELERATION from rest through

gears: 0-30, 4.0s.; 0-40, 6.2s.; 0-50, 9.4s.; 0-60, 13.0s.; 0-70, 18.4s.; 0-80, 26.0s.

BRAKING: 31ft. to stop from 30 m.p.h. in neutral.

FUEL CONSUMPTION: 26 m.p.g. overall.

SPEEDO: Accurate at 30 m.p.h.; 2 m.p.h. fast at 60, 3 m.p.h. fast at 80.

PRICE (approx.): £2500 including tax

SPEEDY SWEDE

revs for long periods without exhaustion.

The massive five-bearing crankshaft plays a part here; and Volvo's engineers have kept test units running at 5500 r.p.m. for 500 hours under full load — i.e., giving out 100 horses!

This output, coupled with four gears and Laycock overdrive, gives a cruising speed close to the car's maximum. The red warning markings on the rev-counter start at 5500 — and after 6000 the red warning is a solid block to the end of the scale at 7000. Using 6000 revs as our maximum, the speedo indicated 160 k.p.h. (just on 100 m.p.h.) in 4th, 120 (75) in 3rd and 80 (50) in 2nd.

On a long, level road in overdrive it is possible to hold 4500, which gives 100 m.p.h. on the clock — and any undulation will put you up to the factory's claimed maximum of 105.

This sort of performance puts the P1800 right in the fast coupe class (if not in the sports-car category), along with Porsche 1600 and Mercedes 190 SL. As a matter of fact, the Volvo has a lot of Porsche feel about it on the road in its flat, hugging ride.

To cope with the performance, the coupe has magnificent brakes—discs front and drums rear. I've never cared much for the mixture, but on the Volvo the balance seems perfect, and the brakes give that same wonderful sense of security as on a Jaguar.

The system is servo-assisted, and the discs are protected against rain, mud and dirt — a legacy of Sweden's unmade roads which will be appreciated in Australia.

Sydney-Melbourne

There was a surprise in store when we began to load the car for our interstate trip. My wife and I were going for over a week, and we were dropping our small daughter off with my family along the way. That meant plenty of luggage, plus my usual racing paraphernalia.

Our child had a comfortable seat on the "occasional" bench behind the buckets, while two larger-than-average suitcases went into the boot without any effort.

Behind the occasional seat is a cubby-hole capable of taking a couple of brollies and three airline bags. I can't remember a more spacious coupe of this kind, with the exception of the 190 SL.

The run to Canberra was uneventful, apart from rain. Despite the latter, we put away Moss Vale-Canberra in 90 minutes — after which I took time out to give the car some long overdue service at rally driver Greg Cusack's garage.

With the car up on the hoist, we could see the great attention to detail and the sensible suspension — but ground clearance looked small, despite the advertised 6 inches.

Next day, on the shocking Hume Highway around Gundagai and Tarcutta, the Volvo actually grounded at the exhaust pipe, just as my Jaguars used to do.

It was raining again as we left Canberra at 11.10 a.m. — but we reached Gundagai at 12.50 and Albury by 2.20 p.m. Leaving Albury at 3.25, we ran onto the tramlines at Coburg at 6.15.

I won't say the trip was effortless, because it never is in anything with less than 3 litres under the bonnet. We knew we'd been motoring — but it was thoroughly enjoyable motoring.

High winds in Victoria moved the car around more than I expected — but I fancy the speed and the somewhat fatigued shockers added to the sensation.

Fuel economy was excellent. At no time did it drop below 25 m.p.g., and from Sydney to Canberra we got 27. With less hurry and less use of the gears, 30 m.p.g. or better should be possible.

Peter Antill had been running on super-grade pump fuel; but as the 9.5:1 engine is obviously designed for the 98-octane petrol that's readily available overseas, I gave it a treat and used Methyl benzine in N.S.W.

As this was then unobtainable in Victoria, I broached some 100-octane juice I had at Albury, and the engine showed its appreciation by a fine run into Melbourne. Not that ordinary super is unsuitable for the P1800— it will run on it, and I've run as high as 10.25:1 on super; but if this was my car, I'd use Methyl benzine or "100."

Summing up the P1800, I see it as a fine car and a welcome addition to that select range of 100 m.p.h. coupes. It is handsome, useful, reliable and safe.

Price is still to be finalised — but it looks like being around £2500 tax-paid in Australia, which is lower than previously estimated and real value for the money.

Incidentally, the 1962 model Volvo saloon, with the same 1780c.c. engine as the coupe, 12-volt ignition and disc brakes on the front wheels, is now also available in this country. Price remains at £1775 tax-paid — not a penny more than the old 1580c.c.-engined, drum-braked model!

INTERNATIONAL COUPÉ . . . CONCLUDED FROM PAGE 9

a very even, restful ride. The "mixed" brakes with servo assistance are powerful; they can be applied hard at high speeds without a suggestion of pull to right or left. Quite high geared and reasonably light, the steering has neutral characteristics and is likely to be judged very satisfactory.

Maximum speed is claimed by the manufacturer to be between 105 and 110 m.p.h. in overdrive. Speeds in the gears corresponding to 6,000 r.p.m., which the manufacturers state can be used with safety, are 30, 47, 69 and 94 m.p.h. for first, second, third and top gears. With 5 gallons of fuel aboard the maker's figure for weight is 22cwt, 53.5 per cent on the front wheels and 46.5 per cent on the rear. The performance figures claimed are 0-60 m.p.h. in 12.5sec and 0-70 m.p.h. in 17sec. At a steady speed of 60 m.p.h. the claimed fuel consumption is 34 m.p.g. in top and 40 m.p.g. in overdrive top; these indicate that, as with the 122S, overall consumption should be very good.

This is a car which will be at its best when covering long journeys at higher than normal speeds. Certainly it cruises comfortably at over 80 m.p.h. There is ample luggage space and a lot of room for the driver and passenger to stretch their legs. The seats are not quite as good as might be hoped and the use of imitation leather for trim and upholstery is disappointing.

Details which were approved were the plastic loop guarding the handbrake button, the rubber resting pad for the driver's left foot, the overriders incorporated in the front bumper styling— a Frua speciality—and the clearance between these elegant fittings and the body to avoid transmission of collision damage.

Volvo's three-point safety harness, of course, is a standard fitting and in all respects the interior has been padded and shaped to provide utmost protection.

All desirable detail equipment is included in the standard price, in particular a powerful heater, two-speed wipers and electric screenwasher and high-performance tyres. The cars are available in red, white or grey; the white and grey cars have red upholstery and all have black mouldings and fittings.

Without allowing the price to soar beyond reasonable limits, Volvo seem to have produced a sporting coupé of superior quality and high performance, incorporating components and units from the several countries that have been selected for their merit and value regardless of the usual national and trade influences.

British suppliers of material for the Volvo P.1800 are:—Clifford Covering Co. Ltd., Dunlop Rubber Co. Ltd., Girling Ltd., Imperial Chemical Industries, Jensen Motors Ltd., Joseph Fray Ltd., Joseph Lucas (Electrical) Ltd., Pianoforte Supplies Ltd., Pirelli Ltd., Pressed Steel Co. Ltd., Joseph Sankey & Sons Ltd., Silent Channel Co Ltd., Smiths Motor Accessories Ltd., The S.U. Carburettor Co. Ltd., Triplex Safety Glass Co Ltd., Wilmot Breeden Ltd., Worcester Windshields Ltd. and Vandervell Products Ltd.

VOLVO P-1800

AFTER MUCH DELAY, the eagerly-awaited Volvo P-1800 Grand Touring coupe is beginning to arrive in numbers on our shores. Full production status for this model was originally planned for early 1961, shortly after we tested the prototype car at Volvo's main plant in Gothenburg, Sweden. But, man's best laid schemes "gang aft a-gley," as the Scot poet once said, and so, too, did Volvo's projected time schedule.

Because Volvo's assembly facilities were even then being strained to capacity in the production of its bread-and-butter sedans, the job of supplying the unit-constructed body/chassis had to be farmed out. The Jensen Company, in England (which has done a similar job for BMC in the production of Austin-Healeys), was awarded the contract. Jensen subcontracted the panel stamping to Pressed Steel Co. Ltd., and did the assembling in its own plant. All mechanical elements, such as the engine, drive-train, rear brakes (the front brakes are discs from Dunlop) and all but the instruments and some of the miscellaneous electrical components were to be supplied by Volvo's factories in Sweden. Unfortunately, the conclusion of agreements coincided with a spate of industry-wide strikes, with first one group and then another joining in the general fun, and as a result production was delayed for almost a full year.

In this instance the wait was well worth while. The production-form P-1800 retains all of the good features of the prototype—and is better finished and quieter. The styling, which impressed us only mildly in Sweden, is, as it turns out, an absolute smash hit with the American man-in-the-street. Perhaps our tastes have become too astringent to properly appreciate the P-1800's lines because people generally swiveled right around to watch it go by. It was just like those dear departed days when an MG was enough to wow the peasantry, and we would have been something more than human not to have enjoyed the experience.

Closer inspection would not have disenchanted the most sharp-eyed and picayunish of those distant admirers. The color selection for P-1800s is a trifle basic (our test car was an undistinguished off-white) but the quality of the paint and the manner in which it has been applied cannot be criticized. The same thing applies to the body panels (which are fastened together with a proper regard for tolerances) and the trim.

The layout and finish inside the P-1800 are done with a slightly heavy touch but, whatever one might think of the decor, there's no denying that the car is superbly comfortable. The seats—which usually account for most of the comfort, or lack of it, in any car—were of the well padded semi-bucket type. They could have been more deeply contoured, for better support while cornering hard, but were adequate for most touring conditions.

Large doors make it easy to enter the P-1800, and once inside there is a lot more room than is usually found in a car of this type—in every direction but "up"; the roof is a bit low. The seats are adjustable over an extremely long fore-and-aft travel, making it possible for even the often-forgotten tall man to get enough leg room. Also, while doing some fast driving we discovered that there was enough room to permit the driver a great flailing of arms and some determined leaning about without his making a serious encroachment on the passenger's preserves. More leisurely touring allows this space to be used as sprawl-room, and the faint sensation of entombment often experienced in small coupes was missing.

The instrumentation is futuristic, but very complete. The speedometer and tachometer are set into a hooded section right in front of the steering wheel, on either side of a combination mounting that holds the water and oil temperature gauges. There are also gauges for oil pressure and fuel level, and even a clock. Colored lights are present in abundance too, and there is a multitude of small switches for the windshield wipers and washers, heater-fan and so forth.

The only controls not easily seen and reached were the ones for interior lighting, fresh air and the choke. These are tucked away below the dash and gave us some

trouble at first. However, they have coded-shape knobs and after the initial period of familiarization they were not much bother.

Primary controls, such as the steering-wheel, clutch and brake pedals (of the pendant type) and the accelerator pedal, were placed perfectly. So was the gearshift lever, but it had a stiffness—which may not be typical—that countered its nice positioning.

Volvo's safety-harness arrangement deserves special mention. It consists of an adjustable-length strap, anchored to the floor next to the door, that reaches across one's lap to a clip-fastener on the driveshaft tunnel and then travels diagonally over one's body, back to another anchor near the top of the door-jamb. These belts are widely appreciated and used in Sweden and have an honestly-earned reputation there for allowing people to survive most crashes. Apart from this obvious and essential advantage, they are comfortable (and unobtrusive) to wear and easy to fasten and remove. Their only deficiency is in the positioning of the upper anchor, which tends to pull the belt down from the shoulder and onto the arm.

In the trunk, we noticed that there was—by sports car

VOLVO P-1800 *continued*

standards—an adequate amount of space and that the necessity for carrying a spare tire had compromised what would otherwise have been a very large luggage locker. The compartment is conveniently shaped and could easily accommodate a fortnight's outfitting for 2 if the car's owner could muster enough daring to leave the spare behind in the garage. Lacking this there is, even so, enough room for 1 or 2 medium-to-small bags.

Service accessibility is exceptional. The engine compartment itself is outsized for the amount of machinery it must contain and there is, as a result, very little crowding. Our only adverse comment concerns the location of the battery, which was tucked away up in the right-rear corner where it cannot miss much of the heat from the engine. Should it overflow, there is a strong probability that some of the acid may find its way down onto the passenger's feet.

In the car's various mechanical elements there is considerable evidence of the "strength above all" design-philosophy. The B-18 engine, which will soon be available in the 122-S and PV-544 sedans as well, is a medium-displacement 4, distinguished more by smoothness than vigor and is the most understressed unit we have seen in many years. It has 5 main bearings, and the size of the shaft, bearings and supporting structure seem wasted on only 1780 cc of displacement. Certainly, the engine will take a lot more than is being asked of it at present.

The same thing may be said of the rest of the car. Any place a little bit would have been enough, a lot was used —particularly in the body/chassis structure. In a machine with racing-car pretensions this would be silly, but in the touring-only P-1800 we didn't mind it a bit. Naturally, the Volvo would be faster if it were not carrying all this extra weight around, but the designers have elected, instead, to give us strength and rigidity much above the average—and in that they have succeeded very well.

All cars of this type that come our way for test get a thorough wringing-out on twisty roads and there the Volvo, despite its weight and soft ride, gave a fine performance. There is a dreadful amount of lean while cornering, but the driver can't feel it inside the car and it doesn't seem to affect the handling. Bends, fast or slow,

can be taken with *élan*—just a touch of steadying understeer being present at all times.

Acceleration is nothing to get thrilled about. A great many cars less imposing in appearance and less expensive to buy will hand the P-1800 a terrible drubbing in a contest of speed. The clutch bites well, and the engine pulls strongly at all speeds, but the car's weight defeats their best efforts. The Volvo's *top* speed needs no apology, and the gear ratios are spaced nicely for best performance, but the sheer mass of the automobile prohibits sprinting.

In doing that for which it was intended, fast steady cruising, the P-1800 is superb and it gave us the impression it would run forever at near maximum speed. There is little wind noise at high speed and the coil-sprung chassis gives a good ride at any speed and on any surface. No squeaks, rattles, creaks, groaning or road-drumming was heard while we had the Volvo, and we decided that this is a car in which a good radio would not be wasted. Comfort is provided in excellent measure and, with the gearing given by the overdrive (4th gear, direct, gives a "red-line" maximum of 88 mph), the P-1800 is a far faster cruising car than either our road conditions or laws will allow. The price is high, a factor which cannot be ignored, but there isn't another car on the market today that offers precisely the qualities abundantly present in Volvo's P-1800—the potential buyer of a GT-type automobile certainly should see and drive this car. 🜨

ROAD TEST
VOLVO P-1800

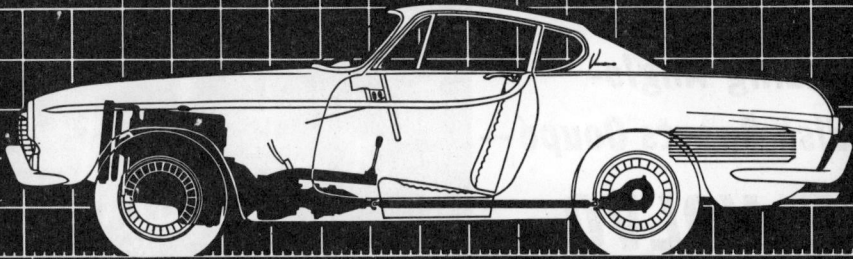

SCALE: 10" DIVISIONS

DIMENSIONS

Wheelbase, in	96.5
Tread, f and r	52.0
Over-all length, in	173
width	67.0
height	51.0
equivalent vol, cu ft	342
Frontal area, sq ft	19.0
Ground clearance, in	5.3
Steering ratio, o/a	15.5
turns, lock to lock	3.5
turning circle, ft	30
Hip room, front	2 x 21
Hip room, rear	50.5
Pedal to seat back, max	43
Floor to ground	10.8

CALCULATED DATA

Lb/hp (test wt)	27.8
Cu ft/ton mile	64.1
Mph/1000 rpm (o/d)	21.2
Engine revs/mile	2840
Piston travel, ft/mile	1490
Rpm @ 2500 ft/min	4760
equivalent mph	101
R&T wear index	42.3

SPECIFICATIONS

List price	$4140
Curb weight, lb	2430
Test weight	2785
distribution, %	54/46
Tire size	165-15
Brake swept area	339
Engine type	4-cyl, ohv
Bore & stroke	3.31 x 3.15
Displacement, cc	1780
cu in	108.5
Compression ratio	9.5
Bhp @ rpm	100 @ 5500
equivalent mph	116.7
Torque, lb-ft	108 @ 4000
equivalent mph	84.8

GEAR RATIOS

O/d (.756)	3.44
4th (1.00)	4.56
3rd (1.36)	6.20
2nd (1.99)	9.09
1st (3.13)	14.3

SPEEDOMETER ERROR

30 mph	actual, 29.8
60 mph	58.4

PERFORMANCE

Top speed (4th), mph	88
best timed run (o/d)	104.7
3rd (5500)	64.5
2nd (5500)	44
1st (5500)	28

FUEL CONSUMPTION

Normal range, mpg	21/28

ACCELERATION

0-30 mph, sec	4.7
0-40	7.1
0-50	10.3
0-60	13.6
0-70	18.7
0-80	25.3
0-100	36.8
Standing 1/4 mile	19.0
speed at end	70.5

TAPLEY DATA

4th, lb/ton @ mph	190 @ 55
3rd	260 @ 48
2nd	380 @ 36
Total drag at 60 mph, lb	115

ENGINE SPEED IN GEARS

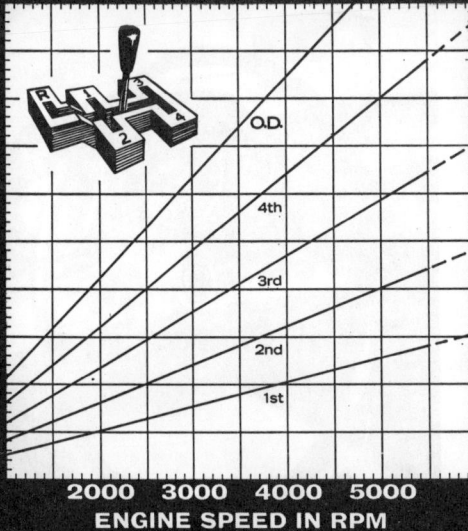

O.D.
4th
3rd
2nd
1st

ENGINE SPEED IN RPM
2000 3000 4000 5000

ACCELERATION & COASTING

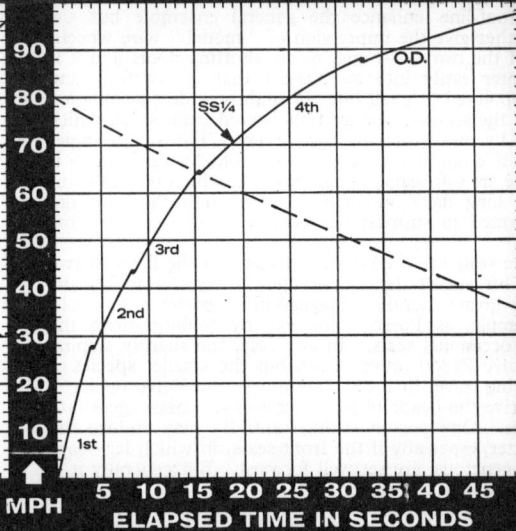

O.D.
SS1/4
4th
3rd
2nd
1st

MPH
ELAPSED TIME IN SECONDS
5 10 15 20 25 30 35 40 45

ROAD TEST REPORT ON—

A Pleasing Anglo-Swedish Sports Coupé—
THE VOLVO P·1800

IN GOOD SHAPE.—The low build and sleek lines of the well-appointed and comfortable Volvo P1800 give it the appearance of faster, more expensive G.T. coupés.

VOLVO cars from Sweden are very conscientiously made and accurately assembled, as readers of MOTOR SPORT's account of a visit to the Göteberg plant (June, 1960) will know. That they go extremely well and possess desirable features of design and equipment has also been made clear in our road-test reports of the 122S and 122S/B18 saloon models.

More recently the long-awaited P1800 sports coupé has been subjected to a 1,000-mile road-test. This is a particularly interesting car, for at the kerb-side it rivals the best Italian G.T. cars for eyeable good looks, being long, low and of wind-defeating form, yet it is really a durable, refined cross between out-and-out *sportswagen* and Grand Touring car, with the additional item of interest that the body is a product of Pressed Steel in Scotland, the P1800 being assembled by Jensen in West Bromwich, using such British components as certain Lucas lamps and electrical equipment, Smiths instruments and Girling brakes.

In appearance the P1800, as I have said, is exciting, although rather less chromium embellishment along the body sides and tail-fins would be an improvement. The Ferrari-like front grille and shapely roof-line enhance the general ensemble but the wheel discs rather give the impression of " model " wire wheels.

Open one of the two well-hung, nicely-shutting doors and it is possible to enter easily into an interior that is tastefully and luxuriously appointed. A tall but not unduly wide transmission tunnel divides the separate leather-upholstered front seats, which are adjustable by means of long base levers. The squab angles are adjustable if a nut at the base of each fold-forward squab is turned. There are soft seats of generous size, which remain comfortable on a long day's motoring even though they are not specifically formed to support the occupants against cornering stresses.

Behind these seats are the occasional seats, in the form of two cushions that lift out of their retaining wells. Presumably the idea is to offer greater depth of luggage but I prefer a flat-shelf, such, for example, as Porsche contrive by folding down the squabs of the occasional seats. In any case, the sharply sloping roof of the Volvo P1800 prevents any but the smaller species of children enjoying travel in these seats unless the Volvo owner is prepared to drive the heads of his " occasional " passengers into their shoulders. One person sitting centrally may endure the experience better, especially if the front seats, in which leg-room is particularly generous, are set well forward. But generally it is better to regard this as a 2-seater car.

Behind the occasional cushions is an arched shelf for parcels, stowage but if suitcases are carried on the rear seats such stowage is rendered inaccessible. Another poor aspect of the car is ventilation. The front doors contain big glasses that wind down with 3¼rd turns of the substantial winders, and quarter-lights that lock with a pip and recess into their rubbers, so that they become very stiff to open. But the back quarter-lights are fixed, so a

flow of draught-free air through the body is difficult to achieve. There is a scuttle intake with small toggle controls under the scuttle but this does not provide any great volume of cold air, and then only to the feet.

The doors have ornate horizontal quadrant-type interior handles that make opening them easy; pushing these knobs forward locks the doors but as the action works if the doors are closed subsequently it would not be surprising to come upon a Volvo owner locked out of his beautiful P1800. The windows are framed only as far back as the quarter-lights; they have good sealing rubbers.

The interior of the body is upholstered in plastic material matching the red leather seats and black facia trim. The doors have curious " pulls " in the form of curved shelves that would scarcely hold a cigarette packet. These have a drain hole, so presumably Pressed Steel are aware that rain is going to seep past the quarter-lights when these are shut and run in when they are

CONTROL LAYOUT of the Volvo P1800 includes hooded speedometer and tachometer before the driver, with vertical thermometers between and two-tiered instrument and control panels. Note the remote gear-lever and drilled spokes of the steering wheel.

This view of the Volvo coupé shows how the tail-fins continue the plated embellishments that run along the sides of the body.

open, as no gutters are provided! In any case, the purpose of these " pulls," which could so easily have constituted pockets or arm-rests, is obscure.

The instrumentation is in keeping with the demeanour of this Volvo coupé. The well padded facias are on two planes, the top one recessed further forward than the lower one. The lower carries two panels, of which the central one contains the overdrive-switch (found only on Home Market cars) flanked on its left by a cigarette-lighter and drawer-type ash-tray; on its right by knobs controlling a quiet 2-speed heater fan, and the 2-speed wipers-cum-washers, with, in addition, a rather unnecessary mauve warning-light to show when overdrive is in use.

The r.h. panel has on it pull-out lamps knob (foot dipper) and Assa ignition-key-cum-starter control.

The top panel has provision for a radio on the left and three Smiths dials, of rather ugly protruding type, covering clock, fuel gauge and oil pressure. Hooded before the driver are the Smiths speedometer and tachometer with a vertical thermometer unit, like a child's barometer, between them. The thermometer records water temperature with a vertical yellow ribbon in the upper scale (marked at 90, 160, 212 and 230° F.) and oil temperature with a blue ribbon in the lower scale (marked at 140, 212, 265 and 280° F.). The speedometer incorporates trip and total with decimal mileometer, warning lights, labelled with symbols, for generator and (sensibly subdued) main-beams. The dial is rather casually calibrated every 20 m.p.h. to 120 m.p.h. The tachometer again, is crudely marked in steps of ten, to 7,000 r.p.m., with a red warning between the 5,500 and 7,000-r.p.m. points. The dials are neat, with white figures on a black background and all, with most of the knobs, are neatly marked as to purpose. The knobs, as I have found on other Volvos, are apt to unscrew, but a far more serious short-coming was failure of the screen-washers to function. The petrol gauge is marked E, ½, F but the " E "

The performance of the Volvo P1800 is somewhat restricted by use of a similar engine to the B18 unit used in the 122S saloon, but raised compression-ratio increases the output from 90 to 100 b.h.p.

THE VOLVO P1800 COUPE

Engine : Four cylinders, 84 × 80 mm. (1,780 c.c.). Push-rod-operated overhead valves. 9.5-to-1 compression-ratio. 100 b.h.p. (net) at 5,500 r.p.m.

Gear ratios : 1st, 14.3 to 1; 2nd, 9.1 to 1; 3rd, 6.2 to 1; top, 4.56 to 1; overdrive top, 3.5 to 1.

Tyres : 165–15 Pirelli Cintura on bolt-on steel disc wheels.

Weight : Not weighed (maker's figure : 22 cwt. (kerb weight)).

Steering ratio : Just over 3 turns, lock-to-lock.

Fuel capacity : 10 gallons. (Range approximately 249 miles.)

Wheelbase : 8 ft. 0½ in.

Track : 4 ft. 3¾ in.

Dimensions : 14 ft. 5¼ in. × 5 ft. 7 in. × 4 ft. 3 in. (high).

Price : £1,335 (£1,836 12s. 9d. inclusive of purchase tax. and import duty).

Makers : AB Volvo, Göteberg, Sweden.

Concessionaires : Volvo Concessionaires Ltd., 28, Albemarle Street, London, W.1.

is set away from the faint pip indicating empty, which can thus be mistaken for the ¼-full mark, causing one driver to run out of petrol in one of August's severe rain-storms.

Up under the scuttle, somewhat inaccessibly placed, are the aforesaid toggles for the fresh-air intake, flanked on the left by a lever-switch for a map-light and on the right by a matching switch for the interior lamps in the back of the body, with a setting for courtesy action. Under the centre of the facia are three neat, labelled levers controlling demisting, ventilation and heating, these being flanked by a zero-setter for the trip odometer and a toggle controlling the mixture enrichener for the twin S.U. HS6 carburetters.

There are no door pockets or cubby-hole but rigid map carriers are provided on both sides of the scuttle and there is a wide but only slightly lipped rear shelf for more bulky objects. The roof is low, so that the soft swivelling anti-dazzle vizors come close to the driver's head. The pedals, of which the accelerator is of treadle type, are of generous size and well placed. An oval rear-view mirror provides an excellent view but, mounted centrally on the screen sill, completely obscures the near-side front wing, which would otherwise just be visible to drivers of moderate height. The test car had streamlined Walpress external mirrors.

The rear boot has a self-supporting, lockable lid, which, however, can be blown down by a gust of wind. The boot is reasonably capacious and adequate if this Volvo is regarded as normally a 2-seater with luggage space behind the front seats. The spare wheel, in a cover, lies on the floor, however.

The exterior of the P1800 is characterised by substantial if flimsily mounted bumpers, upswept at the front, and twin, unplated tail-pipes. The fuel filler consists of a locked flap on the near-side rear panel. This did not seal properly, and a strong smell of petrol invaded the car as the level fell towards empty. Apart from a coloured Volvo motif on the rear quarters and the name Volvo in separate letters below the boot-lid, together, of course, with the Volvo badge, there is no indication to curious strangers, of which I encountered many, that this is the P1800 version of this well-made Swedish motor car.

Push-button exterior door handles are used and all the lamps are Lucas, except for Robo headlamps, which give excellent illumination.

The bonnet opens from the trailing edge to reveal the 1,780-c.c. 5-bearing, twin-carburetter engine with polished valve cover.

Continued

VOLVO P1800 ROAD TEST—continued

Lucas battery, oil filler and dip-stick are accessible but the spare fuse and main fuse-box are tucked too snugly up under the bonnet sill. The wiring is a strange mixture of Bosch and Lucas, the harness being Lucas, the fuse-box Bosch, while the coil and distributor are Bosch. The bonnet is automatically retained in the open position but, irritatingly, the prop needs human aid before it will release. The bonnet-panel seats on a tubular bar but didn't follow the curve of the scuttle as snugly as one would have liked. Volvo safety-belts with good release mechanism are standard equipment.

Driving the Volvo P1800

The Volvo P1800 can claim to have an excellent driving position. The 2-spoke rigid 16-in. steering-wheel is well placed; its spokes have rather dramatic lightning holes. Two slender, slightly too short stalks control, on the right, direction-flashers and daylight full-beam headlamps flashing, on the left the horn. The latter stalk is slightly higher than its fellow and would be more instantaneously available if it were not. The horn note is a depressing growl, matched by that sounded by the steering-wheel hub, the advertised presence of loud and soft horn notes not being apparent.

The short, rigid gear-lever protruding from the transmission tunnel couldn't be better placed. But unless the clutch, which has a very long travel, is fully depressed, the gear-change is affected, and the lever also " hangs up," so that rapid change of ratio are rendered unpleasant. This is a pity, in view of the excellence of the lever and the silence of the indirect gears. The clutch is positive and not heavy but has, as has been said, too long a movement, so those without long legs are obliged to sit closer to the steering-wheel than they would wish in order to change gear cleanly. This apart, the change is acceptable and the synchromesh effective. There is unduly strong spring loading to the right, or high ratios, side of the gate and a heavy spring to be overcome before the lever can be lifted to engage reverse, beyond the 1st gear position.

The Volvo is not a light car and it rides in a " dead " manner. But it is very comfortable, even on bad roads, and roll when cornering ambitiously is consistent and by no means excessive. Only occasionally are you aware that there is a rigid back axle although it does add to the liveliness of the ride; it is sprung on coil-springs and located by radius arms and a Panhard rod. Front suspension is wishbones and coil-springs, with anti-roll bar. The steering, geared just over 3-turns lock-to-lock, with mild but useful return action, is positive and accurate. It transmits no kick-back but " rocks " a little from straight-ahead as the front wheels ride obstructions.

The cornering tendency is towards initial understeer but the throttle can be used to bring the tail out on wet roads and generally the P1800 takes corners very predictably, can be flung about without alarming consequences and normally has neutral cornering, the steering pleasantly light and smooth except at very low speeds.

The handbrake lever, with safety guard for the ratchet-button thumb, lies unobtrusively by the outside of the driver's seat cushion—out of the way, yet very conveniently to hand. The Girling 10.9-in. disc front and drum rear brakes are very powerful, progressive, light and in every way an asset to the car. They are vacuum-servo-assisted, with very slight lag in light applications. Girling make the best disc brakes and they work superbly in this Anglo-Swedish application. Neither under fast cornering nor heavy braking do the British Pirelli Cintura tyres emit any sounds of protest.

Because this handsome coupé is a comparatively heavy car relying on a push-rod o.h.v. 100-b.h.p. engine performance is not particularly noteworthy. In the gears speeds of 28, 45 and 67 m.p.h. are possible at 6,000 r.p.m., and a top-cog cruising speed of 70 m.p.h. is readily attainable, in fact in just over 18 sec. from letting-in the clutch. A rather longer straight road allows this to be extended to 80 m.p.h. but a considerable distance is required in which to attain the top speed, in overdrive, of 105 m.p.h. For some unapparent reason the Volvo feels to be going faster than, in fact, it is, at speeds around 50 m.p.h. The speedometer is not to blame, as it is only 1 m.p.h. fast at 50, two at 60 m.p.h. At 85 m.p.h. in overdrive the engine is lazing at under 4,000 r.p.m., the same crankshaft rate in top equalling 60 m.p.h. In fact, the lower gears are rather too low, and I should be interested to try the P1800 in its native country, where an axle ratio of 4.1 to 1, with or without overdrive, is used, instead of the 4.56-to-1 ratio of the test car. As it is, overdrive is flicked in and out frequently, because at times the normal top gear feels too low, at others overdrive is too high. Its switch is well placed, but if

it and the heater fan knob were changed over it might be possible to flick it without taking the left hand from the steering-wheel.

The Volvo is a smooth-travelling, quiet car for long journeys, ideal for those who want a coupé smacking of a Ferrari and a top speed well clear of the ton if they are prepared to wait for it and can put up with a s.s. ¼-mile time in excess of 19 sec. There is a crisp but never obtrusive exhaust note.

I cannot help feeling ashamed, however, of faults in British workmanship which it is improbable the meticulous engineers at Goteberg would have permitted. Besides the inoperative screen-washers and water leaks (a little more rain appeared to get past the scuttle air-intake), during the test a throttle spring came adrift and the wipers " shorted " and blew a fuse. Examination of the wiring harness in the beastliness of the gales and rain on the eve of August Bank Holiday showed very ragged wiring behind the switch and a red-hot harness, which caused severe burns before the fault was cured. A car costing over £1,836 that had ran only some 7,000 miles should be immune from such faults.

The makers claim a 10-gallon fuel tank and this ran dry from brimful in 248.8 miles, suggesting 24.8 m.p.g. under traffic conditions. A check in similar conditions gave a figure of 24.2 m.p.g. and a long run into mid-Wales returned 26.9 m.p.g., an average of 25½ m.p.g., using 100-octane fuel in deference to the 9.5-to-1 compression-ratio. Premium fuel is, however, quite acceptable. After 1,039 miles most of the sump oil had been consumed and 4½ pints were required to restore the level. Oil temperature was normally 175° F., water temperature 160° F. The engine started promptly without choke and is a smooth, willing power unit. Oil pressure varies from about 30 to 75 lb./sq. in.

In conclusion, there should be a sizeable market for this Volvo coupé on looks alone and many people requiring primarily a 2-seater will not be able to resist it. Thinking in Common Market terms, it is an exceptionally attractive proposition at its basic price of £1,335.—W. B.

Autocar road test 1884

Volvo P.1800 1,780 c.c.

BASED to a large extent on the design of their successful saloon cars, the P.1800 marks Volvo's first essay into the more expensive, luxury market. Right-hand-drive versions have been available only since last March, because previously the company had been concentrating its efforts on transatlantic sales, a fact which has obviously influenced several detail features of this car.

Most of the knowledgeable will be aware already that this car, although of Swedish ancestry, is assembled and finished in the United Kingdom. The bodies are made by Pressed Steel in Scotland, and Jensen in Birmingham, well-known both as coachbuilders and car makers in their own right, assemble the complete car using major mechanical components from Gothenburg. This Anglo-Swedish effort seems a happy compromise and certainly the large proportion of British components incorporated shows a great saving in duty for the British buyer.

Neither a sports car nor, if one is to be a purist, a true Grand Tourer, the P.1800 could well be described as a two-, occasional four-seater saloon with sporting instincts. Rear seat accommodation is mainly restricted by roof height. The high quality fixed-head coupé body allows plentiful room for luggage, and provides comfort far beyond normal

sports car refinement. On the other hand, its road behaviour is better than that normally encountered in a saloon. As an in-betweener it suits many people's needs very well and is the type of car which is oddly rare in world markets.

The power unit, which in derated form appears in what is now known as the 122 saloon, is a four-cylinder pushrod engine of 1,780 c.c., which develops 90 b.h.p. (net) at 5,500 r.p.m. As our earlier road tests have shown, the standard saloons are no sluggards; nor, naturally, is the more sporting coupé. The performance of the P.1800 is slightly handicapped by weight, since it turns the scales at 22 cwt, 0·6 cwt more than the four-door, four-seater saloon.

Compared with the 122 saloon, tested last May, the more powerful P.1800 proves slower up to 40 m.p.h. but after that pulls away to reach 90 m.p.h. in 12sec less time. A standing quarter-mile can be covered in 19·1sec and this coupé is certainly a genuine 100 m.p.h. plus motorcar.

For the four-cylinder power unit, the five-bearing crankshaft engine is adequately smooth in the middle speed range; there is a slight lumpiness at tickover speed, and at higher r.p.m. a throaty but not unpleasant intake roar which is very reminiscent, though not so loud, of the 1,582 c.c. Volvo engine. Even on the chilliest of recent summer mornings, the engine started and ran instantly without need for any choke. It started equally well when hot. The engine is very flexible and one can trickle along quite slowly in either top or overdrive top; for best performance, more-than-usual use of the gearbox must be made.

The handbook recommends an engine speed limit of 6,000 r.p.m., at which the maximum speeds in the four forward gears (all having excellent synchromesh) are 28, 45,

PRICES					
Fixed-head Coupé...	...	...	...	...	£1,335
Purchase Tax	...	...	...	...	£501 12s 9d
			Total (in G.B.)		£1,836 12s 9d

Make · VOLVO   Type · P1800

Manufacturer : AB Volvo, Göteborg, Sweden
Concessionaires : Volvo Concessionaires, Ltd., 28 Albemarle Street, London, W.1.

Test Conditions
Weather ... Dry and sunny with 7-20 m.p.h. wind
Temperature .... 56 deg. F. (13 deg. C.)
Barometer .... 29·9in. Hg.
Dry tarmac and concrete surfaces.

Weight
Kerb weight (with oil, water and half-full fuel tank)
22 cwt (2,464lb-1,118 kg)
Front-rear distribution, per cent F, 54·2; R, 45·8
Laden as tested ...... 25 cwt (2,800lb-1,270kg)

Turning Circles
Between kerbs .... L, 32ft 4in.; R, 33ft. 5in.
Between walls ...... L, 34ft 5in.; R, 35ft. 6in.
Turns of steering wheel lock to lock .... 3·25

Performance Data
Overdrive top gear m.p.h. per 1,000 r.p.m. ... 21·0
Top gear m.p.h. per 1,000 r.p.m. .... 15·0
Mean piston speed at max. power ... 2,887 ft/min.
Engine revs. at mean max. speed ...... 4,880 r.p.m.
B.h.p. per ton laden 72

FUEL AND OIL CONSUMPTION

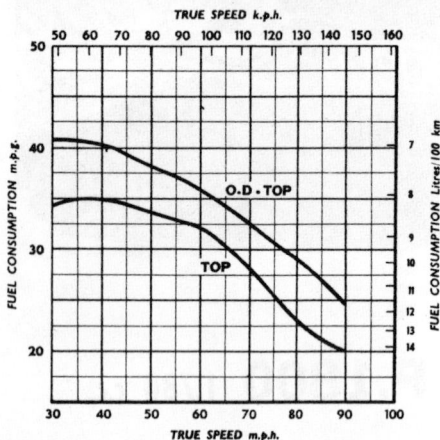

FUEL...................................Premium Grade
(97 octane RM)
Test Distance......................... 1,245 miles
Overall Consumption .... 24·9 m.p.g.
(11·35 litres/100 km)
Normal Range .... 24-32 m.p.g.
(11·77-8·83 litres/100 km)
OIL: SAE 30 ... Consumption: 10,000 m.p.g.

MAXIMUM SPEEDS AND ACCELERATION (mean) TIMES

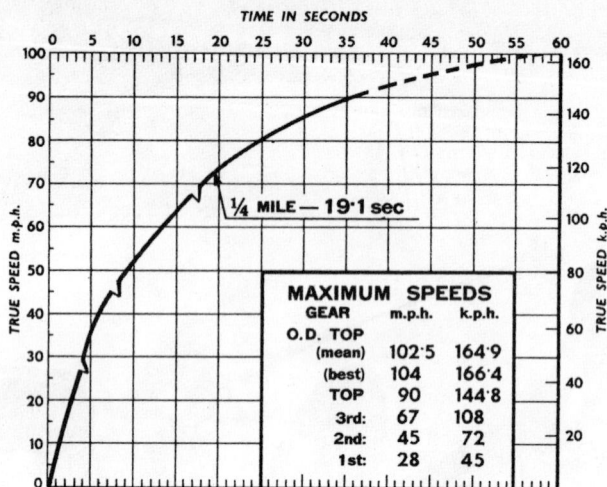

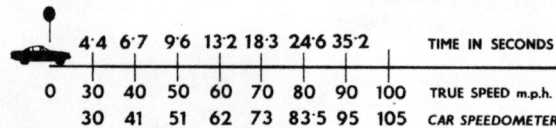

¼ MILE — 19·1 sec

MAXIMUM SPEEDS		
GEAR	m.p.h.	k.p.h.
O.D. TOP		
(mean)	102·5	164·9
(best)	104	166·4
TOP	90	144·8
3rd:	67	108
2nd:	45	72
1st:	28	45

	4·4	6·7	9·6	13·2	18·3	24·6	35·2	TIME IN SECONDS
0	30	40	50	60	70	80	90	100	TRUE SPEED m.p.h.
30	41	51	62	73	83·5	95	105	CAR SPEEDOMETER

Speed range and time in seconds

m.p.h.	O.D. Top	Top	3rd	2nd	1st
10—30	—	8·6	6·2	4·5	—
20—40	—	8·4	5·8	4·1	—
30—50	—	8·3	6·1	—	—
40—60	—	8·3	6·7	—	—
50—70	14·8	9·3	—	—	—
60—80	15·2	11·4	—	—	—
70—90	19·6	16·2	—	—	—

BRAKES	Pedal load	Retardation	Equiv. distance
(from 30 m.p.h. in neutral)	25lb	0·35g	86ft
	50lb	0·65g	47ft
	75lb	0·90g	33·6ft
	Hand brake	0·33g	92ft

CLUTCH   Pedal load and travel   45lb and 5·5in.

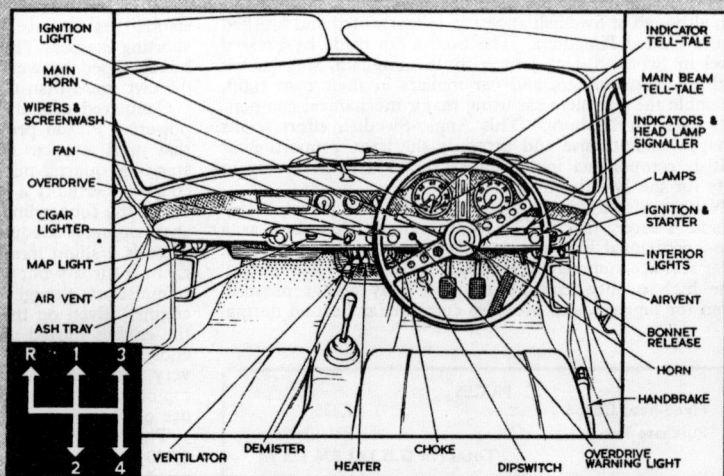

HILL-CLIMBING AT STEADY SPEEDS

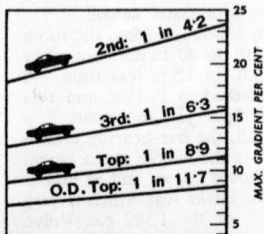

2nd: 1 in 4·2
3rd: 1 in 6·3
Top: 1 in 8·9
O.D. Top: 1 in 11·7

GEAR	O.D.			
PULL (lb per ton)	Top	Top	3rd	2nd
	190	250	350	520
Speed Range (m.p.h.)	54-60	48-53	35-45	28-35

67 and 90 m.p.h. These limits are well spaced but some of the road test staff considered the car to be slightly undergeared. However, the 4·56 to 1 rear axle ratio enables full advantage to be taken of the freely revving power unit, and gives improved acceleration. Overdrive is fitted as standard to the cars sold in this country, although in other markets this component is an option and a 4·1 to 1 axle ratio is the normal fitting. As can be seen from the gap between the maximum speeds achieved in top gear and overdrive, this unit, in fact, is doing duty as a fifth gear.

The short lever of the remote control gear-change has a pleasant action which allows positive and smooth changes. There is a rather strong spring loading towards the upper two ratios and one is initially inclined to select top inadvertently instead of second when coming out of bottom gear. Selection of reverse gear requires an upward lift and a forward and away movement; women, and others with slender wrists, might find it difficult to engage without a struggle. It is obviously much easier with a left-hand-drive version or in the saloon models because of an easier angle of movement. Smooth in its action and tireless under extreme test conditions, the clutch was entirely adequate.

A compression ratio of 9·5 to 1 is used in this engine. It was something of a surprise, therefore, to discover that it operated satisfactorily on premium grades of fuel; only if the engine was allowed to slog at slow speeds could pinking be induced.

Petrol Consumption

Consumption varied considerably with the manner of driving and the conditions encountered. The overall figure for the test was 24·9 m.p.g. and this is below that which the majority of users will return. Numerous fuel checks were taken: keeping mainly in top and overdrive, but not exceeding 60 m.p.h. on a main road, 29·5 m.p.g. was recorded. On the same road, with more frequent use of the gears and performance, this figure fell to 25·8 m.p.g. About 26-27 m.p.g. was the normal consumption for city driving in heavy traffic. On a motorway, cruising round the 90 m.p.h. mark gave a consumption of 23·5 m.p.g.; if the speed were dropped by 10 m.p.h., a consumption improvement of 5-7 m.p.g. was noted.

Girling disc brakes at the front and drums at the rear are used on the P.1800, and a Girling vacuum servo unit is fitted as standard equipment. On the test car the servo was not adjusted correctly and there was a slight lag before it acted. Until one became accustomed to this peculiarity it was difficult not to overbrake. A maximum retardation of 0·9 g was achieved at a pedal loading of 75lb—any greater pressure resulted in the rear wheels locking. The brakes give immense confidence, for they can be used, with minimum effort, hard and frequently to stop from any speed. Mounted between the door and the seat, the handbrake lever is of sufficient proportions for applying considerable leverage. The designer has thoughtfully put a guard round the release button, so that it cannot be accidentally knocked and let off when the driver is climbing in or out. The handbrake held the car on a 1-in-3 test hill, and from this incline the car moved off easily.

Few have ever complained about the roadholding of the Volvo saloons, so it is not surprising to find that the manufacturers have retained, with only detail modifications, a similar suspension layout for their more sporting coupé. In their advertisements Volvo seem to have struck the almost ideal description of their suspension—" soft, yet, at the same time, firm." Ride comfort is certainly the equal of, and perhaps better than, most other cars in this class, and the suspension coped adequately with the various special test surfaces tackled.

There is a certain amount of roll when this car is cornered fast, and it can be cornered very fast indeed. Even a series of twists taken at a speed high enough to foil cars of more sporting pretensions do not disturb the equilibrium of the P.1800. The steering characteristics are almost neutral, with just a faint trace of understeer, which provides a pleasant touch of stability under all conditions.

Light and accurate when the car is moving, the steering needs perhaps too much effort for slow speed manœuvring.

Below: This photograph shows well the compact layout of all the driving controls. The large lever below the handbrake is for the seat fore-and-aft adjustment. Above: When not in use the safety harness can be clipped up out of the way. A good ledge prevents objects sliding off the luggage shelf and the occasional seat cushions can be removed to leave deepish wells

Although the test car had covered some 5,000 miles, there still seemed to be some friction in the steering, which was most obvious through the absence of self-centring action just to either side of the dead-ahead position. On rough roads a certain amount of movement is transmitted to the steering wheel and it seems best, under these conditions, to let the wheel run lightly through the hands and allow the car to pick its own path. At slow speeds, cracks or joints in the road can be felt through the steering wheel and these deflect the car slightly; it seems possible that this may be attributable to the square-shouldered Pirelli Cintura tyres (of British manufacture) which are standard on the P.1800. Apart from this, the tyres are quiet, free from squeal and possess a most tenacious grip on the road.

On the test car the decorative wheel discs were inclined to revolve relative to the wheels and hide the tyre valves. Even when these discs were correctly positioned it was not easy to reach the valves.

Although added weight means loss in performance, this is compensated for by the fact that the body is well built, rattle-free and gives an impression of considerable strength and longevity. Astonishingly, it did not rain during the time the car was on test, but after an immersion at one of the automatic car washes the interior was found to be bone dry. Considerable quantities of sound-deadening material are used and there is a pleasant absence of road and mechanical noise, with the exception of a pronounced whine from the back axle of the test car.

Volvo were one of the pioneers of safety harness and all their cars are fitted as standard with their own combined

At present the P1800 is offered in red, white or dark grey finish. The thin, pressed wheel trims are a standard fitting

Volvo P.1800 . . .

diagonal and lap-strap type which has a sensible one-hand securing clasp. In the P.1800 the absence of rear doors allows the shoulder strap to be anchored at a better angle than in the majority of cars and the harness is thus even more comfortable than in the saloon models.

One criticism made by antagonists of seat belts is that one cannot always reach all the driving controls when strapped down. No such complaint can be levelled at the Volvo P.1800 for everything required when on the move

Although moderately crowded, there is plenty of room in the engine compartment for easy access to all items requiring any routine attention. Note the sound deadening material in the bonnet lid

is within easy reach. There is the short gear lever on the central transmission tunnel and the handbrake immediately down to the right of the seat. On the steering column to the right hand side is the trafficator switch and headlamp flasher lever and to the left one that operates the loud horn, the softer horn having a button in the hub of the steering wheel. The headlamps are adequate for normal night use, and the dip switch is on the floor.

On the facia, to the right of the steering wheel, are the ignition-cum-starter switch and the side and headlamp control incorporating the facia lighting rheostat. To the left there are switches for the excellent two-speed wipers and windscreen washers, two-speed ventilation fan and overdrive. A slightly longer lever on the overdrive switch, or interchanging it with the one for the fan, would make it much easier to flick on and off without taking one's hand from the steering wheel. All these switches are of the pull-push type, except that for the overdrive.

Powerful Heater

Beneath the facia are other controls; in the centre there is the choke and those for air-demist and heat. On the extreme right and left are those for individual control of fresh air vents located above the occupants' legs. As might be expected from a car of Scandinavian origin, the heater and demister are extremely powerful. To obtain a good supply of fresh air, one of the windows needed to be open slightly. It is a pity that the manufacturer has not chosen to make the little rear windows of extractor type, with overcentre catches. If the main side windows are opened when travelling fast, the ears of the occupants are subjected to unpleasant reverberations.

Instrumentation is complete, but unfortunately the designer has succumbed to fitting rather gimmicky dials instead of straightforward and legible faces. Immediately in front of the driver are a large revolution counter and speedometer, with oil and water thermometers set between them. The mileage recorder mounted in the face of the speedometer is almost entirely obscured by the hub of the needle. To the left there are a petrol gauge, oil pressure gauge and a clock. None of these instruments is easy to read by daylight and night makes it somewhat more difficult. The petrol gauge is so scaled that one needs to look very carefully even to get a general indication and this, coupled with a 10-gallon fuel tank, means that a normal safe driving range is just over 200 miles. There are all the usual warning lights, as well as one to indicate that overdrive is in operation.

Visibility is only moderately good, and to the front a view of the left wing is obscured by the facia-mounted driving mirror. The waistline of the body is rather high, so that most people found they were sitting a little too low in relation to it. On the other hand, the roofline is also low, so that their heads were too close to it. Someone with long legs and a shortish body seems to fit the P.1800 best.

Getting in or out of this car is naturally not so easy as with a normal saloon.

The seats are comfortable but provide limited lateral support, especially for the shoulders. The squabs are adjustable through a narrow angle, and seat trim is in leather. The floor is covered with carpet and with rubber matting where the occupants' feet lie. Over the rest of the interior the trim is of various types of synthetic material, which are of pleasing appearance except for that used to cover the cushions of the rear occasional seats, which has a peculiarly unpleasant and coarse texture. The facia and sun vizors are well padded.

There is a fair amount of room behind the front seats and it is possible to carry four adults in the car over short distances. When not used for passengers, this part provides very useful extra luggage accommodation. There are two rear parcel shelves, and small items can be stowed in little buckets on the sidewalls forward of the doors.

Large by two-seater coupé standards the boot is partly occupied by the spare wheel. To the left is the lockable fuel filler cap

The rear boot is quite capacious and has a self-supporting lid. It is necessary to move the spare wheel to take out the jack. A small kit of good-quality tools is provided.

This car is out of the ordinary in being completely free from any vice. While it is difficult to pick on any one outstanding virtue, the formula seems ideal and even at £1,850, the coupé is very well equipped. Volvo may very well have difficulty in meeting the demand.

Specification

ENGINE

Cylinders	...	4 in line
Bore	...	84·1mm (3·31in.)
Stroke	...	80·0mm (3·15in.)
Displacement	...	1,780 c.c. (108·5 cu. in.)
Valve gear	...	Overhead, pushrods and rockers
Compression ratio		9·5 to 1
Carburettor	...	Twin S.U. HS6
Fuel pump	...	AC mechanical
Oil filter	...	Full flow
Max. power	...	90 b.h.p. (net) at 5,500 r.p.m.
Max. torque	...	108 lb. ft. at 4,000 r.p.m.

TRANSMISSION

Clutch	...	Borg and Beck, single dry plate, 8·5in. dia.
Gearbox	...	Four-speed, all synchromesh
Overall ratios	...	O.D. Top 3.5, Top 4.56, 3rd 6·2, 2nd 9·1, 1st 14·3, reverse 13·34
Final drive	...	Hypoid bevel 4·56 to 1

CHASSIS

Construction	...	Integral with steel body

SUSPENSION

Front	...	Independent with coil springs and wishbones. Delco telescopic dampers. Anti-roll bar
Rear	...	Rigid axle; coil springs, radius arm, Panhard rod, Delco telescopic dampers
Steering	...	ZF cam and roller Wheel dia., 16in.

BRAKES

Type	...	Girling hydraulic; discs front, drums rear, with Girling vacuum servo
Dimensions	...	F, 10·9in. dia. R, 9·0in. dia., 2in. wide shoes
Swept area	...	F, 226 sq. in.; R, 113 sq. in. Total: 339 sq. in. (271 sq. in. per ton laden)

WHEELS

Type	...	Pressed steel, 5 studs, 4·5in. wide rim
Tyres	...	165—15in. Pirelli Cintura

EQUIPMENT

Battery	...	12-volt 57-amp. hr.
Headlamps	...	45-40 watt
Reversing lamp	...	None
Electric fuses	...	3
Screen wipers	...	2, two-speed, self-parking
Screen washer	...	Standard, Bosch electric
Interior heater	...	Standard, fresh air, two-speed fan
Safety belts	...	Standard, 3 point diagonal and lap
Interior trim	...	Leather and plastic
Floor covering	...	Carpet and rubber mats
Starting handle	...	No provision
Jack	...	Scissor type
Jacking points	...	Four points under body sills
Other bodies	...	None

MAINTENANCE

Fuel tank	...	10 Imp. gallons (no reserve)
Cooling system		15 pints (including heater)
Engine sump	...	6-8 pints SAE 20. Change oil every 3,000 miles; change filter element every 16,000 miles
Gearbox and overdrive		3·3 pints SAE 80. Change oil every 12,500 miles
Final drive		2·3 pints SAE 80. Change oil every 12,500 miles
Grease	...	8 points every 3,000 miles
Tyre pressures	...	F, 26; R, 28 p.s.i. (normal driving) F, 30; R, 32 p.s.i. (fast driving and fully laden)

Scale: 0·3in to 1ft.

Cushions uncompressed.

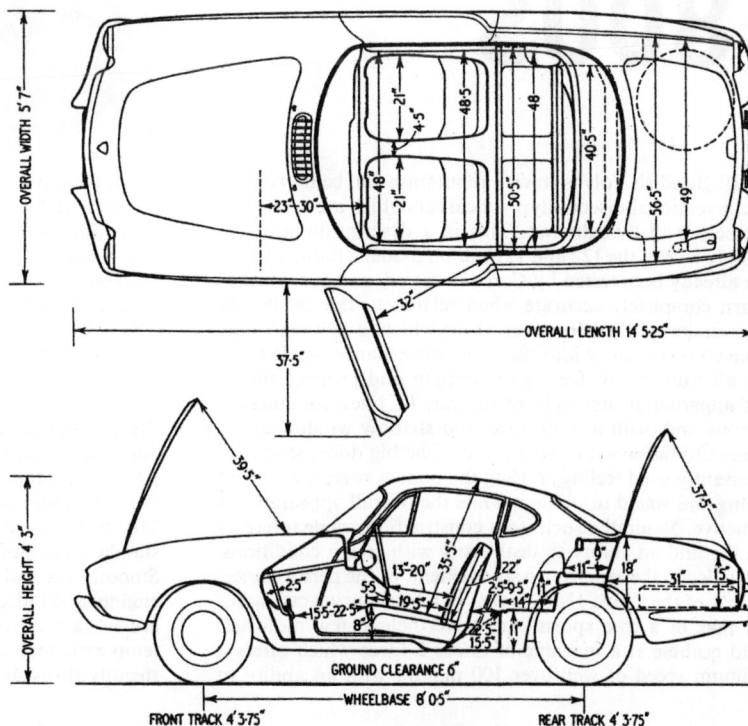

OVERALL WIDTH 5' 7"

21" 48·5 48
4·5
48" 40·5
23"-30" 21" 56·5
50·5 49
32'
OVERALL LENGTH 14' 5·25"
37·5"

OVERALL HEIGHT 4' 3"
59·5" 57·5"
13-20" 35·5" 22" 6"
2·5" 55 19·5" 11" 18" 31" 15
15·5-22·5" 2·5-9·5" 14·7"
8" 22·5" 11"
15·5

GROUND CLEARANCE 6"
WHEELBASE 8' 0·5"
FRONT TRACK 4' 3·75" REAR TRACK 4' 3·75"

VOLVO 1800S

THE Swedish Volvos have a reputation for being rugged, conventional, essentially practical cars which are in all cases extremely well thought out. This is a description which is certainly true of the 122 and 121 saloon models, both of which have already been tested by *Cars Illustrated*, and one which is in turn completely accurate when related to the 1800S, the latest version of the two-seater coupe which, a few years ago, marked Volvo's entry into the high-performance bracket.

Like all Volvos, this feeling of strength and purpose makes itself apparent at first sight of the car. Its lines are graceful, vigorous and, with a high waist and shallow window areas, slightly old-fashioned in appearance. The big doors shut with a pleasantly solid feeling; raising the bonnet reveals extensive bracing and sound insulation, while the overall appearance is distinctive. Naturally, such stout construction, while inferring long life and an ability to deal easily with rough conditions, is provided at the expense, to some extent, of the performance, and that of the Volvo 1800S is that of a fast touring car rather than that of a true sports car. Nevertheless, few motorists would quibble at a machine of under 2 litres which offers a maximum speed of well over 100 m.p.h., with an ability to

reach 60 m.p.h. from a standstill in less than 12 seconds. The mastery of the Volvo, however, is in its untiring ability to cover long distances at high speed, than in its vivid acceleration: this it does in full measure, and there can be few more comfortable cars in which to enjoy high-speed touring with a moderate fuel consumption.

The power unit is the well-known Volvo 4-cylinder engine, in 1·8 litre form, with cylinder dimensions of 84·14 mm. × 80 mm. (1,780 c.c.). As fitted to the 1800S, there are twin S.U. carburettors; overhead valves are operated by push-rods, and the crankshaft runs in five main bearings. Modified exhaust and inlet systems result in the development of slightly more power than the present model's predecessor, the P1800, and the maximum output is 108 b.h.p. at 5,800 r.p.m., with 110 lb./ft. torque at 4,000 r.p.m. An oil cooler is fitted as standard equipment.

Smoothness and flexibility are outstanding attributes of this engine, and indeed at times one can scarcely believe that there are in fact only four cylinders. There is nothing harsh or temperamental about the unit, and it develops its power steadily through a usefully wide range. Hot or cold, the test car was always easy to start, and the engine pulled well from cold, with a commendably short warm-up period: in the warm weather of the test the choke was seldom necessary for "cold" starts. An excellent top gear performance is a feature of the car, and speeds as low as 20 m.p.h. can be used in direct top gear without fuss or snatch from the transmission. At the other end of the scale, prolonged cruising at around 100 m.p.h. in the overdrive ratio optionally fitted to top gear resulted in no significant increase in water temperature, nor drop in oil pressure.

A single dry-plate clutch mates the engine to a four-speed and reverse gearbox, with synchromesh on all four forward ratios and, on the test car, the optional overdrive which operates on top gear alone. The clutch is light to use, and grips firmly and progressively, with sufficient bite to allow some wheelspin on fast take-offs. The transmission is silent in operation and the gear-lever, a short rigid control mounted on the floor, is light and has a short travel, permitting extremely fast gear changes at high r.p.m. At lower speeds the synchromesh which is powerful and effective, occasionally impedes the change of ratio, and imparts a notchy feel to the lever. The switch controlling the overdrive is mounted on the dashboard, and rapid selection of third gear occasionally caused the knuckles to foul and operate the switch inadvertently. The gear ratios are well-spaced, and with a maximum speed of only just under 80 m.p.h. third gear is particularly useful for overtaking.

The suspension, independent, with wishbones and coil springs at the front, and with a rigid rear axle sprung on coil springs and located by radius arms and a panhard rod, emphasises the fact that the Volvo is a "grand touring" car, in the widest sense of the phrase, rather than a sports machine. By sporting standards the ride is soft, a feature which is particularly noticeable at low speeds on rough surfaces. At faster gaits, however, the suspension seems to "toughen up", and even at over 100 m.p.h. there is relatively little body movement. Fast corners produced only small amounts of body roll, and on rough surfaces wheel movement is well controlled by telescopic shock absorbers. The car's steering is curiously susceptible to road camber, and needs a surprising amount of correction on steeply-cambered surfaces. For comfortable, fast touring, however, it is hard to think of a more satisfactory compromise, and the Volvo's suspension endows it with extremely likeable handling qualities, aided by pleasantly-direct, light steering which enables the car to be placed accurately. On dry roads all four wheels remain on their chosen path until the limit of the car's high cornering power is reached, with detectable understeer on fast bends. In the wet, this understeer becomes rather more pronounced, but can be readily overcome by judicious application of power, by which means the tail can be "prodded" round evenly and progressively. Directional stability is good, and the body is little affected by gusty side-winds. Excellent stopping power is provided by splash-protected disc brakes at the front and large-diameter drums at the rear, with vacuum servo assistance. Pedal pressure is light, and repeated applications from high speed produced no indication of fade or uneven pulling, despite the fact that the task of stopping this fairly heavy car gives them a good deal of hard work.

The interior of the car is laid out almost ideally for transporting two people over long distances in comfort and with convenience. In fact, the seating arrangements provide for the occasional transport of four people, and during the test four adults were in fact carried on a journey of some eighty miles, in hot weather, without discomfort other than restricted head-room in the rear. The rear seats are rather more generously provided with padding than is usually found in similar circumstances, and the cushions are supported on hammocks of rubber straps. The front seats, with adjustable back-rests and a generous range of fore and aft adjustment, are extremely

compared with similar machines more directly intended as sporting vehicles. A mean maximum speed of 108·7 m.p.h., together with the optional overdrive on top gear which provides 100 m.p.h. at just over 4,000 r.p.m., gives a cruising speed which, at somewhere in the upper nineties, is well within the car's compass. In actual fact, the 1800S can be cruised extensively at three-figure speeds without any sign of distress, lubricant and coolant temperature and pressure gauges continuing to show encouraging readings. The gear ratios are well-spaced, and third provides a maximum speed of 78 m.p.h., while the suitability of the other ratios is indicated by acceleration figures from rest to 60 m.p.h. in 11·9 seconds, and from rest to 80 m.p.h. in 20·9 seconds. During our performance test we recorded an unusually fast time for the standing-start quarter-mile, a searching judge of the car's acceleration, with a mean time of 17·9 seconds—the best one-way time recorded was 17·5 seconds, both worthy of much faster cars.

The Volvo is an unusually non-tiring car to drive fast for long distances: its rugged strength, and a complete absence of rattles or draughts, combines with a lusty character which makes the car seem to enter into the spirit of things. There is generous luggage space, and for long-distance fast touring the car would be difficult to improve. Despite the car's weight of over 22 cwt., with driver and fuel aboard, it remains economical even when the performance is fully used. Our overall consumption figure for the test mileage was exactly 24 m.p.g., and this could be improved, under less vigorous driving, to 28 m.p.g.

comfortable, and provide adequate lateral support as well as being well-upholstered. With the Volvo's rather high scuttle and waist lines, the driving position is rather low in the car for optimum visibility, and this is further impaired by the standard scuttle-mounting of the rear-view mirror. Most owners would probably re-locate this fitting, possibly suspending it from the top screen-rail. In other respects, however, the Volvo's driving position is good: the adjustment of the seat cushion and squab combines with a well-angled steering wheel and sensibly laid-out controls to provide an arrangement which is comfortable and efficient. Pedals are well-arranged for heel and toe operation, and the instrumentation is adequately full. A matching speedometer and rev-counter, the former incorporating trip and total mileage recorders, as well as warning lights for ignition and headlamp main beams, are set immediately in front of the driver with, between them, water and engine oil temperature gauges. A fuel contents gauge (its dial occasionally obscured by the steering wheel rim), oil pressure gauge and a clock are located in the centre of the facia, while along the lower edge of the dashboard are switches controlling the two-speed screen wipers and washers, lighting, ventilation and heating, overdrive and the ignition/starter switch. Two stalks protruding from the steering column operate flashing direction indicators, headlamp flashers and a loud-tone horn: this latter control is handily-placed and, on fast journeys on crowded roads, much appreciated. Instrument needles are well-damped and easily read.

In terms of performance the Volvo must be judged on fast touring standards, although it shows up far from badly when

Cars on Test

VOLVO 1800S

Engine: Four cylinder; 84.14 mm. × 80 mm. (1,780 c.c.); pushrod-operated overhead valves; compression ratio 10.0 to 1; twin S.U. carburetters; 108 b.h.p. at 5,800 r.p.m.

Transmission: Single dry-plate clutch; four-speed and reverse gearbox with synchromesh on all four forward gears and central remote-control gearlever; overdrive on top gear only.

Suspension: Front, independent, with wishbones, coil springs and anti-roll bar; rear, rigid axle with torque tube and coil springs. Telescopic dampers front and rear. Tyres: 165 × 15.

Brakes: Front, 11 ins. discs; rear, 9 ins. drums.

Dimensions: Overall length, 14 ft. 5¼ ins. overall width, 5 ft. 7 ins; overall height, 4 ft. 2¾ ins; turning circle, 30 ft; dry weight 23.5 cwt.

PERFORMANCE

	m.p.h.			secs.
MAXIMUM SPEED	—109.1	ACCELERATION	0–30 —	3.9
(Mean of 2 ways)	—108.7		0–40 —	6.1
			0–50 —	8.6
SPEEDS IN GEARS	First — 33.0		0–60 —	11.9
			0–70 —	15.8
	Second — 50.0		0–80 —	20.9
			0–90 —	26.8
	Third — 78.0		0–100 —	41.0
	Direct Top —106.0	Standing quarter-mile		— 17.9

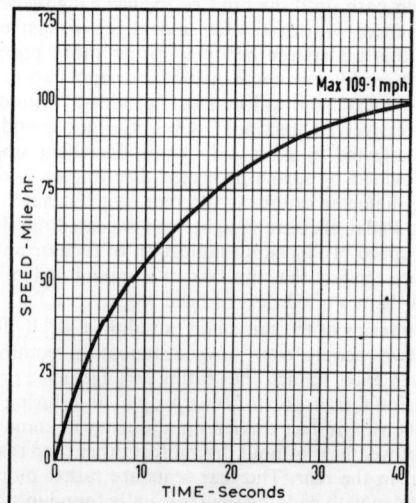

Max 109·1 mph

Concessionaires: Volvo Concessionaires Ltd., 28 Albemarle Street, London, W.1.
Price: £1,651 2s. 11d. including purchase tax.

VOLVO 1800 S *(Continued from page 44)*

(particularly between 1st and 2nd), there's no annoying wait for things to get stirred up and ready to go. You don't need to keep it wound up like you have to with one of those funny little foreign cars in order to get anywhere.

The Volvo people told us we wouldn't be able to lock up the rear brakes. A new relief valve mechanism has been added that balances braking force between the front discs and the rear drums, to help prevent locking the rears as weight transfers forward during hard braking. Thus challenged, we set out to lock up the rears, even going so far as to make panic stops on ice and rain-slick surfaces. To our chagrin, we failed. We could lock up all four wheels easily enough, but we could never lock up the rear alone.

There is some nose dive under hard braking, which surprised and annoyed us at first. Thirty miles of bashing about and we'd forgotten about it. The car stops straight and true, very securely. And we failed to fade the brakes, either. But believe us, we tried.

The nose dive, combined with a fair amount of body lean during cornering, helps form one of the strongest impressions the 1800 S left us with: its Alfa-ish nature. The car is like a heavier, solider, very torquey Alfa. Other aspects contribute: the high winding, throaty-sounding 4-cylinder engine; the excellent sound-damping (in contrast to Volvo sedans, the 1800 suffers very little from road noise); and the unattractive, dumb, and distinctly vague instrument panel design. Thick, chrome bezels adorn small controls, and the speedometer's numbers are too large and too few. In this last respect, the Volvo may be even worse than the last Alfa we looked at. It's a jarring note in an otherwise tasteful interior.

While we're carping, we'd like the car better if there were a little more clearance between steering wheel and padded dash. A horn button that didn't require removing one hand from the steering wheel would be nice. The window cranks are very awkwardly located. Trunk space could be larger, although the car is so obviously a two-seater that we presume it will seldom be used on long trips in such a situation that the luggage space behind the fold-down rear seat back wouldn't be available.

Another complaint, minor but unfortunately difficult to remedy, is the angle at which the suspended clutch pedal meets the floorboard—right at the juncture with the firewall. With pedal fully depressed, your shoe sole is horizontal, but your toe is bent back at a 45° angle. It's uncomfortable, and gives you crap-shooter's toes.

And that's *it,* in the complaint department. We couldn't figure out another change that would add to the livability of the car. Nice touches abound: the seats, for example, are adjustable back and forth, up and down, and in the angle of both the seat back and the seat cushion itself. *And,* by virtue of a screw slot adjustment in the back of the seat back, rubber bands within the seat back can be tightened or loosened at will to give a softer or harder seat back. The people from Volvo designate this infinitely variable lumbar support.

The first 6000 Volvo 1800s were assembled in England by the Jensen people. After Serial Number 6000, assembly was moved back to Sweden (although the bodies are still made in England), where the 1800s are put together on an assembly line alongside the trusty 122 S. Detail work, finish, and overall solidity of the final product have all improved markedly since Swedish assembly was started.

Those first 1800s (called the P-1800 originally) were a trifle overweight, a bit underpowered, and suffered from a drastic lack of head room. By contrast the new version is scrumptuously comfortable, and will hold its own with any GT car made, in that crucial (to Grand Touring) 60-90-mph range. What it lacks in acceleration, it makes up in controllability; what it doesn't have in brute horsepower, it more than compensates for in rugged strength and longevity. The latest Volvo 1800 S is a marvelous combination of well-tried ideas which have been lovingly executed.

And if a single feeling can sum up a car, our reaction to the 1800 is this: it has all the stability and solidity and creature comfort of a large car; it has all the controllability and verve of a small car. You don't pay the small-car price of nervous, dodgy, down-the-road handling and enervating noise levels. You don't pay the big car price of ponderousness, lack of operating economy, and wasted space. All you give up are that last, delicate, road-racing grade of handling sophistication on one hand, and that last, awe-inspiring, dragstrip grade of raw power on the other. There are some of us who can live quite happily without either one. **c/o**

THE Volvo 1800S is an unusual car. Though it is a sporting fixed-head coupé, with an occasional rear seat, it is very solidly constructed and most luxuriously equipped, with no thought of weight saving. It is fairly costly, but by employing a four-cylinder engine the makers have kept down the fuel consumption to a figure which is acceptable on the Continent.

The engine is an orthodox five-bearing unit with pushrod-operated overhead valves, but it differs from typical modern practice in having a gear-driven camshaft. Twin SU carburetters are fitted. The Volvo gearbox was one of the first to have synchromesh on bottom gear (no, I haven't forgotten Alvis!), and it has a pleasantly short lever mounted on a remote control tunnel. The propeller shaft is divided, with a central steady bearing, and the hypoid axle is positively located both fore and aft and laterally, the suspension being by helical springs.

An orthodox wishbone front end also has helical springs and a torsional anti-roll bar, with cam and roller steering. The Girling brakes have discs in front and servo assistance. The Pirelli Cinturato tyres are fitted with inner tubes.

The body is of an attractive shape, though the low roof line entails the use of a rather shallow screen and windows. One seems to sit low down inside the car but the all-round view is nevertheless perfectly satisfactory. A delightful instrument panel carries such dials as oil pressure *and* temperature gauges, as well as the more usual one for water temperature. The upholstery and carpets are of the highest grade.

The big four-cylinder engine of the Volvo is quite flexible and will pull strongly at low speeds. It revs. very freely, running well past the 6,000 r.p.m. mark as a matter of course, but it gets pretty busy as the revs. rise. There is some vibration, which is usual with a four-cylinder unit of 1,800 c.c., but the overdrive permits fast cruising with the engine running below its busy speed. This gives the easy and effortless running that a big four can so well provide.

The gearchange is excellent and the gears are quiet, while the clutch grips well after a quick change. A very good feature is the use of direct connection by rods of the accelerator, without any flexible cable. Flexible cables usually give a sticky, jerky movement, and to eliminate this source of trouble is to guarantee a permanently smooth operation. The brakes are also sweet in action, though they are powerful when a panic stop is demanded.

Fairly wide spacing of the gears is not noticeable with this flexible engine. I went a little over the 6,000 r.p.m. mark to reach 50 m.p.h. in second gear and 70 m.p.h. in third, to the benefit of the acceleration graph. Curiously enough, the well-located rear axle hops

JOHN BOLSTER
road tests
the

VOLVO
1800S

a bit during a rapid getaway, but it behaves very well on bumpy corners. It is possible to touch 97 m.p.h. on the direct top gear, but most people would prefer to use the overdrive above 80 m.p.h., in the interest of smoother and quieter running.

The steering is quite light to handle, in spite of the fairly substantial weight of the car. The handling characteristic is neutral, though the tail can be hung out on power. This is a car which never does anything unexpected, nor does it suddenly change its handling in the middle of a corner. The comfortable seats give good support but the scuttle and bonnet line are rather high for a short driver. There is some roll during fast cornering.

Giving plenty of space, the boot is partly occupied by the spare wheel, though this is enclosed in a cover. There is useful additional space on a shelf behind the folding rear seat back, but there is a shortage of storage room for odds and ends in the front compartment, there being no glove locker or map shelf. Laminated glass is standard, so a suddenly opaque screen need not be feared. Much of the detail work repays close study, the method of pulling down and securing the bonnet without slamming it being worthy of praise. The doors shut nicely but the rear quarter lights do not open. The controls of the heating system are sensibly arranged.

The 1800S is not really a sports car, but it will exceed 100 m.p.h. with something in hand. It would be a pleasant vehicle for long journeys, though it is also suitable for shopping as the large doors make entry and exit quite easy, in spite of the low roof line. Safety is very much to the fore, for Volvo was one of the first manufacturers to standardize safety belts. The car is also thoroughly safe in its handling, and the immensely strong and rigid steel structure would be a splendid protection.

The Volvo 1800S is a thoroughly well-made medium-sized car with many luxurious appointments. Its unusual appearance singles it out from the rows of ordinary saloons, and if it is rather costly for a four-cylinder machine it has an individuality that will appeal particularly to the fair sex. It has obviously been built to have a very long life and to stand up to the toughest conditions. It carries an honoured name which is respected all over the world.

SPECIFICATION AND PERFORMANCE DATA

Car Tested: Volvo 1800S fixed-head coupé, price £1,814 1s. 3d.

Engine: Four-cylinders 84.14 mm. × 80 mm. (1,780 c.c.). Pushrod-operated overhead valves. Compression ratio 10 to 1. 108 b.h.p. (gross) at 5,800 r.p.m. Twin SU carburetters. Bosch coil and distributor.

Transmission: Single dry plate clutch. Four-speed all-synchromesh gearbox with central remote control and Laycock-de Normanville overdrive, ratios 3.34 (overdrive), 4.56, 6.16, 9.07 and 14.27 to 1. Divided propeller shaft. Hypoid rear axle.

Chassis: Combined steel chassis and body. Independent front suspension with wishbones, helical springs and anti-roll bar. Cam and roller steering gear. Rear axle on two pairs of radius arms, Panhard rod and helical springs. Telescopic dampers all round. Servo-assisted hydraulic brakes with discs in front and drums at rear. Bolt-on pierced disc wheels, fitted 165-15 in. Pirelli Cinturato tyres.

Equipment: Twelve-volt lighting and starting. Speedometer. Rev. counter. Water and oil temperature gauges. Oil pressure and fuel gauges. Clock. Cigar lighter. Heating, demisting and ventilation system. Two-speed windscreen wipers and washers. Flashing direction indicators. Seat belts.

Dimensions: Wheelbase, 8 ft. 0½ in.; Track, 4 ft. 3¼ ins.; Overall length, 14 ft. 5¼ ins.; Width, 5 ft. 7 ins.; Weight, 1 ton 2 cwt.

Performance: Maximum speed, 104.6 m.p.h. (overdrive). Speeds in gears: direct top, 97 m.p.h.; third, 70 m.p.h.; second, 50 m.p.h.; first, 31 m.p.h. Standing quarter-mile, 18.6 secs. Acceleration: 0-30 m.p.h., 3.6 secs.; 0-50 m.p.h., 9 secs.; 0-60 m.p.h., 13 secs.; 0-80 m.p.h., 23.2 secs.

Fuel Consumption: 23 to 27 m.p.g.

ACCELERATION GRAPH

VOLVO 1,800S

Vunderful Volvo

Barry Cooke tries stretching the long legs of Sweden's P1800S, and finds it very classy indeed. As it ought to be, at $5300 . . .

ONE thing about television. At least the kids are getting to know their cars.

There I was the other day driving the Volvo P1800S coupe past a very posh private school on Sydney's North Shore. One Billy Bunter type shouted, "There's the Saint!" and the entire school — which was at recess — turned and watched as the Volvo whispered past.

I'd have been something less than an ordinary human being not to derive pleasure at the sidelong glances which came the way of the Volvo while I had it.

It's that sort of car — sleek, unusual looking, and not sufficiently well known yet to arouse anything but interest, curiosity and envy in the average bystander.

I found it a car that takes time to learn. The controls don't encourage sloppy driving techniques, although once you get the hang of things it is really an easy and forgiving car to operate.

Consequently, I found the concentration it demanded to be well driven awakened in me much of the traditional pleasure of motoring, dulled by a long string of lesser cars.

Learning the Volvo is a problem which can't be solved in a hurry. The low seating position, combined with high waistline and low roofline, restricts visibility to such a degree that, for the first few hours of driving, you're not sure of the precise position of the car's extremities.

Learning to use the gears is another thing. There is very little movement between positions, either fore and aft or across the gate.

This proves to be a good thing if correct techniques are used — such as palming the lever backhand for a change from first to second or third to second. Do it any other way, and it's odds on that you'll find top, accompanied of course by some embarrassing coughing and spitting from the motor.

Once you realise that the Volvo is a car that demands correct driving techniques, it responds perfectly and does everything asked of it.

Styling

I've - said - it - before - and - I'll - say - it - again: styling likes and dislikes are very much a matter of taste.

The P1800 has the sort of looks that are universally impressive to the uninitiated: low, streamlined, rakish, functional — sexy, if you like.

Aerodynamically it is first-class, with that near-perfect wedge shape designed for good penetration.

Appearance of this model is only slightly changed from its predecessor.

Most obvious difference is the wheels, which are now distinctively slotted to improve brake cooling.

There are also rubber bumper overriders front and rear to improve protection. The bumpers themselves are more solidly constructed and firmly braced, so they should be some help in the event of a biff.

Slight changes to the grille give the P1800 a slightly smiling countenance, and the egg-crate insert of yore has been replaced by a metal mesh stamping.

Inside, seats are modified to improve comfort and support. They do both, although there is still room for improvement in the latter department.

Comfortwise, they have no peer, and even include an adjustable

TOP: *The classically sleek profile of the P1800S.* LEFT: *Front view shows essential simplicity of line.* ABOVE: *Rear doesn't quite reach the same standard, and vision isn't all it could be.* BELOW: *Those seats are very comfortable — but they could give more support.*

VUNDERFUL VOLVO

lumbar support that slides up and down inside the backrest.

Instrumentation is very comprehensive, includes a speedo, tacho, oil pressure gauge, oil temperature gauge, water temperature gauge, and fuel gauge. There is no ammeter, just a warning light marked "Gen."

There are simple button controls for two-speed wipers (with integrated washer), manual choke, lights, and a very efficient heater-demister unit.

The whole effect of the cockpit is spoiled to some extent by rather "stylistic" dash decor. The instruments are sparsely calibrated, and stand proud from the instrument panel in chunky chrome-plated surrounds.

However, in their favor is a very good lighting system that brought an envious comment from an overseas airline pilot friend. He wished the 707 layout was as well lit as the Volvo's.

Driving position is very good, and, thanks to infinite seat adjustment possibilities, should fit everyone. Foot pedals are well spaced, and big.

In addition to individual front seats, there is a small upholstered bench in the rear. Rakish angle of the rear roofline cuts down headroom severely here, but it is nonetheless a useful area for two small children.

Its usefulness is further enhanced by provisions which allow the seat to be folded flat and converted into a luggage compartment to supplement the boot.

The latter, incidentally, is quite a reasonable size, but spoiled by the spare wheel laid flat on the floor. If you're game to travel without a spare, it will take quite a good load.

Mechanicals

Volvo's power unit is a thoroughly refined ohv water-cooled four. Originally a 1.5-litre, it was enlarged to 1780c.c. for inclusion in the P1800 and 122 sedan series.

So massively strong is it that considerably more boring and stroking could be done without risk.

It is quite conventional in layout, using in the coupe a compression ratio of 11 to 1 and twin 1¾in. SU's. It develops 115 bhp at 6000 rpm and 112 ft./lb. of torque at 4000 rpm. That compression ratio makes the addition of a high-power additive like methyl benzine almost arbitrary.

If you're stuck, it will run on straight super, but not very quietly.

Most striking aspect of the motor is its almost indecent smoothness, which is superior to any other four I've ever driven. It will trickle down to 20 mph in top and accelerate away almost like a turbine. Very impressed, I was.

The generous proportions of the five-bearing crankshaft, which has a huge inbuilt safety margin, account for much of this.

Gearbox, as already mentioned, encourages correct usage. But it, too, is very smooth when mastered, the short lever with its contoured knob slicing through the gate like the proverbial hot knife.

Fully synchronised, the ratios are

SPECIFICATIONS

ENGINE: 4 cylinders in line, o.h.v.; bore 84.14mm., stroke 80mm., capacity 1780c.c.; compression ratio 11:1; maximum bhp 115 (gross) at 6000 rpm; maximum torque 112 ft./lb. at 4000 rpm; twin 1.75in. SU carburettors, mechanical fuel pump, 12 volt ignition.

TRANSMISSION: Single dry-plate clutch, 4-speed, all synchro gearbox with electric overdrive on top; ratios: 1st, 3.13; 2nd, 1.99; 3rd, 1.36; 4th, 1.00; 5th o/d 0.756. Final drive 4.56:1.

SUSPENSION: Independent front by coils, wishbones and hydraulic telescopic dampers; rigid rear axle by longitudinal support arms, longitudinal torques arms, track rod, coil springs and hydraulic telescopic dampers.

STEERING: Cam and roller; 3½ turns lock to lock; 32ft. 10in. turning circle.

BRAKES: Disc/drum, servo assisted; 339 sq. in. of swept area.

WHEELS: Steel disc with 165 by 15 tubed tyres.

DIMENSIONS: Wheelbase 8ft. ½in.; track, front, 4ft. 3¾in.; rear 4ft. 3¾in.; length 14ft. 5¼in.; width 5ft. 7in.; height 4ft. 2½in.; clearance 6in.

FUEL CAPACITY: 10 gallons.

KERB WEIGHT: 23 cwt.

PERFORMANCE

CONDITIONS: Fine and hot; two occupants; 100 octane fuel.

BEST SPEED: 108 mph.

FLYING ¼-mile average: 105 mph.

STANDING ¼-mile average: 18.2 sec.

MAXIMUM in gears: 1st, 33 mph; 2nd, 50; 3rd, 70; 4th, 96.

ACCELERATION from rest through gears: 0-30 mph, 3.7s.; 0-40, 5.8s.; 0-50, 8.2s.; 0-60, 12.0s.; 0-70, 15.8s.; 0-80, 20.9s.; 0-90, 27.3s.

ACCELERATION in top (with third in brackets): 20-40 mph, 8.8s. (6.1s.); 30-50, 9.1s. (6.2s.); 40-60, 9.5s. (6.5s.); 50-70, 9.6s. (7.5s.); 60-80, 10.2s.; 70-90, 10.3s.

BRAKING: 33ft. to stop from 30 mph in neutral; 144ft. to stop from 60 mph in neutral.

FUEL CONSUMPTION: 27.1 mpg over 245 miles, including all tests.

SPEEDOMETER: ½ mph fast at 50; 1 mph fast at 70.

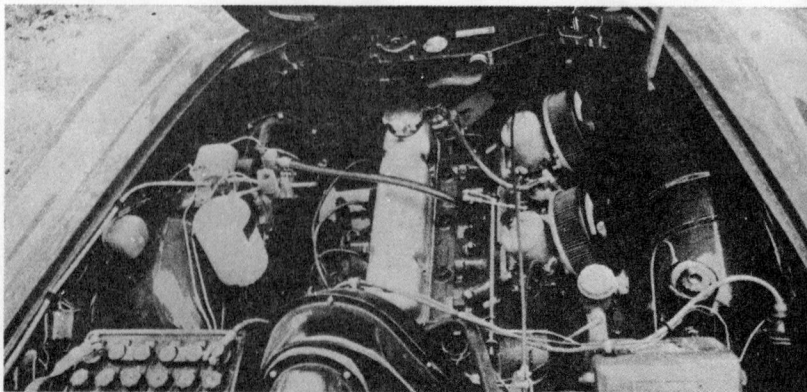

well chosen, and have the added attraction of an electric overdrive on top gear. This overdrive, operated by a small wand on the steering column, has a ratio of 0.756 to 1, and is good for 21.2 mph per 1000 rpm.

Clutch is one of the sweetest I've ever used, is gradual in take-up, and reasonably light in operation.

Suspension is a conventional coil and wishbone set-up at the front. The rigid rear axle, however, is located by a complex system employing two longitudinal support arms and two longitudinal torque arms. Transverse location of the axle is taken care of by a track rod attached to the axle near the nearside coil spring and to the chassis just inside the offside wheelarch.

Very effective, too.

Big discs are fitted on the front, and they are heavily shrouded to protect them from dust and rubbish thrown up by the wheels. Rear drums complement the discs.

Swept area of the brakes is 339 sq. in. A brake servo unit is standard equipment, although its effect is so well controlled that it is virtually undetectable in use.

Pedal pressures are light, but not so light as to suggest servo assistance, and for that reason I like it.

On the Road

The P1800 is at its best on the open road, where its fairly soft ride and long overdrive legs make it ideal for really swift cruising.

Ninety mph can be maintained quite comfortably in overdrive, this being equivalent to about 4300 rpm.

At these speeds the springy, responsive cam-and-roller steering gives precise control, and the excellent

brakes are a considerable reassurance.

Ride is surprisingly soft, and there is also a considerable amount of body lean.

As is often the case, though, it's not really noticeable from inside the car, although on one or two occasions I partially slid from the seat.

Lateral location of passengers is greatly helped by the excellent three-point safety belts which are standard.

Vigorous cornering on loose surfaces is great fun, thanks to the absolute predictability of the Volvo's behavior. Under such circumstances all cars can be made to oversteer in the sense that the tail will hang out.

Not all, however, will respond with the rapidity and precision of the P1800.

On sealed surfaces we never once succeeded in getting the back end unstuck. An acceptable degree of understeer was evident in all the corners we tackled, no matter how fast.

Travelling fast over rough surfaces produced only subdued noise from the suspension, and at all times the car seemed to have all four feet well and truly planted on the ground.

Not until we came to our performance tests were we troubled by fierce wheelspin and back axle tramp — all this despite the track rod and torque rods.

We solved the problem (only partly the fault of the Volvo, for the bitumen of the strip was very hot and consequently sticky) by popping the clutch on about 2500 rpm.

The motor would die momentarily, then pick up and spin right out — well into the red zone above 6000 rpm unless we were very quick with the gear-change.

Turbine-smooth right through the

range, the motor is one of the mo outstanding features in an altogeth outstanding car.

But the other components — gearbox, clutch and brakes—have a brand of excellence seldom experienced these days. They operated smoothly and without complaint throughout the pretty merciless pounding.

The effectiveness of our methods of getting it off the line is amply demonstrated by the figures in the performance panel. They're very good.

Keeping all this performance potential company is a set of brakes which are altogether excellent. As mentioned, pedal pressures, despite servo assistance, aren't so light that the brakes are grabby.

They retain a surprising amount of "feel" and consequently can be used with great precision.

Noise is not obtrusive until the motor is revved hard, although I feel sure this series of the coupe is not as well insulated as earlier models.

With all the windows in place, wind noise is very subdued, a tacit comment on the car's excellent streamlining.

Returning to the city from our out-of-town test strip, we were able to stretch the Volvo's long legs on some of N.S.W.'s fastest rural roads.

The car demonstrated that it has all the ingredients necessary for hour after hour of effortless high-speed motoring. It remained balanced and poised throughout the journey, out-braking, out-accelerating, and out-handling every other car we came across.

It left an indelible impression on my mind, just as I'm sure it will do on anyone else who is lucky enough to drive it. •

Instrument layout is handsome and legible.

Tuned intake tracts, plenum chamber, injector tubes and vacuum plumbing can be seen in this view of new engine.

80▶ found it capable of taking the fastest slam shifts without a crunch. The linkage was a bit stiff on the test car but this should improve with more miles. Overdrive, the Laycock-de Normanville unit which shifts hydraulically and without lifting of the throttle foot, gives high cruising speeds with little mechanical strain although it engages jerkily.

Driving the 1800 always takes us back in time. The windshield and steering wheel (a nice new one with padded rim) are extremely close, putting the doors so far back that one has to reach across himself with his inboard arm to wind the windows; and the windowsills are so high as to make us feel as if we're sitting in a deep bathtub. The control layout isn't bad, nor are the instruments which are handsomer than ever; however, the speedometer in the test car was outrageously optimistic. Nice touches, like the good 3-point belts and the excellent seats (which, incredibly, on our test car didn't have the legally required seatback locks) with their adjustable lumbar section, are offset by poor assembly and detail design here and there—for instance, terrific wind noise caused by poorly sealing windwings or an overdrive light that's blindingly bright.

Over all kinds of roads the 1800E has a good ride though it is prone to pitching on gently undulating pavement; there is adequate vertical suspension travel so that it takes large bumps and dips in stride, and well designed linkage for the rear live axle minimizes the usual failing—primarily wheel hop—of this type of suspension. The steel-belted Michelin radials, replacing Pirelli Cinturatos used before, give noticeably increased cornering power but transmit considerable drumming to a body structure already prone to rattles.

Handling is smooth and predictable. The steering has a great feel to it that really tells the driver what's going on and to boot it's light and quick—classically good sports-car steering. In enthusiastic driving it's possible to hang out the tail by a twitch of the wheel and then keep it out by application of power—all with little danger of overdoing anything because the car is so stable—but most drivers will be content to enjoy the pleasant response that the 1800E exhibits when merely being driven briskly. It's a good car for the novice driver, but an experienced and capable one can enjoy its handling as well.

The new disc brakes are a definite improvement over our last 1800S; panic-stop capability is up from 68% g to 81%. Fade is a moderate 25% but we really expected no fade at all in the tests; pedal effort is light but not too light and in the all-out stop the car stays in a straight line even though there is a mild tendency to wheel lockup.

To summarize, Volvo has kept the performance, handling and braking of the 1800 up to date. But in style, accommodations, refinement of running and the use of available body space, it has fallen 'way behind the times, and though it costs over $4500 it doesn't even have outstanding assembly quality to offset these drawbacks. If we were to·ask for a new model from Volvo—and we sincerely hope that they aren't giving up on the sports/GT market when the 1800 runs down—we'd request a car about the same size as the 1800E but with true 2+2 seating rather than the "2+1" it now has, better noise and vibration isolation and assembly quality, and the same mechanical package underneath. *Then* we might have a Volvo GT worth $4600.

COMPARISON DATA

	Volvo 1800E	Alfa Romeo 1750 GTV	Lotus Elan S4	MGB GT (overdrive)
List price	$4655	$4681	$5133	$3628
Curb weight, lb	2535	2350	1630	2310
0-60 mph, sec	10.1	9.9	9.4	13.6
Standing ¼-mi	17.5	17.3	16.8	19.6
Speed at end	80	80	83	72
Panic stop from 80 mph, % g	81	90	87	80
Fade in 6 stops from 60 mph, %	25	nil	nil	20
R&T wear index	39	60	60	69
R&T steering index	0.97	1.26	0.79	0.93
Fuel economy, mpg	20.9	21.5	27.2	23.5

CAR AND DRIVER ROAD TEST

VOLVO 1800 S

Drive it like you hate it and
ten to one you'll end up
loving the car we used to call
the Swedish Karmann Ghia

There is a certain kind of semi-sports car that has always elicited faint praise from the automotive press, particularly the purist wing. The old Mercedes-Benz 190SL best typifies that kind of car—the sort of elegant but effete conveyance that is marvelously suited for suburban—or society—wives, but really doesn't seem to have any, well, guts.

For some reason C/D has often been guilty of lumping the various past versions of the Volvo 1800 into that category. Good field, no hit. The car is beautiful, very well finished, and based on components we know and love—components that, from long and arduous duty on Volvo sedans, have proved near the ultimate in sheer rock-ribbed strength and durability, if not sophistication.

Yet the car has always seemed stolid. Very Swedish, but in the by-yumpin'-yimminy, Minnesota-lumberjack stereotype, rather than in the good-design-and-exquisite-metallurgy sense that more properly characterizes modern Sweden. A Swedish Karmann Ghia, we tended to say. After all, you can (or could, back in the Model 356 days) buy a Porsche for the same money. The car is heavy (3000 lbs.). It is conventional (4-cylinder, water-cooled front engine, rear drive, live—albeit excellently located—axle). It never seemed to promise much performance. A nice, solid GT car, we said, and dismissed it.

Cruise the new 1800 S about the boulevards—well below the new 6500-rpm red-line—and you'll never get any other impression. For this road test, we drove the 1800 a sedate 350 miles on major highways

away from New York. We also drove it a sedate 350 miles back again. Speed limits, and all that.

But in between those two sedate stints, we spent two full days of pure, plain and simple, elbows-to-the-wall bashing. We careened around narrow, back-country roads at double the speed limit, ran screaming acceleration tests and shrieking brake tests, crashed over frost heaves on seldom-tended farm roads, and generally alarmed the surrounding population (and, occasionally, our passenger). We can't recall ever giving a car such a thrashing for an ordinary road test. We also can't remember having so much sheer, uninterrupted fun with an automobile.

Maybe it's the new horsepower. The car started life as the P-1800 back in 1960, with 100 SAE horse-

power at 5500 rpm. An increase from 9:5:1 to 10:1 in compression ratio in 1964 gave eight more horsepower at 5800 rpm. Now, judicious tuning, particularly in the induction system, has raised the output to 115 at 6000 rpm. The increase doesn't do that much for acceleration times (down 1.2 seconds from 0-60), but the character of the car is subtly elevated. If you really drive it.

You sit in an almost-therapeutic leather-covered bucket seat (a couple of years ago Volvos had just about the worst seats in the automobile industry; now they're right in there in the running for the best), firmly anchored by the excellent 3-point Volvo seat belt. Your knees are bent comfortably—the seat is raked well back, giving a more chair-high effect than usual for a car this low in overall height. Your

CONTINUED

VOLVO 1800 S CONTINUED

arms are nearly straight, and you feel like Ascari already. The pedal placement is right: when the brake pedal is depressed it is on the same plane with the accelerator. The steering wheel rim is thick and solid. And right behind that rim are two stalks, one on each side, little levers that add immeasurably to the pleasure of driving fast.

The left stick is a combination turn signal and light flasher; the right is the overdrive control. Each is positioned so that you need only extend one finger from the steering wheel rim to flick it. The light flasher/turn signal control is just the thing for waking up drivers who might otherwise be startled at your rapid overtaking. The overdrive is something else again. When you are entering a fast bend just a little faster than you feel absolutely secure, and you want the reassuring support of a little more rpm and a

side loading. Nothing else happens. The car gets such fierce bite, so securely and gradually made evident to the driver, that driving it hard is a process of steadily increasing your confidence and your speed until you almost begin to feel ridiculous. You get the impression that the faster you go, the further the limit of adhesion dances on ahead of you, until finally the only factor limiting speed on winding roads is the horsepower, not the roadholding. It's a very comforting balance, particularly after trying to hurry in a big-engined American car.

The overdrive unit is worth some comment. The 1-to-1 final drive, with 4.56 rear end, gives nearly 16 mph per 1000 rpm—a fairly low ratio even for an 1800cc car. Overdrive provides a .756-to-1 final ratio, giving over 20 mph per 1000 rpm—and effortless, loafing cruising as a result. For passing, aforemen-

With a few horsepower here, some judicious tuning there, the conservative men at Volvo have broken loose and improved a GT car that turns on a nickel and stops on a dime.

little more horsepower at the rear wheels, you just touch the lever, and zap, you swap a 3.45 rear axle for a 4.56. Control. Comforting noise. And that much more punch coming out the other end of the turn to boot. It's wonderful.

It is definitely in the high speed stuff that the car comes to life. At low speeds, it's a bit heavy—a combination of steering that is a trifle stiff and considerable initial understeer make you work to hurry the car along in tight turns. But get it up above 60 mph, and you get a transformation. Bend it hard into a turn; and there is neither the scruffly scrambling of tires wanting to let go, nor any refusal to go in a new direction. You simply get a moderate body lean and a gradual increase in side loading from centrifugal force. Turn the wheel more and get more

tioned flick of the overdrive control stalk downshifts to a passing gear (true fourth) that's good to 103 mph. Overdrive gives a theoretical top speed (6500 rpm) of 136 mph. The car is, in overdrive, overgeared; it won't go that fast, but it'll get far enough over the century mark to get you into trouble on almost any highway in the United States.

The only thing we could possibly ask for in addition to this transmission/overdrive set-up would be an overdrive that is operative on third gear also, to give a ratio in the neighborhood of 5.11:1. It'd be fun, but it really isn't necessary. The B 18 B engine (Volvo's designation) is blessed with plenty of torque, despite peaking at 4000 rpm. Although the spacing of the fully synchronized transmission ratios is wide

(Text continued on page 35)

PHOTOGRAPHY: GENE BUTERA

SPECIFICATIONS OVERLEAF

VOLVO 1800S

Importer: Volvo, Inc.
Volvo Drive
Rockleigh, New Jersey
Price as Tested: $4190.95 East Coast POE

ACCELERATION

Zero To	Seconds
30 mph	3.3
40 mph	5.3
50 mph	7.2
60 mph	10.0
70 mph	15.5
80 mph	17.2
90 mph	22.1
100 mph	28.4
Standing ¼ mile	80 mph in 17.2

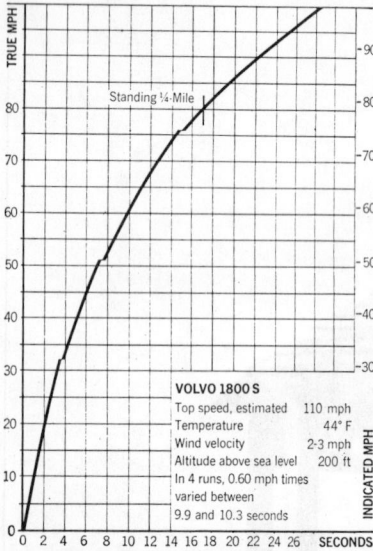

VOLVO 1800 S
Top speed, estimated 110 mph
Temperature 44° F
Wind velocity 2-3 mph
Altitude above sea level 200 ft
In 4 runs, 0.60 mph times
varied between
9.9 and 10.3 seconds

ENGINE

Water-cooled four-in-line, cast iron block, 5 main bearings
Bore x stroke........3.313 x 3.150 in, 84.14 x 80.00 mm
Displacement........108.6 cu.in, 1780 cc
Compression ratio........10.1 to one
Carburetion......Two twin-choke SU sidedraft
Valve gear...Pushrod-operated overhead valves
Power (SAE)........115 bhp @ 6000 rpm
Torque........112 lbs-ft @ 4000 rpm
Specific power output......1.06 bhp per cu.in, 64.6 bhp per liter
Usable range of engine speeds.900–6500 rpm
Electrical system...12-volt, 60 amp-hr battery, 360W generator
Fuel recommended................Premium
Mileage........................22–26 mpg
Range on 12-gallon tank.......264–312 miles

DRIVE TRAIN

Clutch........8.5-inch single dry plate
Transmission......4-speed, all synchro, plus overdrive

Gear	Ratio	Overall	mph/1000 rpm	Max mph
Rev	3.25	14.82	−4.88	−32
1st	3.13	14.27	5.07	33
2nd	1.99	9.07	7.98	51
3rd	1.36	6.20	11.65	76
4th	1.00	4.56	15.87	103
5th	.756	3.45	20.98	110

Final drive ratio................4.56 to one

CHASSIS

Wheelbase........................96.5 in
Track....................F 51.8 R 51.8 in
Length...........................173.2 in
Width.............................66.9 in
Height............................50.6 in
Ground Clearance..................6.1 in
Curb Weight....................2650 lbs
Test Weight....................3061 lbs
Weight distribution front/rear.......52/48%
Pounds per bhp (test weight)........26.6
Suspension F: Ind., unequal-length wishbones, coil springs, anti-sway bar
R: Rigid axle, radius arms, torque rods, Panhard rod, coil springs
Brakes.......F: 10.9-in. discs, R: 9-in. drums 339 sq in swept area
Steering....................Cam and roller
Turns, lock to lock.....................3.5
Turning circle......................32 ft.
Tires and wheels..........165–15 on 4.5J rim

CHECK LIST

ENGINE
Starting...........................Fair
Response..........................Good
Noise.............................Fair
Vibration.........................Fair

DRIVE TRAIN
Clutch action.................Very Good
Transmission linkage.......Very Good
Synchromesh action..........Excellent
Power-to-ground transmission..............Very Good

BRAKES
Response..........................Good
Pedal pressure....................Good
Fade resistance..............Very Good
Smoothness...................Very Good
Directional stability..............Good

STEERING
Response..........................Good
Accuracy..........................Good
Feedback..........................Fair
Road Feel....................Very Good

SUSPENSION
Harshness control.................Good
Roll stiffness.....................Good
Tracking..........................Good
Pitch control.....................Good
Shock damping....................Good

CONTROLS
Location.....................Very Good
Relationship......................Good
Small controls....................Fair

INTERIOR
Visibility........................Good
Instrumentation...................Good
Lighting.....................Very Good
Entry/exit........................Fair
Front seating comfort........Excellent
Front seating room..........Very Good
Rear seating comfort..............Poor
Rear seating room................Poor
Storage space....................Fair
Wind noise.......................Good
Road noise.......................Good

WEATHER PROTECTION
Heater.......................Very Good
Defroster....................Very Good
Ventilation.......................Good
Weather sealing..............Very Good
Windshield wiper action.....Very Good

QUALITY CONTROL
Materials, exterior...........Very Good
Materials, interior...........Very Good
Exterior finish..............Very Good
Interior finish..............Very Good
Hardware and trim................Good

GENERAL
Service accessibility..........Excellent
Luggage space....................Good
Bumper protection................Fair
Exterior lighting............Very Good
Resistance to crosswinds.....Very Good

Volvo 1800S 1,778 c.c.

AT A GLANCE: Swedish GT sports car with occasional back seats. More powerful engine gives extra performance without heavier fuel consumption. Standard overdrive provides economical cruising. Light brakes not entirely fade free, but powerful and progressive. Very safe roadholding; light, positive steering with too much feed-back. Seats mounted too low and instruments vague. Good solid car, rather expensive in the U.K.

MANUFACTURER

A.B. Volvo, Gothenburg, Sweden.

U.K. CONCESSIONAIRES

Volvo Concessionaires Ltd., Tower Ramparts, Ipswich, Suffolk.

PRICES

Basic	..	..	..£1,500	0s	0d
Purchase Tax	..	..	£314	1s	3d
Total (in G.B.)	..	..	£1,814	1s	3d

PERFORMANCE SUMMARY

Mean maximum speed	..	107 m.p.h.
Standing start ¼-mile	..	18·6 sec
0-60 m.p.h.		11·9 sec
30-70 m.p.h. (through gears)		11·4 sec
Overall fuel consumption		24·0 m.p.g.
Miles per tankful ..	..	240

SWEDISH engineering has a reputation for being sound and reliable. It is not inspired, perhaps, but it does go on and on giving unfailing service. The Volvo 1800S is a good example of the Scandinavian way of looking at sports cars, even though this particular model has strong roots and associations in England. Since the right-hand-drive versions first became available in the spring of 1962 this Volvo has not changed its appearance, yet under the skin there have been several important alterations.

Earlier this year the engine and braking system were improved, following some detail revisions to the trim and embellishments in the latter part of 1965. Production is now centred on the main Volvo plant at Gothenburg, with bare metal body pressings being shipped from the Pressed Steel Company. A lot of the transfer plant and control machinery at the factory is British, and such components as carburettors, clutch, brakes and instruments are imported from the U.K. Originally, Jensen assembled the complete car in Birmingham, but production was transferred to Sweden about three years ago.

The engine is basically the same as that used in the saloon Volvos, only in this more sporting version the peak power is boosted to 103 b.h.p. net at 5,600 r.p.m. However, this is far from just a hotted-up derivative, for it runs more quietly and more smoothly than any of the saloons we have tried recently, with no temperament and lots of low-speed flexibility. There are no difficulties in pulling away from 10 m.p.h. in third gear, and the engine really has two distinctly different characters. For gentle pottering around town and relaxed driving with no urgency, one tends to keep the rev counter needle below 3,000 r.p.m. and enjoy a kind of executive GT without sacrificing too much performance. But with the bit between one's teeth, an extra 3,000 r.p.m. up to the peak gives real bite to the acceleration and enables one to hustle along to the accompaniment of a deep throbbing intake roar and some tappety sewing-machine noises from the pushrod valve gear.

Compared with the last Volvo 1800 we tested on 20 July 1962, performance has been increased quite substantially. For example, acceleration through the gears from rest is 1·3sec quicker to 60 m.p.h., and 6·6sec quicker to 90 m.p.h. Maximum speed in overdrive top, a standard ratio installed as a usable fifth gear, has increased from 102 to 107 m.p.h. with a new best of 111 m.p.h. in the favourable direction.

According to the handbook and the markings on the rev counter, maxi-

Autocar Road Test 2088

MAKE: **VOLVO**

TYPE: **1800S**

WEIGHT

Kerb weight (with oil, water and half-full fuel tank): 21·3 cwt (2,383lb–1,085kg)

Front-rear distribution, per cent   F, 54;   R, 46

Laden as tested   ..   24·3 cwt (2,719lb–1,237kg)

TURNING CIRCLES

Between kerbs   ..   L, 31ft 8in.; R, 30ft. 11in.

Between walls   ..   L, 33ft. 11in.; R, 33ft 3in.

Steering wheel turns lock to lock   ..   3·3

PERFORMANCE DATA

Overdrive top gear m.p.h. per 1,000 r.p.m.   21·1

Top gear m.p.h. per 1,000 r.p.m...   ..   15·9

Mean piston speed at max. power   2,935 ft/min

Engine revs. at mean max. speed..   5,070 r.p.m.

B.h.p. per ton laden   85

OIL CONSUMPTION

Miles per pint (SAE 20)   500

FUEL CONSUMPTION

At constant speeds

	OD Top	Top
30 m.p.h.	45·0 m.p.g.	39·2 m.p.g.
40 ,,	44·0 ,,	37·0 ,,
50 ,,	39·6 ,,	34·5 ,,
60 ,,	35·8 ,,	31·3 ,,
70 ,,	32·0 ,,	28·4 ,,
80 ,,	27·6 ,,	23·5 ,,
90 ,,	23·8 ,,	20·2 ,,
100 ,,	19·8 ,,	—

Overall m.p.g.....24·0 (11·8 litres/100km)

Normal range m.p.g. 20-28 (14·1-10·1 litres/100km)

Test distance   ..   ..   ..   1,136 miles

Estimated (DIN) m.p.g.   25·8 (10·9 litres/100km)

Grade   ..   Super Premium (99·4-101·7 RM)

TEST CONDITIONS

Weather   ..   Showering with 10-15 m.p.h. wind

Temperature   ..   ..   12 deg.C (53 deg.F)

Barometer ..   ..   29·5 in. Hg.

Surfaces   Dry concrete and tarmac with damp patches

Speed range, gear ratio and time in seconds

m.p.h.	O.D. Top (3·45)	Top (4·56)	Third (6·21)	Second (9·08)	First (14·27)
10—30	—	—	6·5	4·5	3·6
20—40	12·1	8·7	5·7	3·6	—
30—50	12·8	8·3	5·6	4·5	—
40—60	13·2	8·0	5·8	—	—
50—70	13·7	8·9	6·8	—	—
60—80	16·3	9·9	—	—	—
70—90	21·4	12·8	—	—	—

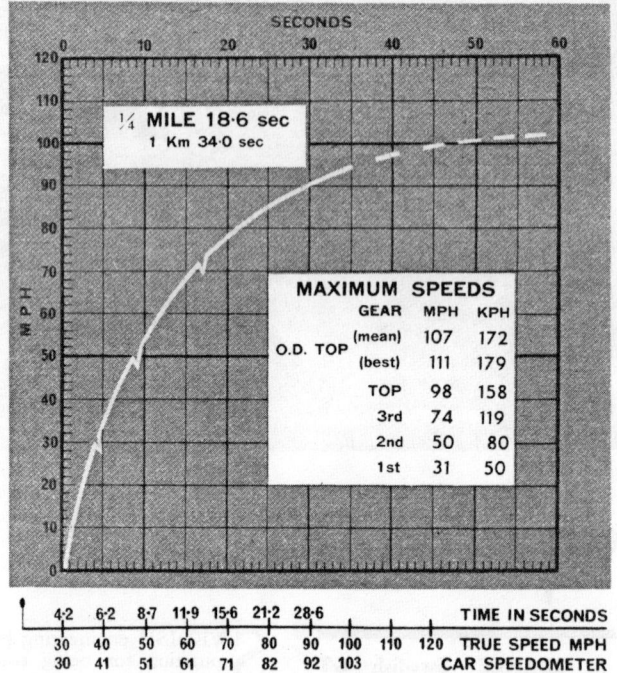

¼ MILE 18·6 sec
1 Km 34·0 sec

MAXIMUM SPEEDS			
GEAR		MPH	KPH
O.D. TOP	(mean)	107	172
	(best)	111	179
TOP		98	158
3rd		74	119
2nd		50	80
1st		31	50

										TIME IN SECONDS
4·2	6·2	8·7	11·9	15·6	21·2	28·6				
30	40	50	60	70	80	90	100	110	120	TRUE SPEED MPH
30	41	51	61	71	82	92	103			CAR SPEEDOMETER

BRAKES

	Pedal load	Retardation	Equiv. distance
(from 30 m.p.h.	25lb	0·30g	100ft
in neutral)	50lb	0·60g	50ft
	75lb	0·90g	33·4ft
Handbrake		0·30g	100ft

CLUTCH Pedal load and travel—40lb and 5in.

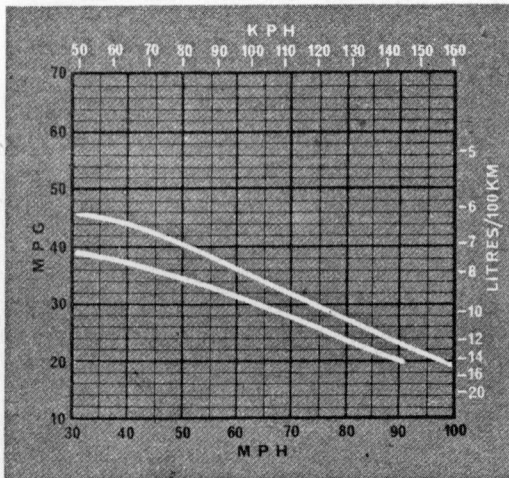

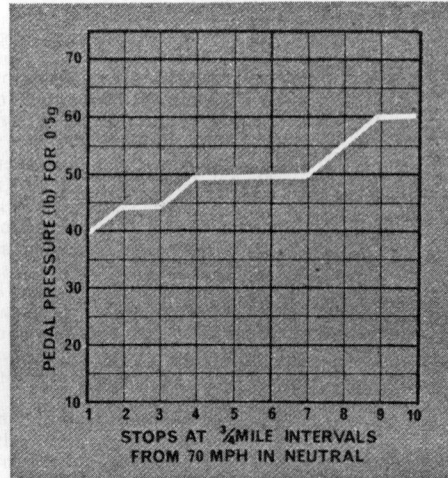

STOPS AT ¼ MILE INTERVALS FROM 70 MPH IN NEUTRAL

AUTOCAR, 15 July 1966

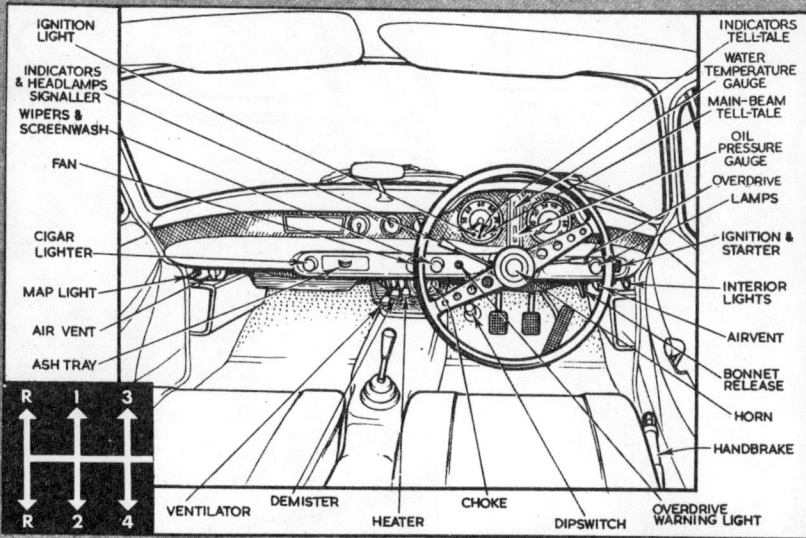

mum revs should be 6,500. Using this as a limit gave times about 1sec slower than going on to 7,000 which the engine seemed very content to do without getting harsh or sounding distressed. For normal road use, of course, 6,000 is plenty and, in fact, during our testing we found that by keeping to this lower limit only 2sec were added to the times right through to 90 m.p.h.

Overdrive Included

Gearbox ratios are well spaced out up to almost 100 m.p.h. in direct top, and overdrive can only be engaged with this ratio. A stalk on the right-hand side of the steering column just under the wheel rim operates the solenoid when moved in any direction, on the repeater principle. A purple warning lamp on the facia lights when overdrive is selected and it is possible to set the control before engaging top if one wants. On our test car this touch-switch did not always contact immediately, and as the warning lamp was mostly masked by a steering wheel spoke, there were times when we were not sure whether we were in overdrive.

Upward changes into overdrive were smooth with the throttle open for acceleration, but changing down, either on the over-run or with power on, proved so jerky that we usually stabbed the clutch at the appropriate moment to cushion the change.

The gearbox itself is operated by a very positive and stubby little lever in a nice position on the tunnel and close to the wheel rim. There is strong spring loading towards the top and third gear plane which helps fast upwards changes when accelerating. The synchromesh (on all ratios, incidentally) could never be beaten, and the shiny black plastic knob is thoughtfully shaped to fit the palm of one's hand.

The steering of the 1800 is very quick and precise, but there is a lot of feed-back to the driver's hands. We took the car abroad to measure maximum speed, and on French roads the driver finds the rim continually sawing through quite large arcs as the front wheels follow the bumps and gulleys on the road surface. The steering column is mounted almost horizontally, which puts the wheel within comfortable reach at an easy angle to wind on.

This quick steering response and its associated effects could be ultra-sensitive if the suspension of the Volvo were not set up very carefully.

Within normal bounds the handling is neutral, with a balanced and taut feel that encourages one to toss it through bends with confidence. On a wet test track we were surprised at how stable the car remained towards the limit of adhesion, with no tail swing at all even when applying power to the rear wheels suddenly in the middle of a turn. More extensive examination from outside on a steering pad showed the car to be under-steering predominantly under these extreme conditions to the extent of practically dragging the tyres sideways off the rims of the front wheels. With the excellent grip of the Pirelli

Accessibility is good with all fillers easy to reach. The bonnet has a self-supporting strut and positive locks

Left: Seats are comfortably padded, but lack lateral support. Floor covering is stout woven carpet. Doors are wide for easy entry and exit.
Right: The rear seat backrest folds down to provide a carpeted platform for luggage which can be secured with the leather straps provided

Volvo 1800S . . .

Cinturatos this characteristic never reached the stage where we found ourselves running out of road, and the Volvo is the kind of car that helps you out of trouble should an emergency arise, or over exuberance get the better of the driver.

Spring rates are rather soft, too soft for a GT car in the opinion of some of our testers. The ride, on the other hand, is comfortable and quite firmly damped although there is quite a lot of body roll on corners. The radial tyres rumbled on certain types of road surface, but otherwise suited the suspension characteristics very well indeed.

The Girling braking system is the conventional mixture of discs at the front with rear drums and it works with the aid of a powerful vacuum servo. Pedal pressure is therefore light and it took only 75lb load to lock the wheels on a damp surface for an ultimate stop of 0·9g. On a dry road we could undoubtedly have bettered this figure and probably achieved 1g or more. The fade tests showed some loss of efficiency as the temperatures rose, but this was a gradual and progressive process with an increase in load from 40 to 60lb over 10 stops. Recovery was very quick.

With a big, pull-up lever on the right of the driving seat, the handbrake held securely facing either way on a 1-in-3 test hill and stopped the car with 0·3g when used on its own from 30 m.p.h. Moving off again on the test hill was easy.

Fuel economy does not seem to have been affected at all by the extra engine power and our overall consumption for 1,136 miles in this country and abroad worked out at exactly 24 m.p.g. In our test four years ago the corresponding figure was 24·9, and even the steady-speed consumption graph has not changed signi-ficantly. The economy of having an overdrive for cruising is well illustrated by this graph, the saving at 70 m.p.h. being 3·6 m.p.g. or nearly 13 per cent.

A lot of the original P.1800 was the work of stylists rather than designers and the instruments are an example of their misguided efforts. These have not changed on the latest model and are still a confusing collection of colourful gauges, difficult to read and even harder to interpret.

For a sports car the boot is large. The lid is counterbalanced, and the fuel filler has a separate locking flap

Latest cars have rear bumpers without wrap-round corners to protect the wings, and a rubber insert across the full width

HOW THE VOLVO 1800S COMPARES:

TOTAL PRICE		
£1,814		
£998		
£878		
£2,498		
£2,387		

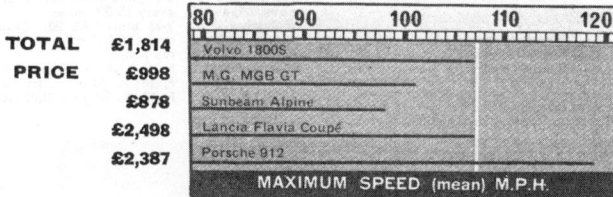
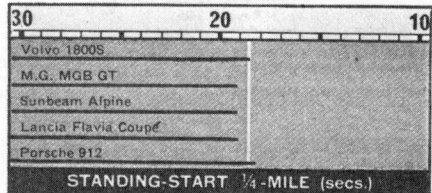
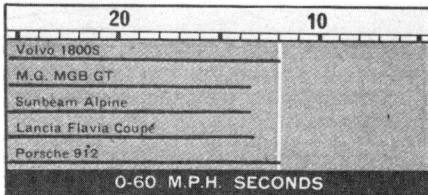
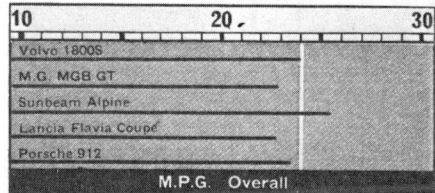

MAXIMUM SPEED (mean) M.P.H.
STANDING-START ¼-MILE (secs.)
0-60 M.P.H. SECONDS
M.P.G. Overall

(Volvo 1800S, M.G. MGB GT, Sunbeam Alpine, Lancia Flavia Coupé, Porsche 912)

In front of the driver are a large speedometer and matching rev counter with two manometer-type temperature gauges for oil and water in between. Over to the left are three more circular dials for fuel tank, oil pressure and a clock. These all have sunken faces and vague calibrations that are practically impossible to read without bending down and peering into them. Even then the fuel gauge appears to have two different and conflicting scales, so one can never rely on it.

Minor Controls

The switches are scattered across the facia below the instruments and work on combined push, pull and twist principles rather than those of the more modern flick toggles. There are two-speed wipers which we timed at 77 and 43 sweeps per min, and pushing this knob works the electric screenwash, with very powerful jets. There is a three-speed heater fan and a really high-output hot

matrix designed to cope with sub-zero winters. Little T-handles under the dashboard each side are supposed to open cold air vents to the footwells, but we never succeeded in getting more than a dribble of ram air through.

By far the loudest and most universal complaint from all our staff concerned the seating position, which is much, much too low. An average 5ft 9in. man getting in and settling back finds his eyes on a level with the instruments, so he must sit up and crane over the scuttle to see the nearside wing in traffic. Even our tallest six-footer would have liked to be higher and although there is a small vertical adjustment provided, we could all have been sitting at least 2in. up without coming near the limit of headroom. We did in fact drive a similar car with blocks under the runners last year, and found it transformed. Even the passenger has trouble seeing out, and the scuttle is lower that side.

The seats themselves have been

reshaped recently and they give good support in the small of the back, but have little sideways location. This is not so important if the standard seat belts are worn, although one gets stiff on a long fast journey when bracing against cornering forces all the time. The backrests can be adjusted over a small angular range, but as mentioned earlier, we mostly set them upright to see out.

With difficult access and thin padding only, the back seats are of the plus-2 variety intended mainly for children or occasional short runs for adults bending over to clear the roof. The backrest can now be dropped down to form a large carpeted luggage shelf in addition to the very roomy boot.

Although we had yellow bulbs fitted for our Continental trip, the headlamps were extremely impressive in their powerful throw on main beams and their good spread when dipped. The foot dipswitch, however, is rather a stretch to reach and not nearly as convenient as a finger-tip lever when there is gear changing to be done. Pulling up on the indicator arm, by the way, flashes main beams any time.

During our fortnight with the car, and especially when making trips, we found the lack of stowage space inside the car an annoyance. The two big boxes on the sides of the footwells have shrunk to tiny elastic-topped pockets on the latest models, and that is the total extent of locker space.

There is no cubby-hole in front of the passenger, no hollow armrest between the seats, no door pockets and no under-facia shelf.

This latest Volvo 1800 is still much the same car as it has always been, but now are several worthwhile improvements to keep its performance well up with the competitors in its class, as our charts show so well. The price in the U.K. is now almost the same as four years ago, largely be-

cause purchase tax has decreased by as much as the basic price has been forced up. At over £1,800 it is not a cheap car, and although well equipped it somehow seems lacking in the luxury touches one would expect for the money. Nevertheless the quality of engineering can be taken for granted, and this Volvo can still offer the performance and reliability which are so important to many motorists.

SPECIFICATION : VOLVO 1800S, FRONT ENGINE, REAR-WHEEL DRIVE

ENGINE

Cylinders	4, in line
Cooling system	Water; pump, fan and thermostat
Bore	84·1mm (3·31in.)
Stroke	80mm (3·15in.)
Displacement	1,780 c.c. (109 cu. in.)
Valve gear	Overhead, pushrods and rockers
Compression ratio	10-to-1
Carburettors	2SU HS6
Fuel pump	AC mechanical
Oil filter	Full-flow, Wix or Mann
Max. power	103 b.h.p. (net) at 5,600 r.p.m.
Max. torque	108·5 lb. ft. (net) at 3,800 r.p.m.

TRANSMISSION

Clutch	Borg and Beck, diaphragm spring 8·5in. dia.
Gearbox	4-speed, all-synchromesh
Gear ratios	OD Top 0·756; Top 1·0 Third, 1·36; Second, 1·99; First, 3·13; Reverse 3·25
Final drive	Hypoid bevel, 4·56 to 1

CHASSIS AND BODY

Construction	Integral steel body

SUSPENSION

Front	Independent, coil springs and wishbones, telescopic dampers
Rear	Live axle, coil springs, trailing arms, Panhard rod, telescopic dampers

STEERING

	Gemmer, cam and roller wheel dia. 16in.

BRAKES

Type	Girling disc front, drum rear
Servo	Girling vacuum
Dimensions	F, 10·88in .dia.; R, 9in. dia; 2in. wide shoes
Swept area	F, 226 sq. in.; R, 113 sq. in. Total 339 sq. in. (279 sq. in. per ton laden)

WHEELS

Type	Pressed steel disc, 5 studs, 4·5in. wide rim
Tyres	Pirelli Cinturato tubed 165-15in.

EQUIPMENT

Battery	12-volt 60-amp. hr.
Generator	Bosch 240 watt d.c.
Headlamps	Bosch sealed 45/40 watt
Reversing lamp	Standard
Electric fuses	3

Screen wipers	2-speed, self parking
Screen washer	Standard, electric
Interior heater	Standard, fresh air
Safety belts	Standard
Interior trim	Leather seats, pvc headlining
Floor covering	Carpet
Starting handle	No provision
Jack	Screw pillar
Jacking points	4 next to wheel arches
Other bodies	None

MAINTENANCE

Fuel tank	10 Imp. gallons (no reserve) (45 litres)
Cooling system	15 pints (including heater) (8·5 litres)
Engine sump	6·5 pints (3·75 litres) SAE 20 or 10W/30. Change oil every 3,000 miles; change filter element every 6,000 miles.
Gearbox and overdrive	2·9 pints .SAE 30. Change oil every 25,000 miles
Final drive	2·25 pints SAE 90. Change oil every 25,000 miles
Grease	No points
Tyre pressures	F, 26; R, 28 p.s.i. (normal driving). F, 28; R, 30 p.s.i. (fast driving). F, 28; R, 30 p.s.i. (full load)

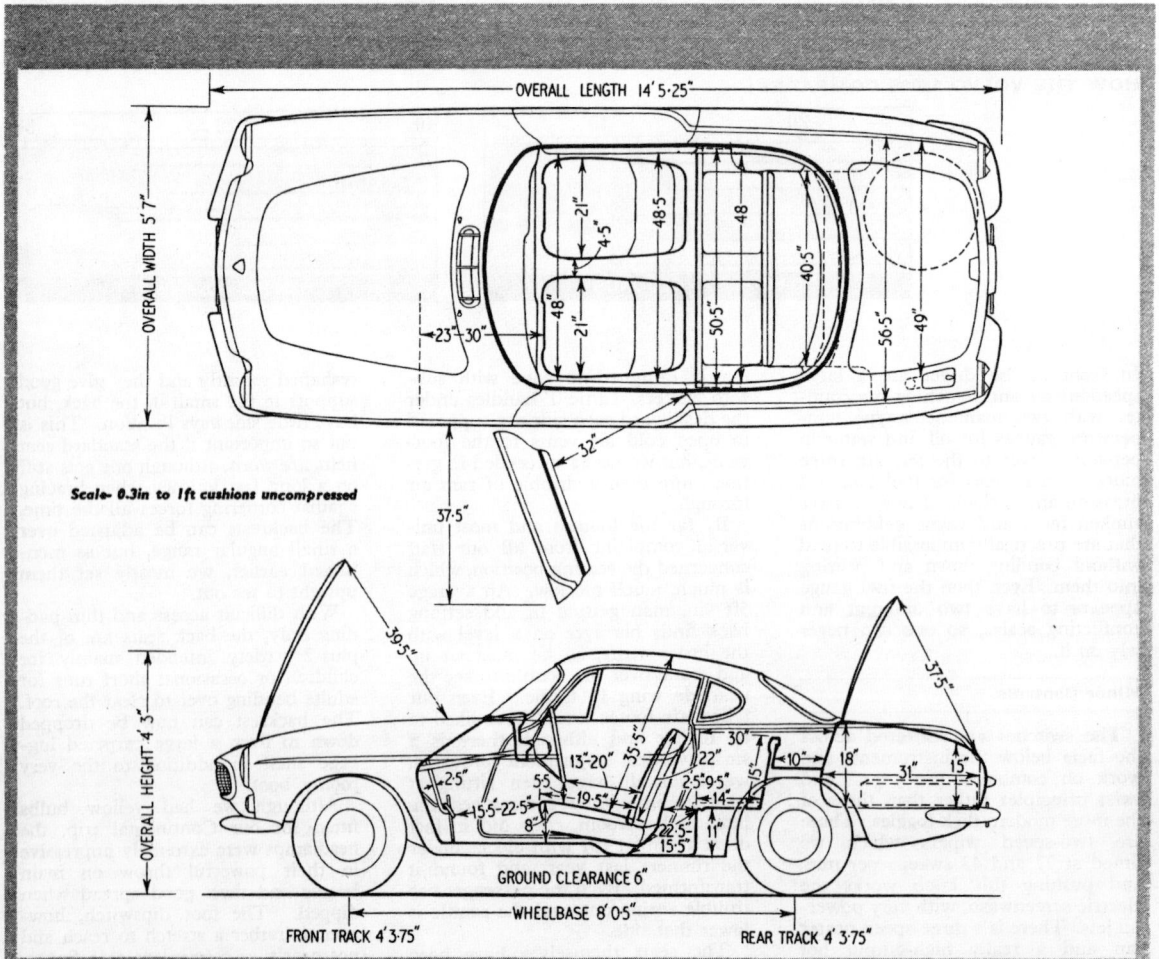

Scale- 0.3in to 1ft cushions uncompressed

Cars on Test

VOLVO 1800S

Engine: Four cylinders, 84·14 mm x 80 mm 1,778 c.c.; compression ratio 10·1 to 1; twin S.U. HS6 carburettors; push-rod overhead valves; 115 b.h.p. at 6,000 r.p.m.

Transmission: Four-speed and reverse gearbox with synchromesh on all forward gears. Overdrive on top gear.

Suspension: Front, independent with wishbones, coil springs and anti-roll bar. Rear, live axle with coil springs, located by panhard rod and radius arms with torque arms. Pirelli Cinturato tyres as standard.

Brakes: Front, disc; rear, drums. Vacuum servo assistance, and limiting valve to balance front and rear brakes.

Dimensions: Overall length, 14 ft. 5¼ ins; overall width, 5 ft. 7 in. overall height, 4 ft. 2½ ins; ground clearance (unladen) 6 in.; weight, 2,625 lb.

PERFORMANCE

	m.p.h.		secs.
MAXIMUM SPEED	110	ACCELERATION 0–30—	3·3
Mean of two ways	110	0–40—	4·3
SPEEDS IN GEARS	First—33	0–50—	7·1
	Second—53	0–60—	10·0
	Third—80	0–70—	15·5
	Direct 4th—98	0–80—	21·2

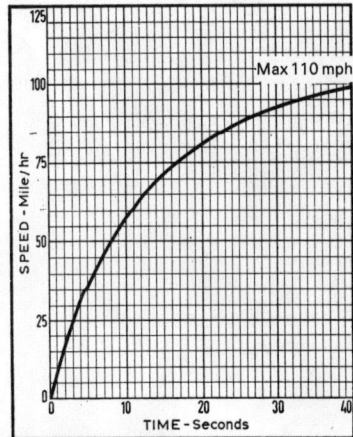

Max 110 mph — SPEED - Mile/hr vs TIME - Seconds

Manufacturer: Volvo AB., Gothenburg, Sweden
Price in U.K.: £1,845 including purchase tax

SPORTS CAR ROAD TEST ▶ # VOLVO 1800S

IT CAN'T *ALL* be due to the Saint and that sort of thing— the Volvo 1800S obviously has charm of its own. We must admit that during our test we didn't manage to pack the car with half as many gorgeous females as Simon Templar regularly seems to on the telly, but we didn't hold that against it.

Volvos have always appealed to us, and the 1800S, for obvious reasons, more so than the others. Whether or not you think it is good-looking depends, presumably, on your taste: speaking for ourselves, we reckon that the styling is by current standards a bit long in the tooth, and while this may or may not matter all that much it does carry with it a slight disadvantage in that visibility is not, perhaps, all that it might be. Mind you, the inside of the thing is well up to date in terms of roominess and comfort, you can pack a lot of luggage into it and although it is only really supposed to be a two-seater you can pack four adults into it, although so far as the bodies in the back seat are concerned it might be kind not to go too far in one hop without giving 'em a chance to stretch the old legs.

The latest 1800S is still largely the same as it has been for a number of years now, but the current version has more power and a revised braking system: from the garage-on-Sunday-mornings aspect, there are fewer points you have to plug in a grease-gun and among other things the front suspension is "lubricated for life". As soon as you hop in you realise that this is one of those cars designed by a driver. Getting in with the window wound down needs just the tiniest bit of care if you are not going to take your eye out on the top of the quarter-light frame, but once you're in you've got it all—it is a beautifully-equipped car. Once again, the elegance of the instrument panel is a matter of taste, but like it or not no-one can deny that the instruments are all there and are easily read at that. There's even an oil-temperature gauge.

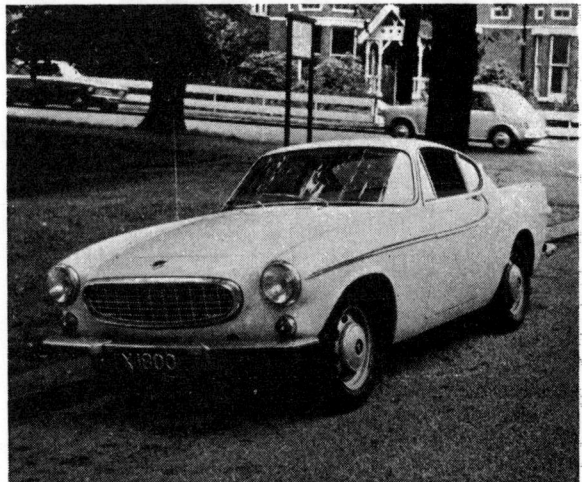

Well it's ugly or just plain beautiful, all depending on your point of view.

The engine is the B18 B type power unit, which means that it is the four-cylinder o.h.v. job, with a five-bearing crank, which you find all over the Volvo range. In 1800S form, this unit has a 10·1 to 1 compression ratio and its 1,778 c.c.s push out a total power output of 115 b.h.p. at 6,000 r.p.m. Five bearings on the crank and oversquare proportions (bore and stroke are 84·14 mm x 80 mm) give a hand in letting it run up to this speed with unusual smoothness for a "big four." Maximum torque of 112 lb. ft. arrives at 4,000 r.p.m. and on the overdrive model, direct top gives you 15 m.p.h. per 1,000 r.p.m. and overdrive top (fourth, by

▶ 60

VOLVO 1800S

And if 115 bhp isn't enough, there's a hop-up kit that offers more

HAVING BEEN WITH us since early 1961, the Volvo 1800 coupe has attained Old Friend status. A conservative design when it first appeared, it has become comparatively more so over the years, but it still holds a lot of appeal for many people and it's still a soundly constructed, rugged car that offers decent value for the money.

Over its years of production the 1800S has remained very much the same but has been refined in small details, such as a change to small hub caps from the original, over-styled wheel covers; a simpler, more pleasant front bumper; some interior changes including new seats; and two power increases with the latest (as of 1966) bringing the output of the coupe's engine to 115 bhp at 6000 rpm. Another significant change to appear in the 1966 car is a front/rear brake proportioning valve to reduce the chance of rear brake lock-up in hard braking—a laudable improvement that is also applied to the rest of the Volvo line this year.

Getting behind the wheel of the 1800S, one is immediately aware of a rather old-fashioned atmosphere about the seating position. You sit low in the car, the steering wheel is as nearly vertical as any we've tried lately; headroom is a little restricted and the windows seem like narrow slits compared with those in some of the low-waisted cars of today.

This classical feeling in the driving position is visually counterbalanced by an instrument panel that smacks of American Contemporary circa 1955. It's a handsome enough layout but a bit more stylized than many sports car drivers

would care for, with heavy chrome bezels for each instrument and a speedometer that has only 10-mph increments marked out. All the information is there, though—tachometer, speedometer, trip odometer, oil temperature gauge along with the water temp, clock—and in addition to the expected warning lights, a bright red telltale reminds you when overdrive is engaged.

Seats are sufficiently adjustable for fore-and-aft position and rake, and in addition have the novelty of a variable lumbar support. A small hole in the outboard side of the back rest gives access to the large Phillips-head screw that turns a pivoted lateral frame from which are stretched india rubber straps: turning the frame tightens or relaxes the straps to make the seat back stiffer or softer. These seats are covered with real leather and are comfortably soft, vertically and laterally. The lateral softness does not make for sidewise security, but the seats seem comfortable for all, and lateral location of the driver and passenger has been left to the excellent seat belt-body harness arrangement.

Behind the two main seats is a generous luggage area, with leather straps for holding the cargo in place, that doubles as minimal extra seating space. The trunk itself is generous for the size of the car.

Sweden is a country of severe climate, and hence the design of Volvos is influenced by the need for rugged, all-weather cars that will perform reliably and keep the occupants happy in all kinds of weather. Because America is

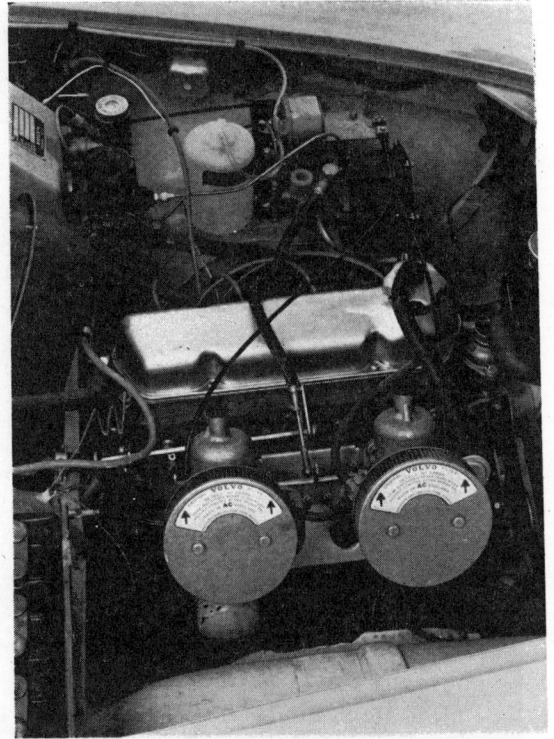

also a land of extremes in weather, the Volvo is better suited to American use than are many imports. There has been more than token attention to rustproofing of the body, for instance, and Volvo heaters are in a class with their American counterparts, as evidenced by a recent test conducted by a Finnish magazine which showed a Volvo 122 to be capable of raising interior temperature from 9°F to over 80°F in 40 min. Too, Volvos have a reputation for living a long time, and their claimed 11-year car life may not be far off.

Sweden also has bad roads in abundance, as do so many European countries. Again the local influence shows to advantage: the 1800S is very much at home on the worst kind of roads with the staunch body structure and fairly soft springing making the road surface a [relatively] negligible factor in determining driving speed. The live rear axle can be made to hop, but the provocation must be severe. On smooth roads where the cornering properties can be evaluated separately, we found moderate understeer, moderate body roll, good directional stability and light, positive steering. Volvo engineers consider radial-ply tires essential to the design and install Pirelli Cinturatos as standard equipment; these combined with tight shock control give the low-speed firmness one expects in this kind of car, but with increasing speed the ride improves. In fact, there are few sports cars with a more satisfactory ride for the long haul. Along with the radial tires, however, comes the slight vibration problem inherent in such tires: our car had a slight resonance coming through the steering wheel at around 70 mph, and careful re-balancing didn't eliminate it completely.

Along with all the rock-solidity comes high weight and modest performance. an 1800-cc engine pulling 2410 lb of curb weight is somewhat restricted by Newtonian physics. The latest power increase shows in the performance figures, but the acceleration of the 1800S is still on the leisurely side. The engine is a most impressive unit, of itself, for a four: vibration periods and power throb are at a minimum and it starts easily, idles smoothly, and runs quietly. To answer

the demand for a little extra, Volvo has worked out a hop-up kit for the B-18 engine and after completing our road test of the standard version we returned it to the distributor's technical center for installation of the kit.

Not a factory-installed option yet, the kit is part No. 419350 and it can be applied to all B-18 engines. For the latest 1800S engine, no changes are required before installing the kit, and it consists of the following pieces:

-Cylinder head, compression ratio 11.1:1 with 1.65-in. intake valves and 1.38-in. exhaust valves (standard 10:1, 1.97 and 1.65-in. respectively)
-Camshaft with 0.406-in. lift
-Lighter flywheel (17.6 lb with ring gear)
-Oil pump and timing gear covers
-Pulley hub
-Carburetor needles, richer than standard
-Lighter springs for carburetor damper pistons
-Bosch W280 T 13 S spark plugs
-Bosch TK 12 A10 ignition coil
-Sheet metal exhaust header (tuned for extraction)

VOLVO 1800S
AT A GLANCE...

Price as tested	$4280
Engine	4 cyl in line, ohv, 1780 cc, 115 bhp
Curb weight, lb	2410
Top speed, mph	109
Acceleration, 0-60 mph, sec	13.9
50-70 mph (3rd gear)	8.0
Average fuel consumption, mpg	24.5

VOLVO 1800S

In order to install the kit on earlier 1800S cars and B18D engines (122S) certain other preparatory modifications are called for, such as installing correct pistons and/or the oil cooler. The hopped-up engine output is 135 bhp at 6000 rpm, and there is a modest and noticeable increase in performance through the gears without a serious loss in flexibility. Idling speed went up from 700 rpm to 1000 with the kit, but overall noise level didn't increase. The kit will be available through Volvo dealers and will cost $299; installation should run about $100 on current 1800S models.

Staff opinions on the 1800S styling were generally unenthusiastic, with low marks going to the chromium sweepspear and the semi-finned rear fenders, both cliches of a bygone American era. The formerly expensive-looking eggcrate grille has been superseded by a stamped affair that doesn't affect the basic styling but does look less elegant.

Good marks go to the shift linkage on this car for precision, easy reaches and low shift efforts. In addition to the good shift linkage, we also liked the method of engaging the overdrive, a handy directional-like lever on the right side of the steering column that's pushed toward the dash to either engage or disengage the overdrive. The unit does not cancel itself when the shift lever is taken out of 4th (the only gear to which the od is applied). Personal taste decrees whether this is an advantage or not, but it didn't seem a bad thing to just leave it on for leisurely driving, going directly from 3rd to 4th od. The overdrive is standard on the 1800S. All indirect gears are quiet and the ratios seem appropriate for the car. Brake, clutch and accelerator efforts are all light and their action smooth, and the whole drive train was tight and slack-free after being attended to by the technical center.

We understand that pops and clunks from the rear suspension and/or axle have been a common occurrence with the model, and our car was delivered to us with a rather severe pop. However, we were pleased to know that the trouble could be (and was) corrected. A small gripe was an oily film deposited on the windshield by the defroster.

To summarize, the 1800S is for the man who wants a solid, conservative and durable car with a little verve and good road manners. Set up properly it gives a feeling of pleasant precision in its responses to driver demands; servicing should be inexpensive, fuel economy is good (24 mpg in all-round driving) and 100,000 miles should be the rule rather than the exception.

ROAD TEST
VOLVO 1800 S

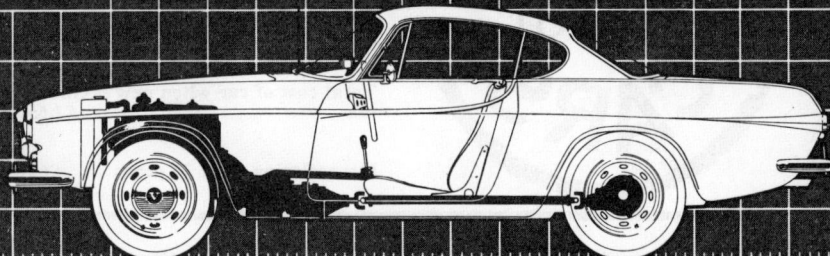

SCALE: 10" DIVISIONS

PRICE
Basic list.................$4200
As tested................$4280

ENGINE
No. cyl & type......4 in line, ohv
Bore x stroke, mm...'...84 x 80
In.................3.31 x 3.15
Displacement, cc/cu in...1780/109
Compression ratio.........10.0:1
Bhp @ rpm.........115 @ 6000
  Equivalent mph...........135
Torque @ rpm, lb-ft...112 @ 4000
  Equivalent mph............83
Carburetors.................2 SU
No. barrels, dia.......1 x 1.75
Type fuel required......premium

DRIVE TRAIN
Clutch type.......sdp diaphragm
  Diameter, in............8.5
Gear ratios: od (0.756)....3.45:1
  4th (1.00)............4.56:1
  3rd (1.36).............6.19:1
  2nd (1.99)............9.07:1
  1st (3.13)...........14.24:1
Synchromesh............on all 4
Differential type..........hypoid
  Ratio.................4.56:1
Optional ratios...........none

CHASSIS & SUSPENSION
Frame type.......unit with body
Brake type...........disc/drum
  Swept area, sq in.........339
Tire size............165 x 15
  Make.........Pirelli Cinturato
Steering type........cam & roller
  Turns, lock-to-lock........3.2
  Turning circle, ft........31.2
Front suspension: independent
  with unequal A-arms, coil springs,
  tube shocks, anti-roll bar.
Rear suspension: live axle on trail-
  ing arms with Panhard rod, coil
  springs, tube shocks.

ACCOMMODATION
Normal capacity, persons.......2
  Occasional capacity..........3
Seat width, front, in......2 x 18.5
  Rear...................39.5
Head room, front/rear...38.0/28.0
Seat back adjustment, deg......10
Entrance height, in..........46.6
Step-over height...........13.7
Door width................38.0
Driver comfort rating:
  Driver 69 in. tall.........90
  Driver 72 in. tall.........85
  Driver 75 in. tall.........65
  (85-100, good; 70-85, fair;
  under 70, poor)

GENERAL
Curb weight, lb..........2410
Test weight.............2770
Weight distribution (with
  driver), front/rear, %....52/48
Wheelbase, in............96.5
Track, front/rear.....51.8/51.8
Overall length..........173.2
  Width................67.0
  Height...............50.5
Frontal area, sq ft........18.8
Ground clearance, in........6.0
Overhang, front/rear...31.2/45.5
Departure angle, deg.......14
Usable trunk space, cu ft.....8.1
Fuel tank capacity, gal........12

INSTRUMENTATION
Instruments: 120-mph speedometer, trip odometer, 7000-rpm
  tachometer, water & oil temperature, oil pressure, fuel level,
  clock.
Warning lights: generator, high
  beam, directional signals, overdrive on.

MISCELLANEOUS
Body styles available: coupe only
Warranty period: 6 mo/unlimited
  mileage

CALCULATED DATA
Lb/hp (test wt)..........24.1
Mph/1000 rpm (overdrive)...19.7
Engine revs/mi (60 mph)....3040
Piston travel, ft/mi.......1595
Rpm @ 2500 ft/min.......4760
  Equivalent mph.........102
Cu ft/ton mi............69.0
R&T wear index...........48.5

EXTRA COST OPTIONS
Radio, limited-slip differential.

MAINTENANCE
Crankcase capacity, qt.......4.0
  Change interval, mi......3000
Oil filter type..........full flow
  Change interval, mi......6000
Chassis lube interval, mi....3000

BRAKES
Panic stop from 80 mph:
  Deceleration, % G.........68
  Control..............good
  Parking: hold 30% grade......yes
  Overall brake rating........good

ROAD TEST RESULTS

ACCELERATION
Time to speed, sec: standard kit
0-30 mph........... 4.1... 3.8
0-40 mph........... 6.8... 6.3
0-50 mph.......... 10.3... 9.4
0-60 mph.......... 13.9..12.7
0-70 mph.......... 18.5..17.4
0-80 mph.......... 24.5..23.2
0-100 mph......... 51.5..49.0
50-70 mph (3rd
  gear)............ 8.0... 7.8
Time to distance, sec:
0-100 ft........... 3.6... 3.6
0-500 ft.......... 10.2... 9.8
¼-mile........... 19.0..18.4
Speed at end, mph... 71.0..72.0
Passing exposure time, sec:
  Car ahead going 50
  mph............. 6.4... 6.8

SPEEDS IN GEARS
                   normal with kit
Overdrive mph.......109...114
4th (6000).........100...100
3rd (6000).......... 66...66
2nd (6000)......... 44...44
1st (6000)......... 29...29

SPEEDOMETER ERROR
30 mph indicated.....actual 30.0
40 mph.................40.0
60 mph.................58.6
80 mph.................76.9
90 mph.................86.0
Odometer correction factor...1.006

FUEL CONSUMPTION
                   standard with kit
Normal driving, mpg.24.5...23.5
Cruising range, mi...294.....281

ACCELERATION & COASTING

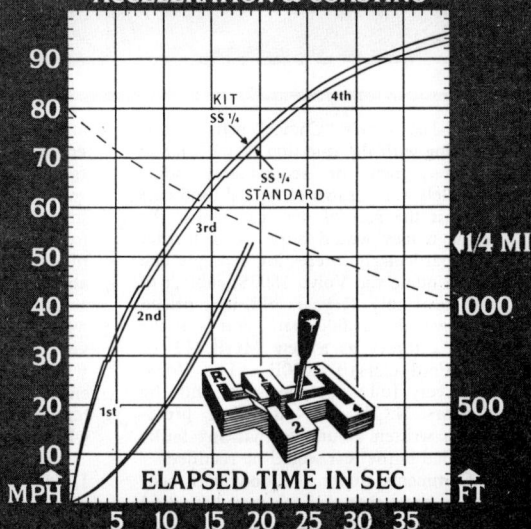

AUGUST 1966

USED CARS ON TEST

PRICES

Car for sale at Nottingham at £1,025

Typical trade advertised price for same age and model in average condition £1,050

Total cost of car when new including tax £1,652

Depreciation over 2½ years £627

DATA

Date first registered 9 October

Number of owners

Tax expires   30 September

Fuel consumption   23-26 m.

Oil consumption   600 m.p.

Mileometer reading   22,

No. 265 1964 Volvo 1800S

Left:
From the extent of rust and chipping aro edges of wheels and bodywork it may be presumed that the car has stood out quite a lot in its short life. The rear quarter windows are fixed

Below left:
Although with evidence of reasonable wear, the interior is very clean. This is a particularly comfortable car for long journeys

Below:
A true enthusiast would want to start at once on thorough cleaning of the under-bonnet compartment. A new battery filler cap is needed—a detail, but still a fault especially for an expensive quality car

IN last week's "Choice" article dealing with the question of whether to buy new or secondhand, some parallels were drawn of typical used cars against the sort of new car which the same money would buy. As a further and particularly interesting example one could quote the Volvo 1800S, subject of this test; only 2½ years old, it is priced just over the £1,000 mark, and is in the same category as a new MGB GT or the Ford Corsair 2000E. The Volvo is a very fully equipped car, and the vendors, N.C.V. of Nottingham, provided a written assurance that any faults revealed in the test would be rectified.

Comments under the bodywork section suggest that this car may have had a fairly hard life, and is not one which has been "kept in mothballs" and had care lavished on it; yet it is very fit mechanically. The only slight need for

attention is for a general tune-up of the engine, as response to the throttle is rather hesitant below 3,000 r.p.m. In spite of this, the performance is fairly impressive, with acceleration from rest to 60 m.p.h. in 14.7 sec, and a 0 to 90 m.p.h. time of 34.6 sec. Top speed is above 100 m.p.h. in overdrive. The acceleration figures do not compare too well with the Road Test published last year, but the latest car had more power which accounts for much of the difference. The performance is slightly better than that of the original P1800, which we tested in July 1962.

The engine is a 4-cylinder unit of 1,778 c.c. It always starts promptly, with ample rich mixture when cold, and is quiet even when taken up to high revs; oil consumption is low although there are signs of leakage. This engine is renowned for long life.

An almost embarrassingly lo crackle and rort from the exhaust w found to be caused by a fracture of t pipe just after the first silencer b putting the second one out of action al gether.

Good synchromesh on all gears, a a crisp change—with very small trav of a short lever mounted at the end the transmission hump—match t sporting character of the car. Ove drive engages very smoothly, works top gear only, and allows 90 m.p. cruising at 4,250 r.p.m. Provided t throttle is opened at the right momen a tendency to snatch on cutting out ove drive can be avoided, and there is a ti purple tell-tale ahead of the driver show when overdrive is engaged. T clutch takes up smoothly, and althou the travel is rather long it is not t heavy in traffic.

PERFORMANCE CHECK

Figures in brackets are those of the slightly more powerful model—103 b.h.p. (net)—introduced in 1965; Road Test published 15 July 1966)

0 to 30 m.p.h. 4·2 sec (4·2)
0 to 40 m.p.h. 7·0 sec (6·2)
0 to 50 m.p.h. 9·9 sec (8·7)
0 to 60 m.p.h. 14·7 sec (11·9)
0 to 70 m.p.h. 19·6 sec (15·6)
0 to 80 m.p.h. 26·5 sec (21·2)
0 to 90 m.p.h. 34·6 sec (28·6)

In direct top:

20 to 40 m.p.h. 10·2 sec (8·7)
30 to 50 m.p.h. 10·1 sec (8·3)
40 to 60 m.p.h. 10·2 sec (8·0)
50 to 70 m.p.h. 10·2 sec (8·9)
60 to 80 m.p.h. 11·0 sec (9·9)
70 to 90 m.p.h. 13·3 sec (12·8)

Standing quarter-mile 19·7 sec (18·6)

TYRES

Size: 165-15in. Pirelli Cinturato on all wheels. Approx. cost per replacement cover £8 6s 6d. Depth of original tread 9 mm; remaining tread depth: 8·5 mm (front); 7 mm (rear, right and spare); 4 mm on irregularly worn left rear.

TOOLS

Original tool kit complete, and handbook with car.

CAR FOR SALE AT:

N.C.V. of Nottingham, Ltd., Bulwell Forest Works, Bulwell, Nottingham. Telephone: Nottingham 271272-3.

CONDITION SUMMARY

Bodywork

The white paintwork is original, but in relation to a life of only 2½ years, its condition is a little disappointing. There are a few small blemishes, and more rust than would be expected, particularly along the sills and around the inside edges of the wings. The chromium also has not lasted too well, and speckles of corrosion are noticed, particularly on the side trim strips. The interior is finished in maroon, and the seats are upholstered in leather; they are fairly well creased, but sound. The carpets, and most of the trim show little wear, except for a few marks on the p.v.c. roof lining, and the driver's heel mark on the carpet at one point. There is also an ugly hole on the arm rest of the driver's door where the p.v.c. covering has broken up and the foam padding is showing through. There is little underbody corrosion.

Equipment

Everything including the clock is in working order, but the fuel gauge occasionally sticks at E. Original equipment included a heater which is highly effective, but difficult to adjust for mild warmth. The windscreen washer is electrically operated, and there are two-speed windscreen wipers. A good area of the screen is cleared but—a common used car fault—new blades or rubber inserts are needed. The instruments are all somewhat difficult to read, with calibrations vaguely embossed on the background. An oil temperature gauge is included, mounted between the speedometer and rev counter. ROBO headlamps fitted as standard give extremely good range and spread for fast, confident night driving.

Accessories

A Lucas FT6 fog lamp on the left and LR6 spot lamp on the right have been added and there is also a fine Motorola push-button radio with the car. Safety belts, fastening to a common anchorage between the seats, are standard with every Volvo.

ABOUT THE 1800 SPORTS

Though the exciting Volvo sports car was first shown to the public at the Brussels Show in January 1960, it did not actually go into production until May 1961. Under a unique manufacturing agreement, the bodies were built by Pressed Steel (Linwood), and the cars were assembled with Volvo mechanical parts and many British accessories at the Jensen factory in West Bromwich.

The early cars, chassis numbers 1 to 8,000, had a 100 b.h.p. (gross) engine of 1,778 c.c. For the British market a Laycock overdrive was standard, with a rear axle ratio of 4·56 to 1. After the first 6,000 P1800s had been assembled at Jensen, there was a short hiatus as production was transferred to the Volvo factories at Gothenburg, and the 8,000th car was built in August 1963.

From chassis number 8,001, the car's power output was increased to 108 b.h.p. (gross) and the car was renamed the 1800S. Production continued unchanged until the end of 1965, when a further power increase was made—to 115 b.h.p. (gross)—and minor styling changes made. The front bumper is now straight (whereas earlier cars had swept up bumpers near the grille) and there have been some instrument panel styling changes. The overdrive switch on the current cars is now a self-centring prong; on earlier cars this was a small switch hidden among other minor controls.

The 1800S is still in full production at Gothenburg. Many components are British made; bodies are still made at Linwood, now owned by Rootes (Pressings) Ltd.

Steering, ride and roadholding are still up to the high standard remembered from our comparatively recent Road Test of the 1800S, but although extremely comfortable over all surfaces the car suffers from a tiresome vibration period caused by out-of-balance wheels. It begins to be noticed above 60 m.p.h. and one has to go right up to 80 m.p.h. before it is completely smooth again.

The ride is well-damped and extremely comfortable over all surfaces, and the car retains the splendid feeling of rigidity and strength which characterizes all Volvos. The handling is well-balanced with only slight understeer, and the car can be cornered hard with confidence, but the steering transmits too much reaction. All the time the wheel seems to be trying to turn one way or the other against the driver's hands, calling for a lot of correction; however, it provides excellent response to small movements, and the car can be held to a dead straight course at speed. Side winds have little effect.

Slight sag of the driver's seat makes even more noticeable the excessively low seating position criticized in all tests of the 1800 so far, and we had to resort to using a cushion to obtain high enough eye level for good visibility. Even then, the exact position of the front of the car is difficult to judge when parking, and the severely restricted headroom does not allow one to sit much higher. In other respects the seats are comfortable; they have reclining backrests. The rear seat squab can be dropped as a tray for extra luggage, or with the seat in use there is room for two children, or for one adult to sit in a rather cramped sideways position.

Very effective servo assistance on the brakes gives good response to light pedal pressures (disc at the front only), and the handbrake is unusually effective. The tiny guard has been broken, but still surrounds the button to prevent accidental release when the driver is getting out of the car.

Volvo engineering has the reputation of quality and long life which leads one to expect to find everything in peak condition, and although it has admittedly seen little service, the test car's mechanical condition lives up to expectations, and there are no faults in any of the mechanical components or electrical equipment, other than the need for engine tuning and exhaust repair mentioned. The quality of construction, and the high initial cost, need to be borne in mind when considering the value now offered on the used car market.

53 ▶ the way, is the only gear it works on) puts this up to 20 m.p.h. per 1,000 r.p.m., which means that 80 m.p.h. cruising in overdrive works out at exactly the maximum torque figure, and you can stay there with complete effortlessness all day long. Or you can abroad, we hasten to add before we offend Our Babs.

Twin S.U. HS6 carbs are fitted on the inlet manifold, and the exhaust system ends in a twin outlet. Everything is nice and easy to get at; a full-flow oil filter and an oil cooler as standard equipment help to keep you out of trouble in that department, too.

The transmission starts off with an 8½ in. single-dry-plate clutch which links up with a four-speed, all-synchromesh gearbox with, in the case of the test car, the optional overdrive on top only. This in fact provides you effectively with five well-spaced ratios which give over thirty in bottom, fifty in second, eighty in third and just under the ton in direct top, overdrive allowing the car to go on to 110 m.p.h. (which is a bit slower than Volvo claim, but to balance that we got better acceleration figures than they talk about!) Fifty in second is obviously a bit low in comparison with eighty in third, but while this a mathematical fact it doesn't seem to worry you when you are actually driving. The gear-lever works beautifully, with absolute precision, and there is no doubt that this is one of the nicest gearboxes in current production. Mated to the Volvo engine, they form together an unbeatable partnership, and there's no question of one being let down by the other as is the case with one or two other motors in a similar capacity class and of similar type that come to mind.

Another good thing about the Volvo is that it has the road-holding to match. Mind you, this is essentially a touring car and in no sense a racer, and so perhaps the cornering power isn't as high as it could be made to be. But there's no point in all this because the car is too heavy for success in that direction anyway, so why bother altering it all and probably spoiling it? There is independent front suspension with wishbones and coil springs in the usual way, and at the back the live axle is also coil sprung and is satisfactorily located, so that you don't get fussed about with axle tramp and all that nonsense. It gives a smooth ride, comfortable without being sick-making, and on rough surfaces the radius arms and panhard rod keep it in one place, while torque arms stop it from winding up just as they do in acceleration. The handling is damn near neutral: if you press the car to the limit it is the back which goes first, but you get plenty of warning and it is easily controlled. Corner it at a more gentlemanly pace — you must be really pressing on if you lose it—and it simply goes round the corner, with no fuss and no drama.

Stoppers are self-adjusting discs on the front and drums at the back, with a balancing valve linking them to stop the drums locking up first. There is a fairly powerful servo, and in exchange for light pedal pressure the car comes to a halt. Stamp hard on the pedal and you'll really stop it! They also work well in the wet, and it isn't easy to lock them even under these conditions.

So much for the bits that are out of sight. Inside the car, as we said before, it is all there. There is plenty of room: the upholstered back seat provides more than sufficient room for children or one adult (except that headroom under the rear window can be a bit dodgy) and you can get two adults in if they're willing and easy-going. When no behinds are placed upon it, the back seat folds down to provide additional luggage space in estate car or Hillman Imp style. The front seat's adjustable in all sorts of ways—fore and aft in the usual way, up and down by means of nuts and bolts, and they have adjustable back-rests. The centre of the back rest—what we apparently call the "lumbar support"

in the trade—is separately adjustable if you use a screwdriver and follow the directions in the Book. Front seat safety belts are standard equipment. So is a heater which supplies warmth to front and rear of the car, two-speed wipers, screen washers, fresh-air ventilation and a full-set range of instruments—rev-counter, red-lined at six-five, speedometer, oil temperature and pressure gauges, and water temperature gauge. There is an electric clock, and warning lights for dynamo charge, headlamp-main beams and flashing direction indicators: the indicator lever also flashes the headlights. There is an automatic reverse light, variable instrument lighting and so on.

The steering wheel is pretty large by modern standards, but it provides a light precise control with plenty of feel, and wants just over three turns from lock to lock. Everything is exactly where you want it on the Volvo, which bears out what we said at the start that this is one of those cars designed by a driver.

It isn't the easiest car in the world to get the best out of, we thought. You can go fast with no trouble at all, but to go *very* fast needs a little experience of this particular model. The thing is that it is a better car than you expect it to be, somehow, and you fight a little shy of taking liberties until you begin to realise that they aren't liberties at all. Once you've got this idea in your head the Volvo will cover the ground all right. Pirelli Cinturatos are standard equipment, and the whole thing sticks down in a leech-like manner: when it is going fast it doesn't seem to be, either inside or outside the car. A lot of thought has gone into it, which shows up in the little things, such as the provision of stout leather straps to secure luggage carried inside the car.

So far as performance is concerned you have to bear in mind, as we have already emphasised, that the 1800S is a touring car. And when you bear that in mind add the fact that it is a touring car, moreover, which weighs about 25 cwt, and that this considerable hunk of metal and people has to be shoved around by an engine of under two litres' capacity. Do all this, and you'll very likely be surprised by the fact that it wants only ten seconds to get to sixty, and not much over twenty to reach eighty. This, plus a top whack of 110, adds up to a pretty lively car, and what's more it isn't hard work to make it so. From rest to the legal limit takes fifteen-and-a-half seconds, and this isn't done by being snappy on one occasion, because you can make it do this time after time after time. It's just the way the 1800S likes to get around.

The gearing in overdrive top makes it long-legged, to say the least: at a steady ton you still have a thousand revs to go before the needle gets anywhere near the red, and by making the step between direct and overdrive fourth gears a wider one than is usual the result is not only this long easy stride, but a direct top which is really a bit low. So that the direct top gear acceleration is as sharp as that of some cars in third, and if you need a bit of extra go while you are cruising in overdrive, all you have to do is to wag the tip of a finger at the overdrive switch and brother, you're in business! Naturally, you have to pay a bit for all this. The price of the Volvo 1800S is £1,814 by the time you have added on a good bit over three hundred quid for the tax man. On the credit side, you get the 25 m.p.g. you might expect from less than two litres, and it is possible (though much less fun) to push this up something like 28 m.p.g. The tank holds 10 gallons. We used no oil at all during the test, and so far as reliability is concerned—well, the thing is obviously built to last, it has been in production long enough to have ironed out all the bugs, and anyway they have a wonderful reputation in this respect. A man we know has done over seventy thousand miles of hard driving in a Volvo, and all he's had to replace so far are plugs and tyres!

VOLVO P1800S $4,285
West Coast P.O.E.

*Four cylinder engine, five main bearing crank. 118 HP at 5800 rpm. 1998 c.c.
Compression 9.5:1. Overdrive standard. Engine longevity legendary. Good resale value.
Manufactured by A. B. Volvo, Gothenburg, Sweden.*

Volvo's 1800 S for 1969 is no longer just 1800cc, but bored out to 1986cc. It is a stretch of the existing 4 cylinder engine that has been around for years. Bigger, freely rotating valves, stronger pistons and rods, and various other minor detail changes have gone into the engine. The extra displacement has not been used so much for extra power but to give the torque a bit more boost in the lower to middle speed ranges. Power is increased from 115 bhp at 6000 to 118 bhp at 5800. The peak torque is now 123 lb-ft at 3500 rpm, much more usable than the older 112 lb-ft

at 4000 rpm. The compression ratio is 9.5:1.

Alternators are at last now fitted on all Volvos. This item has been standard on domestic cars for years but is just being introduced in Europe.

The sealed cooling system is retained but the oil cooler has been dropped. Electrics are still Bosch but the British S.U. carburetors have been replaced by the Stromberg-Zeniths, part of the efficient smog system that is standard on all Volvos, regardless of where they are sold.

The independent front suspension

is by coil springs with telescopic shock absorbers. Rubber mounted control arms and an anti-sway bar make up the package. No lubrication of the front suspension or the drive shaft components is required for the life of the car.

The rear suspension is a simple solid rear axle carried by longitudinal rubber mounted control arms and torque rods. The transverse location is done by rubber mounted track rod. Coil springs with telescopic shock absorbers make up the assembly.

The four speed transmission is the same as before with a full synchro-

Despite its low roofline and high, slab sides, the Volvo still contrives to be one of the sleekest sports coupes on the market today.

Fully equipped. The Volvo has it all — air conditioning, tachometer, oil pressure and temperature gauges included.

mesh on all gears. Reverse is hidden on this one and to engage it, the lever must be lifted up and moved over the first slot. The box is rubber mounted and will jiggle noticeably when in use.

Overdrive is available on fourth gear and is engaged by the stalk on the right hand side of the steering column. It is easily operated just by tapping the lever and care must be taken when cornering not to accidentally engage it.

The seating in the 1800 is 7-way adjustable and the seats are the orthopedic type. The lumbar adjustment is excellent and relieves the

fatigue effect on a long trip. The seat travel is 9″ which allows the tallest driver ample room. The controls are still well grouped but the same complaint can still be found with the foot rest beside the clutch. It is possible to catch the side of a large shoe on it and thereby be unable to fully depress the clutch. Most drivers would prefer to have it removed because of this.

Instrumentation is good and fully comprehensive and all the instruments are well recessed. The full shoulder harness has had the attachment point in the floor modified and each belt can be released by the flick

of a small red lever. A much easier operation than the previous 'cheese-cutter' unit. The rear jump-seat is usable only by small children and should be looked upon as bonus luggage stowage. The back of the seat folds down and there are two leather straps for securing luggage in place.

The brake system has gone over to the full safety system that was introduced on the 144 sedan series. The car uses discs on the front and drums on the rear. No matter how the brake line may be cut, the driver will always have two front wheels and one rear wheel brake in operation. The system

ROAD TEST

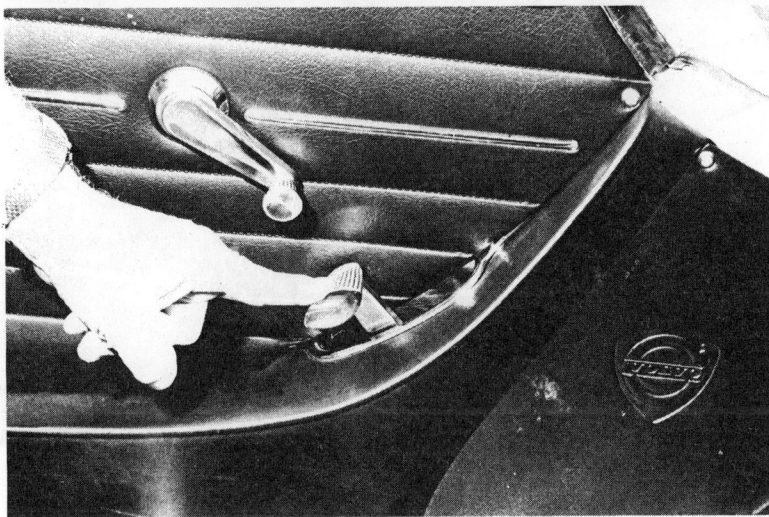

That tail-end design is one of the smoothest yet. Clean, simple and uncluttered by excessive trim.

Volvo has long been big in the field of safety, especially in interior design. This recessed door catch is typical of their thinking.

also has the relief valves that prevent the rear wheels locking up before the front under emergency braking. As this unit is probably the most advanced of its kind in the industry, it is worth a closer look. The front disc pads are operated by separate dual actuating cylinders and the rear discs have the normal single cylinder. The system is designed so that the primary cylinder will operate the lower cylinders on the front wheels together with the right rear wheel; and the secondary system, the upper fronts and the left rear wheel. This will still give 80% of normal braking

efficiency, although, when on the secondary system, the pedal has to be depressed almost its full travel before the brakes will work. This gives the feeling that there is no brake there at all but the car does stop to all intents and purposes as normal. There is a warning light on the dash to indicate that the car is on the emergency system. This is a simple pressure/ micro-switch combination which is actuated whenever hydraulic pressure between the two separate systems is unequal, indicating a leak in one of the lines. If the secondary system has failed, the light is essential

as the braking from the primary system gives the feeling that all is normal. Also included in the system is a pressure relief valve which prevents the rear wheels from locking up before the fronts. To top it off, the car has a mechanical linkage hand-brake to a drum on the left rear wheel. This simplifies the normal difficulty in utilizing the disc system for parking use.

The Volvo 1800 S has never really hit it off strongly with the younger set and unaccountably tends to be likened to the Mercedes 280 SL, big and heavy and alright for older folks.

It is unfortunate that salesmen don't rectify this situation as this car is more than capable of mixing it with Porsche 912 and the Alfa GTV coupes. The car can be really thrown around corners with the radial Pirellis hanging on well and it always comes as a pleasant surprise to glance at the speedometer; the car just doesn't feel that it is going that fast.

As a touring car, the 1800 S really comes into its own and with the judicious use of overdrive, is capable of turning in some pretty impressive gas mileage figures, well up in the high twenties. The orthopedic seats go a long way towards driver comfort and with the new powerplant and overdrive engaged, the previous engine roar has to all intents been eliminated; all tending to reduce driver fatigue.

Availability of 1800 S models has stiffened the retail price of the car and 'deals' are almost unheard of. The car does have a high resale value but the difficulty is in finding a late model car. The only ones around are usually 62/63 vintage thereby indicating a high satisfaction rating by the owners. For someone desirous of Volvo's lasting qualities, the 1800 S deserves a close look and more than a run 'round the block. ♠

Volvo
Data in Brief

DIMENSIONS

Overall length (in.)	182.7
Width (in.)	68.1
Height (in.)	56.7
Wheelbase (in.)	102.5
Turning diameter (ft.)	16.4

WEIGHT, TIRES, BRAKES

Weight (lbs.)	2340
Tires	165 x 15
Brakes, front	disc

ENGINE

Type	4 cylinder
Displacement (cu. in.)	116
Horsepower	118

SUSPENSION

Front	independent coil springs
Rear	coil springs and torque arms

ROAD TEST

IT GOES FASTER WITHOUT THE CARBURETORS.

The Volvo 1800E now has fuel injection.

Which not only makes it go faster, but think.

The system is electronically controlled by a little computer unit that evaluates information on air temperature, altitude, engine speed, load and temperature. Then it "orders" the perfect fuel mixture for the conditions. So the engine always runs smoothly. And doesn't require a tune-up every time the weather changes.

It used to be you'd buy a Volvo 1800 because you wanted a sports car with brawn.

Now when you buy one, you also get a brain.

GENE GARFINKLE DRAWINGS

Road & Track Owner Survey

VOLVO

VOLVO 1800/122/144

OUR VOLVO OWNERS sample didn't include a single 11-year-old Volvo, the average car life claimed in the manufacturer's advertising, but it did contain an unusually high concentration of high-mileage cars and it did indeed show that Volvos are long-lived cars. It also showed that they have at least their share of minor problems to annoy the owner.

There were 134 cars covered in this survey: 77 122Ss, including two of the sporting 123GTs, 29 1800S coupes and 28 of the newer 140 series (the 142S, 144S and 145S wagon). The 122s and 1800s ranged from 1962 to 1968 year models, the biggest concentrations being 1967s in each case; two-thirds of the 140s were 1968s and the rest 1967s. A recent addition to our questionnaire form is to ask whether the car is a "first" or "only" car or a second (third) car: 80% of the 140s are first or only cars, 68% of the 122s, 64% of the 1800s; the rest are members of a multiple-car family. Eighty-eight percent of all the cars were bought new. Another recent addition to the form covers the owner's age, occupation and the state where he lives; the greatest number of our owners, by a wide margin, fell in the 21–30 age bracket and the three most frequently mentioned occupations were engineer, student and technician.

New York was the most represented state, California second; Massachusetts and Florida tied for third.

We eliminated those cars with less than 5000 miles on their odometers from the report. Fourteen percent of the balance had between 5000 and 10,000 miles, 26% between 10,000 and 20,000, 19% between 20,000 and 30,000, 16% between 30,000 and 40,000, and 14% between 5,000 and 10,000. Fully 5% had between 80 and 90,000 miles on them and the highest mileage reported was 104,000. Volvo owners use their cars at about the national-average rate—40% of them travel between 10 and 15,000 miles per year and 36% drive between 15 and 25,000 mi/yr. Ninety-five percent of the cars in the survey are used daily for transportation, 68% of them driven on long trips. Sixteen percent of the owners participate in rallies—21% of the 1800 owners, 16% of the 122, and 14% of the 140 owners; 9% of the total drive in a slalom occasionally. The largest percentage in our survey series to date—56%—say they drive their cars "hard," while 37% drive "moderately" and 7% "very hard."

The fact that Volvo owners tend to drive vigorously is reflected in the reasons they give for having bought Volvos. The most frequently noted reason was durability—39% of them mentioned this legendary Volvo quality. Couple that with the 26% who gave reliability as a decision factor and the 7% who mentioned the "Volvo reputation" and you have a strong indication that Volvo advertising and word-of-mouth are convincing people that Volvos are indeed sturdy, reliable machines. This also means that once the owner has bought his Volvo he expects it to be relatively trouble-free. To quote one, "After having supported a Morgan Plus 4, an MGA Twin-Cam and a Porsche 356, I was duly impressed with Volvo's tank-like qualities."

Handling was next on the list of reasons for purchase, and this factor is getting to be a fixture on these lists already; it seems that nearly anyone buying an import expects it to handle well. Naturally, a greater percentage of the 1800 owners considered handling that important: 34%, vs 32% for the 140 buyers and 21% for the 122s. Volvo also has a reputation for good assembly and finish, and 22% of the owners considered this fact an important reason to buy one. Twenty-one percent also were looking for good fuel economy, 20% for safety (another part of the "reputation") and 19% for a high level of comfort. Performance allied to economy, handling and comfort was considered a Volvo combination by 20% of the 122 owners, 14% of the 1800 owners and 11% of the 140 owners before their purchase. The highest previous-ownership percentage to occur so far in this series goes to Volvo: 13% of the owners reporting had already owned one or more Volvos. "Engines and drivetrains absolutely reliable—all could be driven vigorously with little fear of breaking anything"— owner of 145S and two previous 122Ss. Miscellaneous reasons for buying Volvo: styling (mostly 1800 owners), value for money, family space (122 and 140), engineering.

The care Volvo owners give their cars is, as far as we can tell, about average for an imported car owner; 67% follow the maker's maintenance schedule closely, 25% follow it "mostly" and 8% wait for something to break. Once again a "highest yet" percentage goes to Volvo: 14% of these owners do most or all of their own maintenance, and that's a lot. Perhaps this has something to do with their opinion of the dealers; only 50% of the owners consider their dealer's service to be good. (In previous surveys we have found that 62% of VW owners, 56% of Porsche owners and 39% of MGB owners gave their dealers a "good" rating.) Twenty-two percent of the Volvo owners said their dealer service was "fair" and 19% rated it as "poor." As with other makes, about 10% felt that service was too expensive.

New or Used	
Bought new	88%
Bought used	12%

Miles per Year	
0-5000 miles	1%
5000-10,000	17%
10,000-15,000	40%
15,000-25,000	36%
Over 25,000	6%

How Owners Feel about Volvo Dealers' Service

Rated "Good"	50%
Rated "Fair"	22%
Rated "Poor"	19%
No local dealer	6%
No opinion	3%
Do own work	14%

About Driving Habits

Drivers who said they drove "Moderately"	37%
Drivers who said they drove "Hard"	56%
Drivers who said they drove "Very Hard"	7%

Factory Maintenance Schedule Followed?

Owners who followed schedule completely	67%
Owners who followed it mostly but not totally	25%
Owners who didn't follow it at all	8%

Problem Areas

Mentioned by more than 10% of the owners:
Instruments (mostly 1800s)
Cooling system
Body parts
Clutch

Mentioned by between 5 and 10% of the owners:
Differential — Carburetors
Oil leaks — Exhaust system
Wheel alignment — Running-on (mostly 1968)

Owners Reporting No Troubles ... 10%

How Many Current Volvo Owners Would Buy Another?

Would	83%
Would not	12%
Undecided	5%

Five Best Features
Handling
Comfort
Fuel Economy
Reliability
Durability

Five Worst Features
Lack of Power
Ventilation
Engine Noise
Idiot Lights
Harsh Ride

Road & Track Owner Survey
VOLVO 1800/122/144

Of the qualities the owners liked best about their Volvos, 42% listed handling as a best feature—53% of the 140 owners, 48% of the 1800S and 35% of the 122S owners. Comfort came next on the best-liked list: 41% mentioned it, with 19% specifically giving the credit to Volvo's seats. Surprisingly, those with Volvo's unique lumbar-support adjustment in the front seats (1800 and 140 series) didn't brag any more about the seats than those without.

Fuel economy was the next favorite feature, mentioned by 24%; reliability garnered a 23% mention and so did durability. Fewer owners were impressed by the quality level (17%). Other favorites mentioned were performance, solidity, brakes, high-speed cruising ability and overall safety design.

And what's worst about Volvos? Well, for one thing, we have learned in these surveys that owners are better at picking out "worst" features than they are at naming "best" features. Every owner has some little annoyance, and there were 79, count 'em, different "Worst Features" listed by owners, few of them in any significant quantity. All this proves is that nobody can build a car to please everybody. The grievances that do count are: lack of acceleration, 13% (the new 2-liter engine should improve things here); poor ventilation, 10% (the 140s have better provisions); engine noise, 9%; 8% of the 122-140 owners disliked the "idiot light" dashboard and 9% of the 122 owners thought their cars rode harshly. Seven percent of the 122 owners disliked the rear suspension because it clunks, and 17% of the 1800 owners thought the Smiths instruments in their coupes were a worst feature.

As with MGBs and Porsches, Volvo owners reported that instruments were the most frequent problem area, with 17% of them having trouble. Predictably, the Smiths instruments in the 1800S were the biggest offenders—41% of these owners had trouble of some kind with them. Only 10% of the 122-140 owners had instrument trouble, mostly with speedometers or speedometer cables. Next on the trouble list came the cooling system, 13% of the owners having had some trouble here—8% had water pump trouble specifically. Body parts accounted for trouble for 12% of the owners, and the 140 series, relatively new to production, had a 21% incidence of this sort of thing. Window-winding mechanism was the most frequent body trouble in the 122s; vent windows in the 140 owners were troublesome, again indicating some early production difficul-

ties. Differential trouble and oil leaks (mostly from the gearbox) gave 10% of the owners difficulty, and clutch trouble reported by 12% of the owners was in part due to the gearbox leaks. Sixteen percent of 122 owners had some complaints about their exhaust systems—a tendency for hangers to break seems the most likely trouble here. Sparkplug life was reported to be about 8000 miles by several owners; some said that they could get longer life (more like 15,000 miles) by using an equivalent Champion plug. Running-on was a common problem with 1968s (21%), a by-product of Volvo's otherwise excellent dual-manifold emission control system. (This has been corrected for 1969 by a lower compression ratio.) Ten percent of the owners had no problems at all, other than normal maintenance and wear-tear.

Tire life ranged from 22,000 to 45,000 miles on the 1800s, 25,000 to 58,000 on the 122s; there weren't enough wear-outs on 140s to establish anything. Brake reline jobs came from 20,000 to 66,000 miles on the 122s, with the front disc brakes generally requiring attention before the rear drums—this is normal for disc/drum combinations. Seven percent of the "family" Volvos have been equipped by their owners with radial tires—some don't like the original tires' performance in the rain. (The 1800 models come with radials.) Seven percent of our owners said they had an automatic transmission and most of these made some adverse comment on it.

There wasn't a single engine overhaul reported, and the owner who had racked up 104,000 miles said, "This vehicle still has commendable compression after 104,000 miles; the head has never been off." (Our associate editor's old 544, disposed of at 97,000 miles, hadn't had its head off either— we're going to project 110,000 miles as an average life between overhauls in a Volvo.) There were only three owners who had had valve trouble, and one of those had a faulty camshaft when the car was new. Surely this durable engine is Volvo's prime claim to being an "11-year car," and it's worth noting that the engine does have to work hard most of the time. It also shows that engines don't have to be large, slow-turning and "lazy" to be durable and reliable!

In conclusion, we find that 85% of the 122S owners, 83% of the 1800S owners and 75% of the 140 owners would buy another Volvo; 5% of the 122S and 11% of the 140 owners aren't sure whether they would or not, and the rest would buy something else. Overall, 82% would buy another Volvo, a very respectable comeback potential that has, thus far in our survey series, only been exceeded by the loyalty reported by Porsche owners.

All in all, Volvo owners seem to be a practical lot who are well satisfied that they have made a wise investment in buying a Volvo and very likely will do it again.

Motorway Express

Dated but rejuvenated by fuel-injected engine;
effortless high-speed cruising;
poor visibility; very heavy steering; good ride;
superbly finished but expensive

M
MOTOR TESTED

To many the Volvo 1800 is the ultimate grand tourer. Perhaps frequent appearances on television in *The Saint* series as Simon Templar's personal transport have irretrievably linked the Volvo's distinctive shape with excitement. In this context it is surprising to reflect that the basic design is 10 years old.

Volvos have been available here since 1959, the P1800, as the car was originally known, appearing late the following year. Initially the bodies were built by Jensen Motors but in 1963 Volvo took over, gave the car a more powerful version of the 1780 cc B18 engine and renamed it the 1800S. With only detail improvements, which included a further increase in power

PRICE: £1,725 plus £529 7s. 6d. tax equals £2,254 7s. 6d. Extras fitted to test car: wing mirrors £5 (pair). Total as tested £2,259 7s. 6d.

output, the 1800S continued in production until 1968. That year the whole Volvo range received an engine increase to 1985cc, exhaust emission control equipment was fitted as standard and the engine given the designation B20. The announcement of the 1800E in Sweden last year brings history up to date.

It's basically the same car as its predecessor. Alloy wheels, 'E' badges on the rear panel, and a slightly different grille identify the new model externally; internally the facia has been improved and the seats now have built-in headrests. Under the skin there are now split-circuit brake lines operating all-round discs and of course fuel injection replaces carburetters.

We haven't road tested an 1800 since 1962; even then we thought the driving position rather vintage and the scuttle high. The past decade has seen a dramatic increase in glass area, a general lowering of waist lines and considerable progress in the field of ergonomics. These factors combine to make the substantially unchanged Volvo seem positively old fashioned though the adoption of Bosch electronic fuel injection has certainly give the car a lot more zest.

The increased power, up from 105 to 120 bhp DIN, is reflected by the performance figures—a maximum speed of 108 mph and a 0–50 mph time of 7.1 sec. Even so, the 1800E is still more of a marathon runner than a sprinter. The standard overdrive makes it a very relaxed high-speed tourer and reasonably economical. But its performance on secondary roads is less satisfactory and it doesn't compare well with some of its more modern rivals in the £2300 bracket.

As Sweden is a fellow EFTA country the price is not inflated by import duty. What you pay for is the car's superb finish and general quality feel. Volvo AB are the largest foreign buyers of British-made automobile equipment (about £21 million annually) so patriotic buyers need have few qualms about not buying British. Imports began a couple of months ago but Volvo intend to sell the 1800E in limited numbers only, so if you are prepared to pay Elan or E-type money for Volvo engineering in a sporting tourer then the 1800E is worth short-listing.

Performance and economy

The Bosch electronic fuel-injection equipment used on the 1800E (the E refers to fuel injection) includes an electronic control unit. This picks up signals from various senders in the engine and then regulates the opening time of the injection valves and hence the amount of fuel supplied. The senders transmit information to the control unit on engine rpm, cooling water temperature, inlet air temperature, manifold vacuum and the position of the throttle butterfly which is located at the forward end of the cast alloy inlet manifold. An electric fuel pump, aided by a pressure regulator, maintains a steady pressure of 30 psi to the injection nozzles, themselves located just upstream of the inlet valves.

The cold start procedure is to leave the throttle alone and to keep the starter turning for up to 15 seconds until the engine fires. At each new attempt a starting valve functions and squirts fuel into the inlet manifold. Nevertheless as cold starting is not immediate and the engine hesitates before it runs evenly, it's best to remain stationary until the control unit sorts things out. Then the car will pull away without hesitation. The warm-up period is very brief. For subsequent hot starts, you depress the accelerator half way and let the slow pre-engaged starter turn the engine until it fires.

The additional capacity of the B20 engine was obtained by increasing the bore of the B18 from 84.14 to 89.9 mm, keeping the stroke constant at 80 mm. So in its current 2-litre form the unit is still oversquare. The crankshaft runs in five main bearings, and the engine is normally remarkably smooth, though very rough and tappety at idle. The rev counter has a striped red

PERFORMANCE

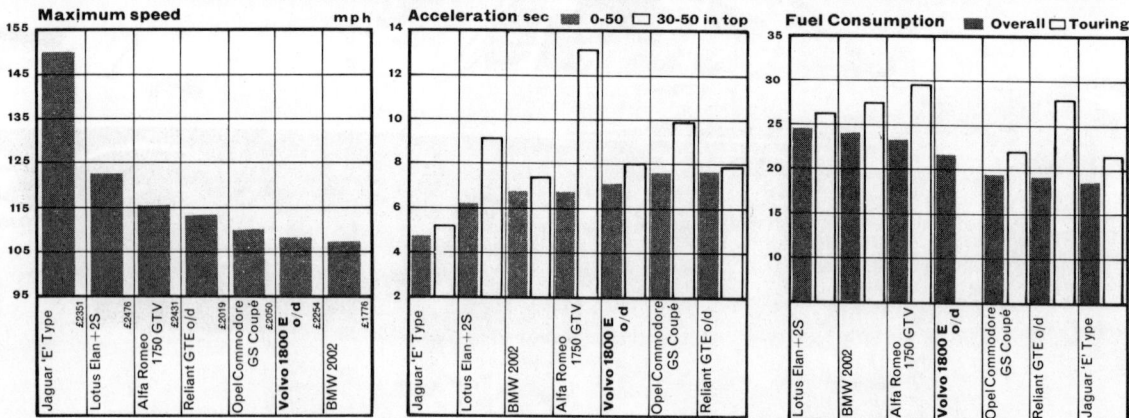

Maximum speed (mph): Jaguar 'E' Type £2351; Lotus Elan +2S £2476; Alfa Romeo 1750 GTV £2431; Reliant GTE o/d £2019; Opel Commodore GS Coupé £2090; Volvo 1800 E o/d £2254; BMW 2002 £1776

Acceleration sec ■ 0-50 □ 30-50 in top: Jaguar 'E' Type; Lotus Elan +2S; BMW 2002; Alfa Romeo 1750 GTV; Volvo 1800 E o/d; Opel Commodore GS Coupé; Reliant GTE o/d

Fuel Consumption ■ Overall □ Touring: Lotus Elan +2S; BMW 2002; Alfa Romeo 1750 GTV; Volvo 1800 E o/d; Opel Commodore GS Coupé; Reliant GTE o/d; Jaguar 'E' Type

Performance tests carried out by *Motor's* **staff at the Motor Industry Research Association proving ground, Lindley.**

Test Data: World copyright reserved; no unauthorized reproduction in whole or in part.

Conditions
Weather: Dry, sunny wind, 0-15 mph
Temperature: 78-92°F
Barometer 29.51-29.46 in. hg.
Surface: Dry tarmacadam
Fuel: Premium 98 octane (RM), 4 Star rating

Maximum Speeds
	mph	kph
Mean lap banked circuit	108.0	173.8
Best one-way ¼-mile	112.5	181.0
3rd gear	76	122
2nd gear } at 6000 rpm	52	83
1st gear	32	52

"Maximile" speed: (Timed quarter mile after 1 mile accelerating from rest)
Mean	109.8
Best	112.5

Acceleration Times
mph	sec
0-30	3.3
0-40	5.2
0-50	7.1
0-60	9.6
0-70	13.0
0-80	16.7
0-90	22.9
0-100	31.4
Standing quarter mile	17.4
Standing kilometre	32.1

mph	O/d Top sec	Top sec	3rd sec
10-30	—	—	6.5
20-40	—	12.0	6.0
30-50	—	11.0	5.6
40-60	—	11.5	5.6
50-70	—	12.2	6.1
60-80	—	13.6	6.7
70-90	—	16.0	—
80-100	—	13.9	—

Fuel Consumption
Overall	21.75 mpg
	(= 13.0 litres/100km)
Total test distance	1532 miles

Brakes
Pedal pressure, deceleration and equivalent stopping distance from 30 mph
lb.	g.	ft.
25	0.27	111
50	0.57	53
75	1.00	30
Handbrake	0.37	81

Fade Test
20 stops at ½g deceleration at 1 min. intervals from a speed midway between 40 mph and maximum speed (=74 mph)
	lb.
Pedal force at beginning	50
Pedal force at 10th stop	65
Pedal force at 20th stop	50

Steering
Turning circle between kerbs:
	ft.
Left	26⅞
Right	28
Turns of steering wheel from lock to lock | 3:6
Steering wheel deflection for 50 ft. diameter circle 1.0 turns

Clutch
Free pedal movement	= 2 in.
Additional movement to disengage clutch completely	= 4 in.
Maximum pedal load	= 40 lb.

Speedometer
Indicated	10	20	30	40	50	60	70
True	9	18	27.5	36	45	55	63.5
Indicated	80	90	100				
True	72.5	81	90				
Distance recorder 5% fast

Weight
Kerb weight (unladen with fuel for approximately 50 miles)
22.25 cwt.
Front/rear distribution	54/46
Weight laden as tested	26.0 cwt.

Parkability
Gap needed to clear 6 ft. wide obstruction in front

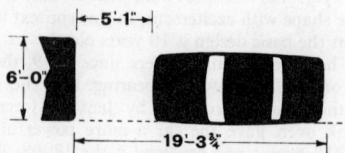

5'-1"   6'-0"   19'-3¾"

line running from 6000–6500 rpm and beyond that solid red defines the prohibited area.

Maximum power of 120 bhp DIN is given at 6000 rpm, but the engine feels delightfully unstrained at 6500 rpm and we used this for the performance tests to accelerate to 50 mph in 7.1 sec. and to the quarter mile post in 17.4 sec.—impressive figures for a 22¼ cwt. car. Over a lap of the banked MIRA track we recorded 108 mph and a best quarter mile of 112.5 mph. On the slowing-down lap the car emitted clouds of oil smoke from the exhaust; presumably oil was being drawn into the combustion chambers through the valve guides. Although alarming it didn't seem to have any detrimental effect on the car's performance and only one pint of oil was needed during our 1500-mile test.

Unfortunately the engine's smoothness at the top end is not matched by low speed flexibility. At low rpm it is snatchy and there are loud unpleasant vibrations from under the dash panel up to 25 mph in top and up to 20 mph in third. The engine is not happy pulling below 2000 rpm in the higher gears, which is reflected in the acceleration times; beyond 2000 rpm it pulls strongly. This high gearing pays off in fuel economy—we achieved nearly 22 mpg overall and an intermediate check showed over 23 mpg; on a long run at a steady 70 mph we recorded 26 mpg. The B20E engine has a higher compression ratio than the B20 as well as larger inlet valves and a different camshaft. But even at 10.5:1 the makers recommend only 97 octane fuel; we used 4-star 98 octane petrol and could detect no pinking.

Transmission

The 1800E excels on long straight-road journeys. This is in no small measure due to the high gearing, which some of our testers thought too high for the car's power output. Nevertheless it just managed to start on the 1-in-3 test hill, though a previous attempt immediately after the acceleration runs had failed. The clutch pedal pressure (40 lbs) is too high and pedal travel excessive—a total movement of 6 in. is required fully to disengage the drive; we suspect the cable needed adjustment.

The ratios are quite well spaced with 70 mph easily attained in third; it is geared to do 76 mph at 6000 rpm. The overdrive operates on top gear only and is controlled by a stalk mounted on the left of the steering column shroud. It engages with a perceptible thump to reveal a really unstrained high-speed cruise capability. Top gear at 1:1 gives a fairly average 16.9 mph per 1000 rpm but overdrive top at 0.797:1 give a really long-legged 21.2 mph. A red light on the facia, which can be distracting at night, shines when overdrive is engaged. The Laycock unit slurs out of engagement with no jarring.

There's an enormous circular knob mounted atop a stout gearlever which is pleasant to grasp, unlike many modern spindly devices, and controls a smooth though rather heavy change. This is particularly noticeable when the gearbox oil is cold—the change from first to second needs a firm hand. It is spring loaded towards third and top and works in a semi-horizontal plane, so you tend to place your hand either on the forward or the under

An imposing front; the B20 badge refers to the 2 litre engine

The rear compartment is best considered as additional luggage space rather than a passengers' seat. Straps are provided to hold luggage in situ. Our 5 ft. 10 in. tester has his head firmly pinned on the roof and little room for his legs

Flat seats set too low do not help to improve basically poor visibility. They don't provide much lateral support either. The circular knob on the side of the seat adjusts a lumbar support pad. The steering is very heavy

side of the knob when preparing to change. The movement from second to third is particularly slick—just a forward prod and it's home—and even a really fierce change won't beat the synchromesh. Both the gearbox and final drive are quiet.

Handling and brakes

One thing that did not endear the 1800E to us was its heavy cam and gear steering. When parking it requires a lot of effort to get any movement at the road wheels; when the car is stationary it is not possible to turn the wheel with one arm. But once it's moving the gearing (3.6 turns lock-to-lock) is good and only one turn is required to scribe a 50 ft. circle—a typical right-angled turn. The turning circle is reasonable for a largish car, which it needs to be as three-point turns soon bring the driver out in a sweat. Out of town the steering is acceptable but ponderous. It's fairly accurate and readily transmits information on front-end breakaway to the driver.

Basically the Volvo understeers and displays quite a lot of body roll. Wishbones and coil springs are used at the front (mounted on a sub-frame) with a substantial anti-roll bar to increase front-end weight transfer and thus promote understeer; but towards the cornering limit controllable roll oversteer predominates. The live rear axle is also coil-sprung and located fore and aft by trailing arms with a Panhard rod to control lateral movements. We think the rather imprecise behaviour of the rear end during high speed cornering may be due to the very large rubber bushes in which the trailing links are located at their forward end.

Our test car was shod with Irish-made Michelin XAS tyres which provided good squeal-free grip in the dry but were prone to rather sudden breakaway in the wet. They are mounted on large handsome five-stud "mag" wheels which have a steel rim and alloy centre; they are made by Cromodora Fergat.

There are servo-assisted discs all round, and dual-circuit hydraulics with three wheels in each circuit so that if one circuit is damaged 80 per cent braking efficiency is maintained. The handbrake operates on separate drums and achieved a 0.37 g stop, but would not hold the car on the 1-in-3 hill. With 25 lb brake pedal pressure we recorded a 0.27 g stop; trebling the pressure to 75 lb gave a creditable 1 g. The car stopping all square.

The brakes are very reassuring during normal driving so we were surprised to find their performance was affected by our fade test. Initially 50 lb pressure was required to give a 0.5 g stop, but after only seven applications (when the brakes began to smell) this rose to 75 lb. They recovered towards the end of the test. The watersplash had no effect on their performance.

Comfort and controls

One of the outstanding features of the 1800E is undoubtedly the ride, which belies its live axle specification. Small ridges and bumps are soaked up without murmur, and no joggling is transmitted to the body. Yet the suspension, though evidently fairly soft (witness the body roll), feels taught and is in no way

The spare wheel occupies much of the boot which only took 5.3 cu. ft. of our test boxes. The pile on the left fits on the ledge behind the front seats giving a total luggage capacity (assuming only two occupants) of 10 cu. ft.

SPECIFICATION

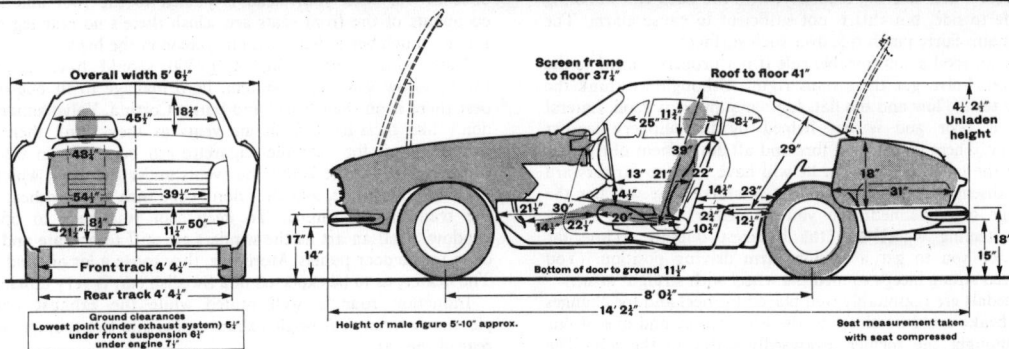

Overall width 5' 6½" · 45¼" · 18½" · 49½" · 54½" · 39¼" · 21½" · 8½" · 50" · 11½"
Front track 4' 4½" · **Rear track 4' 4½"**
Ground clearances — Lowest point (under exhaust system) 5¼", under front suspension 6½", under engine 7½"
17" · 14"
Screen frame to floor 37½" · Roof to floor 41" · 4½' 2½" Unladen height
25" · 11½" · 8½" · 39" · 29" · 13" · 21" · 22" · 18" · 31" · 21½" · 30" · 4½" · 14½" · 23" · 14½" · 22½" · 2½" · 12½" · 2½" · 10½" · 12½" · 18" · 15"
Bottom of door to ground 11½" · 8' 0½" · 14' 2½"
Height of male figure 5'-10" approx.
Seat measurement taken with seat compressed

1985 cc four-cylinder engine with fuel injection; live rear axle; all-round disc brakes

Engine
Block material . . . . Cast iron
Head material . . . . Cast iron
Cylinders . . . . Four in line
Cooling system . . . Water, pump, thermostat and viscous coupling fan; sealed
Bore and stroke . 88.9 mm (3.50 in.) x 80 mm (3.15 in.)
Cubic capacity . . . . . 1985 cc (121 cu. in.)
Main bearings . . . . Five
Valves . . . . Pushrod operated ohv
Compression ratio . . . . 10.5 : 1
Induction . Bosch electronically controlled fuel injection
Fuel pump . . . . Electric
Oil filter . . . . Full flow
Max. power (net) . . . . . 120 bhp at 6000 rpm
Max. power (gross) . . . . 130 bhp at 6000 rpm
Max. torque (net) . . . . 123 lb. ft. at 3500 rpm
Max. torque (gross) . . . 130 lb. ft at 3500 rpm

Transmission
Clutch . . . . . . 8½ in. dia. sdp, diaphragm spring
Internal gearbox ratios
Overdrive top 0.797
Top gear 1.00
3rd gear 1.34
2nd gear 1.97
1st gear 3.14
Reverse 3.54
Synchromesh . . . . . On all forward gears
Overdrive type . . . . . . Laycock J-type
Final drive (type and ratio) . . . Hypoid bevel, 4.30:1
Mph at 1000 rpm in:
O/d top gear 21.2
Top gear 16.9
3rd gear 12.61
2nd gear 8.6
1st gear 5.4

Chassis and body
Construction Unitary

Brakes
Type . . . . . . Split circuit servo-assisted discs all-round. Drum for handbrake
Dimensions . . . . Front 10.59 in. dia. disc, rear 11.6 in. dia. disc
Friction areas:
Front: . . . . . . Effective area 27 sq. in.
Rear: . . . . . . Effective area 15.5 sq. in.

Suspension and steering
Front . . . . . . Coil springs, wishbones with anti-roll bar.
Rear . . . . . . Coil springs, live axle located by trailing arms and a Panhard rod
Shock absorbers:
Front and rear . . . Double acting telescopic
Steering type . . . Gemmer cam and roller
Tyres . . . . . . 165 HR 15 Michelin XAS
Wheels . . . . . Pressed steel · rims with cast-aluminium hubs
Rim size 5J

Coachwork and equipment
Starting handle . . . No
Tool kit contents . . Box spanner for plugs and wheel nuts; tommy bar; adjustable spanner; pliers; plain blade and crosshead screwdrivers
Jack . . . . Scissor type
Jacking points . . . Four
Battery . . . . . 12 volt, negative earth, 60 amp hrs. capacity
Number of electrical fuses 12
Headlamps 45/40W
Indicators . . . . . Self-cancelling flashers
Reversing lamp . . Yes, operated automatically by gear lever
Screen wipers . . Two-speed electric
Screen washers . . . Electric
Sun visors . . . . Two
Locks:
With ignition key . . Steering lock
With other keys . . a. doors and boot; b. central lidded console
Interior heater . . . Fresh air type with booster fan
Upholstery . . . . . Leather
Floor covering . . . Carpet
Alternative body styles None
Maximum load . . . 484 lb. without driver

Maintenance
Fuel tank capacity . . 10 galls
Sump . . . . . . 6.6 pints SAE 20W-50 (incl. filter)
Gearbox . . . . . . 2.46 pints SAE 20W-50 (incl. overdrive)
Rear axle . . . . . 2.28 pints SAE 90 EP
Steering gear . . . . 0.44 pints SAE 90 EP
Coolant . . . . . . 1.87 galls (1 drain tap)
Chassis lubrication . . None
Minimum service interval . . . . . 6000 miles

Ignition timing . . . 10 deg. btdc at 700-800 rpm vacuum pipe disconnected
Contact breaker gap . 0.016-0.020 in.
Sparking plug gap . . 0.028-0.032 in.
Sparking plug type. . Bosch W225T35
Tappet clearance (warm or cold) . . Inlet 0.016 in. Exhaust 0.016 in.
Valve timing:
inlet opens . . . 29° btdc
inlet closes . . . 71° abdc
exhaust opens . . 71° bbdc
exhaust closes . . 29° atdc
Rear wheel toe-in . . 0—.16 in.
Camber angle. . . . 0—+½°
Castor angle . . . . 0—+1°
King pin inclination . 8° with no camber
Tyre pressures:
Front . . . . . . 26 psi
Rear . . . . . . 28 psi

Safety check list
Steering Assembly
Steering box position   Mounted on o/s front inner wing
Steering column collapsible   Yes
Steering wheel boss padded   Yes
Steering wheel dished   No
Instrument panel
Projecting switches   Yes, but of collapsible type
Sharp cowls   None
Padding   Yes, top and bottom
Windscreen and Visibility
Screen type   Laminated
Pillars padded   No
Standard driving mirrors   Day/night interior mirror
Interior mirror framed   Yes
Interior mirror collapsible   Yes
Sun visors   Two
Seats and Harness
Attachments to floor   On slides
Do they tip forward?   Yes
Headrest attachment points   Headrests standard
Safety harness   Static lap and diagonal
Doors
Projecting handles   Window winders
Anti-burst locks   Yes

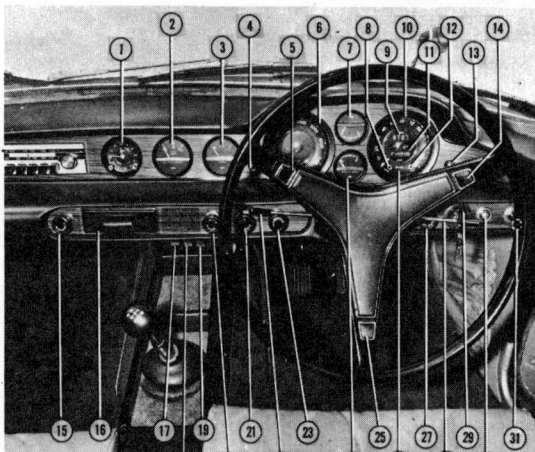

1 clock. 2 oil pressure gauge. 3 fuel gauge. 4 overdrive tell-tale. 5, 14 and 25 horn. 6 tachometer. 7 oil temperature gauge. 8 battery charge warning light. 9 odometer. 10 speedometer. 11 mileometer. 12 main beam tell-tale. 13 handbrake and brake system warning light. 15 cigar lighter. 16 ashtray. 17 and 18 heater distribution controls. 19 heater temperature control. 20 wipers and washers. 21 heater booster fan. 22 indicator/headlamp flasher stalk. 23 hazard warning lights. 24 water temperature gauge. 26 indicator tell-tale. 27 instrument panel lighting rheostat. 28 overdrive stalk. 29 steering lock/ignition/starter. 30 side and headlights. 31 heated rear window

soggy. Over long-wavelength irregularities the car displays a certain rear wheel steering tendency, with the back end waddling from side to side, but this is not sufficient to cause alarm. The body remains fairly pinch free over such surfaces.

Seats can spoil a comfortable ride if not properly tuned to the suspension. Volvo got their sums right. Although we think the seats are set too low and too flat, lumbar support is good. Lateral support is poor and is not helped by the slippery leather upholstery. There is plenty of fore and aft adjustment of the seat for even the tallest person, but he will have to sit so far forward fully to disengage the clutch that it is unlikely he will use the full range of adjustment. So you sit rather too close to the vertical steering wheel and the backrest doesn't recline far enough for you to get a straight arm driving position. (You would need strong biceps to turn the wheel with straight arms.)

The pedals are reasonably well placed for heel and toe changes but the brake could be closer to the accelerator, and one of our testers thought the former awkwardly offset to the left. The handbrake is mounted to the right of the driver's seat with the release button surrounded by a circular ring to prevent accidental operation when climbing in or out—a clever idea.

Minor controls are operated by push-pull switches spread across the facia. Only the indicators and headlamp flashers are controlled by a stalk which is too short and too far from the wheel rim. Wipers and washers are on the left of the wheel, one click for slow, the second fast, and the third for fast and washers. So you merely have to pull the switch right out to get wash and wipe. On the other side of the wheel, which has a horn button mounted in each of its three spokes, a switch operates powerful lights on main beam; the dip is a self-centring micro-switch on the indicator stalk.

The car falls down badly on visibility. Sitting very low down in a car with high sides is not a good starting point; added to this is a very limited glass area (some described the windows as portholes). With high headrests on the front seats you can't see much to the rear either (though the pronounced tail fins are useful parking aids), so the optional wing-mounted mirrors are essential. And the lack of three-quarter rear vision becomes almost dangerous when joining a main road from an oblique junction, such corners must be approached at right angles van-style for a safe exit.

Symmetrical wipers sweep a reasonable arc, but there is a blind spot on the right of the screen. For rear seat passengers the accommodation is claustrophobic—they really can't see anything with the headrests blocking the view forwards and only tiny slots to the side. But the rear seats are not really meant for passengers,

though they're fairly accessible through the wide doors. But once in the back your head is pinned to the roof and if the occupants of the front seats are selfish there's no rear leg room. It's not much better with just one person in the back.

Cars with a price tag of £2300 should have a proper through-flow ventilation system. Ford manage to fit one of the best there is on their bread-and-butter Cortina. Volvo apparently don't like facia-level fresh air vents as they think there is a possibility of, for example, cigarette ash being blown into the driver's eyes. So the 1800E has vents under the dash, which are not really adequate, and they don't cope with radiated heat from the transmission tunnel. To keep cool you have to open a window, itself an art as the winders are stiff to operate and very close to the door panels. Moreover, they cause a lot of wind roar. The heater, as to be expected in a Swedish car, is very efficient.

Induction roar is well muted while the exhaust note is pleasantly 'fruity'. A single exhaust splits into two tailpipes at the rear of the car.

The viscous-coupled fan helps to subdue engine noise, which at 70 mph in overdrive top (3300 rpm) is very low, but the sealing of the frameless windows is not good particularly in side winds. Road noise is low and radial thump almost imperceptible.

Fittings and furniture

An imposing array of instruments, including an oil temperature gauge, faces the driver. Volvo warned us that the speedometer was inaccurate and because no spare was available we had to make allowances for a 10 per cent error. It is matched by a rev counter and the two are separated by oil and water temperature gauges. The oil gauge needle rarely moved but that for the water temperature often approached the red sector; the handbook said this was acceptable for short periods. The facia is attractively laid out and the instruments mounted on a simulated matt wood background with black leathercloth top and bottom. Standard equipment includes a heated rear window (there is an alternator to cope with supply) which has a two-position switch, one for clearing the window and the other for keeping it clear. There are courtesy switches for two rear-mounted interior lights on both doors—the lights can also be operated by a flick switch above the driver's knees or by pulling out the trailing edge of the lights themselves. There is a map-reading light on the passenger's side.

There is plenty of oddment storage space inside the car. Between the seats a carpeted console within easy reach of the driver takes oddments and behind it there is a lidded lockable box. In each footwell there is a map pocket and behind the rear seat a deep full-width shelf for more bulky articles.

We think most prospective buyers will regard the rear compartment as an extension of the luggage capacity rather than potential occupant space. Volvo evidently planned it this way, too, so the accommodation in proportion to total vehicle size is small. The backrest of the rear ledge folds flat and under the squab there are straps for retaining luggage. We got our biggest test box in here though it only just went through the door. Without restricting rear visibility we got a total of 4.7 cu. ft. inside the car and an additional 5.3 cu. ft. in the boot. Much of the boot space is taken by the spare which is concealed in a neat cover. The unlit boot has a rubber mat on the floor.

Volvo's own brand of seat belts are fitted; they are easy to use and adjust.

Servicing and accessibility

The self-propping bonnet (it uses a stay like that on a BLMC 1800) is released by a substantial lever under the dashboard. Most items are readily accessible, though the distributor is rather hidden by the brake servo unit. The labelled fuse box is in the cockpit mounted on the nearside bulkhead above the passenger's legs.

There are now about 300 Volvo dealers and distributors in Britain. After the first 3000 miles the 1800E needs attention at 6000-mile intervals when the oil is changed. There are no greasing points, and there is a towing bracket welded to the front subframe should your Volvo ever break down.

1 oil filler cap. 2 clutch cable. 3 coolant expansion tank with filler cap. 4 brake fluid reservoir. 5 brake servo unit. 6 coil. 7 dipstick (hidden). 8 windscreen washer reservoir

MAKE: Volvo. MODEL: 1800E. MAKERS: Aktiebolaget Volvo Goteborg, Sweden. CONCESSIONAIRES: Volvo Concessionaires Ltd, Raeburn Road, Ipswich, Suffolk

Rob Luck, dodging the crims, reports on 400 Coupe miles . . .

VOLVO P1800E

DIAL 999 999

wheels ROAD TEST

NO, SCOTLAND YARD does not have a Volvo dealership! The familiar digits symbolise Volvo's latest piece of sports car one-upmanship — an odometer that reads to a million miles!

About the closest Volvo has got to the legendary criminal hounds of Great Britain is the equally legendary Saint television series in which dapper Roger Moore private eyes-off crims with great success while punting a Volvo Coupe with true skill and daring.

Despite its idiot-box image, the Volvo Coupe is equally a car for retired businessmen, still-posing managing directors and even wives of the affluent. And it has the

The shadow of a near Melbourne haystack could be the ideal place for a Volvo driver to rest with bird and bottle. Volvo's Coupe puts across ultimate classic luxury image despite ageing body.

durability to go a million miles.

It's not all brawn and brute power but it is a gentle boulevardier in any sensitive driver's hands.

So what else is new? Isn't that the format of the Volvo Coupe that has been around for many years, even on the local market.

Basically it is — but for the 1971 silly season, Volvo has gone the full performance/dress-up package route for the vehicle that has inevitably

been pushed into the high echelon price market by import taxation.

Dare I say, that Volvo Aktiebolaget, Goteborg, Sweden has *injected* the long-lasting coupe with new power from a sohpisticated induction system developed specially for its well-proven four-cylinder engine?

Despite a facial high-rise, the engine boost is the main news. Bosch-developed four-port fuel-injection lifts power on the well-developed B20 engine to 130 (SAE) bhp at 6000 rpm and puts torque at an identical figure (130 lb/ft) at 3500 rpm. It adds up to great performance with flexibility and smoothness.

Your 1971 Volvo Coupe will trot out standing quarters in the low 16-second bracket if you can get the rear skins to break traction, and 120 mph in overdrive top is a pretty casual affair if you have the right road.

The engineers didn't neglect other aspects of the vital torque and

Pleasant place to live/work. Volvo wraps up its front seat passengers in ultimate · seating, with high-sill cockpit and that aircraft-style wrap-around feeling. Instrumentation is complete.

E is for Einspritzen — or fuel injection — and the B20E engine pumps 130 bhp through four speed with O/D for impressive performance and remarkable fuel economy. Engine compartment is ultra-tight but most vitals are accessible.

Perfect profile blends into stubby, finned tail that European-style advocates find appealing. The 1971 style changes include full magnesium road wheels, black air-extractor/fuel filler vents.

power curves and built-in a flat-graph characteristic that gives top gear lugging figures close to V8 times — 20-40 mph in 7.4 seconds, 50-70 mph in 6.4 seconds.

That means the little-old-lady-from-Pasadena can drop it into top and carve up the outbound traffic without having bad moments from the opposite direction. If she does get in a squeeze, four-wheel power-assisted discs will slot her back in a conveniently located space or she can do the full production and stop dead in a straight line with a sickening stomach from the G-loadings. From 60 mph it takes only 3.3 seconds, from 30 mph the car will be stationary in 1.4 seconds — not bad for 2700 lb-plus (unladen).

At first I didn't believe my Breitling. The wrist chronometer may not read to split-tenths but 0-60 mph times in close 9 seconds and standing quarters under the mid-16s looked pretty exaggerated. The next step was a battery of recently-corrected stopwatches and a dead-serious run against the sweep second hand on Calder's main dragway. There is something clinically convincing about figures recorded on a drag strip.

The figures were confirmed — in fact they kept getting better and better. Calder is quite an accommodating place to test a really hot bit of gear — so I ran out another important test time. From a standstill to maximum rpm in top gear (fourth — not O/D fourth) took just 31.6 seconds. That's virtually standstill to 110 mph in just over 30 seconds — a very impressive time for a social boulevardier.

Still on the Calder scene, I put down three laps from a flying start on a surface smattered with the scars of the previous day's rallycross meeting.

VOLVO P1800 E

That meant plenty of slippery dirt and mud in all the tweaky bits, but road pressures and little familiarisation time still brought times crashing to 62.5 seconds on the Michelin XAS tyres which naturally rolled and distorted without pressure to reduce the sidewall loadings. For a stock sporty — any stock sporty — that's a competitive time.

To achieve fast laps, the Volvo has to be punted hard — right to its maximum performance level. But it reaches and holds that level with the greatest safety of any sports car I've driven. The steering was also the best in any road car - light, sensitive, precise with adequate feel, no feedback, and a perfectly balanced castor section that spins the wheel back to neutral without over-handling.

Performance is punched out in short, sharp stabs of power through a beautifully swift gearbox that is controlled in the cockpit by a big-diameter lever with a massive four-ball shifter on top. The overdrive fifth (which you won't use on the circuit) is on a special steering stalk.

The ratios are not close and are definitely not circuit or ultra-performance-oriented — they're meant to provide practical all-round use of an engine built for general purpose motoring. The clutch is disappointingly heavy — for the traffic light grand prix you have to pop it on the yellow, drop it quickly on the green and use as little as possible on the shifts. It seems lighter as you get to know the car. The promised automatic transmission for women drivers has been delayed by the fantastic demand from the American market — we won't see it in Australia until the end of 1971.

Overdrive is a great saver. It slashes engine rpm by an average 1000 rpm, effectively kills the thrashy four's engine noise at medium range speeds and knocks the thirst right back — you can save 8 mpg or more with careful and experienced use of the little steering column stalk. But if you want to drive smoothly, you have to help the O/D in and out with the clutch.

The engine's willing torque is so great it pulls strongly all the way to 5600 rpm in O/D top — and gives the impression it will go further. The limiting factors of wind pressure, and available space is unlikely to allow this on a flat road, but the Volve Coupe gained from 5000 O/D to 5500 in a mile and to 5600 in another mile with the engine still swinging — it could grab another 100 rpm or so but it's not really significant. It will get to 120 mph easily.

Up top, the car has a few problems. Its shape ducks crosswinds beautifully — we had a sidewind factor of 20 mph through hedges, forests and windbreaks without shifting the beast off line at better than the ton, but the wind noise above 90 mph is appalling. The test car had no exterior mirror (which it needed badly) so that can't be blamed — it's simply fussy design around the windows. With through-flow ventilation already installed, Volvo should aim for sealed (or eliminated) quarterlights and better soundproofing.

There are two uncharacteristic hang-ups for high speed work. The wipers float frantically above 70 mph and are never really fully effective in any speed in heavy rain. The lights are stretched to show the way at 80-90 mph. Both problems are clearly easily shelved.

But these points apart, Volvo does get your up in the road-bound jet-set faster, smoother and more comfortably than most other cars.

The cockpit is incredibly compact, detailed and well-equipped. Visually it looks good, with a vast wrap-around console blending into high sills that give a comfortable, ensconced feeling, with obvious safety benefits. Instrumentation is comprehensive, beautifully arranged, visually well-coded and perfectly blended to the interior treatment.

The steering wheel is originally located, perfect for most heights/reaches and gives a good view of the instruments with a ready access to the controls. And all the switchgear and controls can be reached from the driver's seat even when fully buckled-in by the centre-located auto-clip-in lap-sash seat belts.

Visible through the tri-spoke wheel are the main instruments — clear and obtrusive. The tacho is good for 7000 (but you'd best cool it at 6000) and a speedometer runs to a humorous 120 mph and contains the legendary one million mile odometer (plus trip meter).

Between the two master dials are smaller gauges for oil and water temperature. I'd like to see the oil temperature gauge swapped for the more important oil pressure gauge — one of the three other ancillary dials out to the left on the console (oil pressure, fuel level and clock). The oil temperature gauge registers only in extremely hot conditions, or when pushed very hard or subjected to track-type conditions. Water temperature stays constantly in its vital green operation area due to sealed cooling system and a slip-coupling fan that works efficiently down to idle

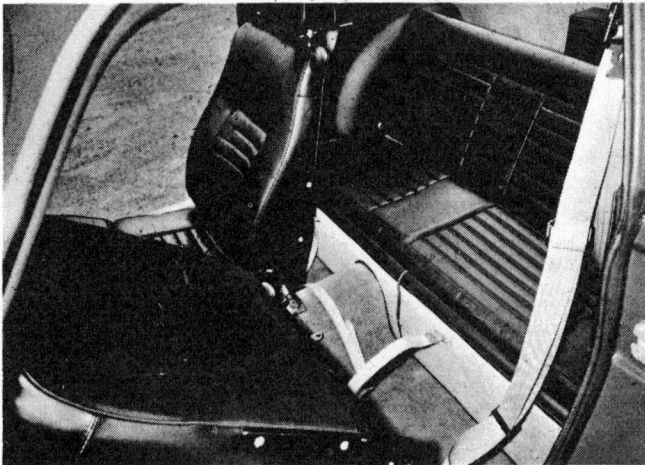

Rear seat is convertible style — folded down there's extra luggage space with locating straps to stop it floating. Lock the rear squab up and you have occasional room for adults, great place for small children.

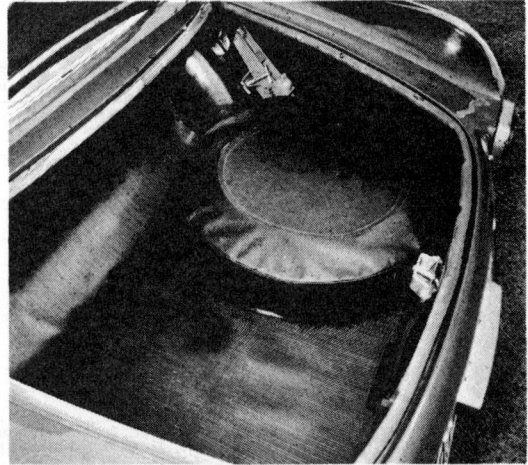

Boot faces the typical sports car problem — with a low-profile shell, where do you put the spare? Volvo laid it on the floor and covered it, but it's greedy for space and a holiday means bootlid racks or gear stacked behind the front seats.

wheels ROAD TEST

TECHNICAL DETAILS

MAKE . . . . Volvo
MODEL . . . . P1800E Coupe
BODY TYPE . . . . .2-door Coupe
PRICE $7125
OPTIONS . . . . Radio
COLOR . . . . Red
MILEAGE START 2271
MILEAGE FINISH 2590
WEIGHT . . . . (1230 kg) 2706 lb

FUEL CONSUMPTION:
Overall . . . . 22 mpg
Cruising . . . . 26 mpg

TEST CONDITIONS:
Weather . . . . hot, dry
Surface . . . . hot mix
Load . . . . 2 persons
Fuel . . . . .pump premium

SPEEDOMETER ERROR (mph):

Indicated	30	40	50	60	70	80	90
Actual	27.8	37.5	46	55	65	75	84

PERFORMANCE
Piston speed at max bhp . . . . . .(960 m/min) 3150 ft/min
Top gear mph per 1000 rpm . . . . . . (5th) 21.6 (4th) 17.2
Engine rpm at max speed 5600
Lbs (laden) per gross bhp (power-to-weight) . .(9.8 kg) 22 lb

MAXIMUM SPEEDS:
Fastest run . . . . 124 mph
Average of all runs . . . . 122 mph
Speedometer indication, fastest runSee text — approx 135 mph

IN GEARS:
1st . . . . (51 kph) 32 mph (6000 rpm)
2nd . . . . (78 kph) 53 mph (6000 rpm)
3rd . . . .(126 kph) 78 mph (6000 rpm)
4th . . . .(172 kph) 108 mph (6000 rpm)
5th . . . .(198 kph) 124 mph (5600 rpm)

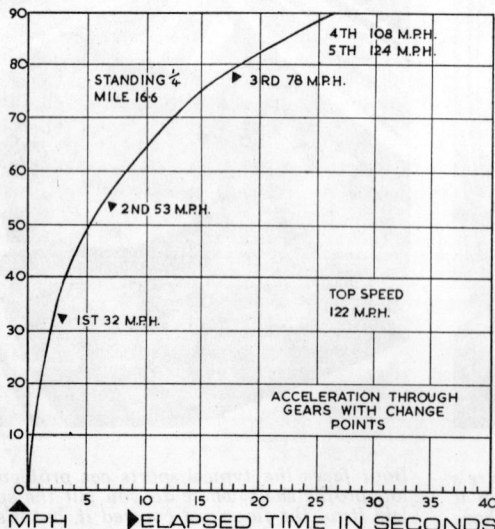

ACCELERATION THROUGH GEARS WITH CHANGE POINTS

ACCELERATION (through gears):
0-30 mph . . . . .2.7 sec
0-40 mph . . . . .4.9 sec
0-50 mph . . . . .6.9 sec
0-60 mph . . . . .9.1 sec
0-70 mph . . . . .11.8 sec
0-80 mph . . . . .15.8 sec
0-90 mph . . . . .19.2 sec
0-100 mph . . . . .21.8 sec

	2nd gear	3rd gear	4th gear
20-40 mph	3.2 sec	5.3 sec	7.4 sec
30-50 mph	3.2 sec	4.9 sec	7.3 sec
40-60 mph	3.6 sec	4.3 sec	6.6 sec
50-70 mph	—	4.5 sec	6.4 sec

STANDING QUARTER MILE:
Fastest run . . . . .16.4 sec
Average all runs .16.6 sec

BRAKING:
From 30 mph to 0 . . . . .1.4 sec
From 60 mph to 0 . . . . .3.3 sec

SPECIFICATIONS

ENGINE:
Cylinders . . . . .Four in line
Bore and stroke . . . (88.92 mm) 3.5 in. x (80 mm) 3.15 in.
Cubic capacity . . . .(1990 cc) 121 cu in.
Compression ratio . . . . 10.5 to 1
Valves . . . . overhead
Induction . . . . .four — port fuel injection
Fuel pump . . . . mechanical
Oil filter . . . . .full flow
Power at rpm . . . . (19.6 kg/m) 130 (SAE) bhp @ 6000 rpm
Torque . . . . . . (19.6 kg/m) 130 (SAE) bhp @ 3500 rpm

TRANSMISSION:
Type . . . . .four speed all syncro with overdrive
Clutch . . . . .mechanical SDP diaphragm
Gear lever location . . . . .floor

Ratios:	Direct	Overall
1st	3.1	13.5
2nd	1.9	8.4
3rd	1.3	5.7
4th	1.0	4.3
5th	0.7	3.4
Final drive		4.3

CHASSIS and RUNNING GEAR:
Construction . . . . unitary
Suspension front . . . . wishbones/coils/anti-roll bar
Suspension rear . . . . live by coils/support arms/
torque rods/track bar
Shockabsorbers . . . . .telescopic
Steering Type . . . . cam and roller
Turns I to I 3¼
Turning circle . . . . (9.5 m) 31 ft 2 in.
Brakes type . . . . servo assisted four wheel discs

DIMENSIONS:
Wheelbase . . . . (245 cm) 96.5 in.
Track front . . . . (131.5 cm) 51.6 in.
Track rear . . . . (131.5 cm) 51.6 in.
Length . . . . (435 cm) 14 ft 3.25 in.
Height . . . .(128 cm) 4 ft 2.4 in.
Width . . . .(170 cm) 5 ft 7 in.
Fuel tank capacity . . . . (50 litres) 11 galls

TYRES:
Size . . . . (55 x 15) 165 HR-15
Make on test car . . . . Michelin XAS

GROUND CLEARANCE:
Registered . . . . (15 cm) 6 in.

speed in traffic and never exceeds 3500 rpm — it saves energy, uses the fan's ideal calculated effective blade angle, and reduces noise.

The oil pressure on the test car was a constantly healthy 70 psi at good operating speeds. It never wavered on the track or during performance runs.

Switchgear covers the usual fuctions, plus a few bonus offerings. There's a special panel switch to mute the instruments when you light them with the headlights. A two-speed fan switch works on the Continental principle of fast speed on the first pull-stop. The washer/wiper switch has two speeds with a third to give great electric gushes of water to the screen and there's a hazard warning flasher (not connected to the test car).

The final touch is the knob for the rear window demister — two stages, with a warning light of varying density for each standard of demisting control. On fast speed, the rear wires cut the fog in 60 seconds with a 150 watt putput. Drop the switch to phase two and 40 watts keep the glass constantly clear on a muted warning light glow. Or you can switch off and call in the demister as you need it. All knobs are soft, pliable crash-proof plastic.

Under the dash, controls in simple slides vary temperature and distribute warm/cool air to face and feet. Supplementary side-panelling booster vents for the through-flow ventilation system combine with this set-up which is great in the cold, but totally inadequate in Australian conditions in a closed Coupe of this type. An engine/transmission tunnel that runs down the centre of the cockpit along the occupants' legs doesn't help and black upholstery as on the test car is the final killer. The answer is air conditioning — and if you can pay seven grand for a Volvo Coupe you can take the jump to full "air" if the heat hurts.

Otherwise, cockpit comfort is plush. The leather/vinyl seats are great — providing three obvious and instantly adjustable positions, plus several others. Basically, rails let the seat slide horizontally, a rake gives you a variety of squab angles (without layback) and a strategically located knurl on the squab will adjust to the individual spine curvature of drivers.

If you want to get highly technical there are special sleeves for extra seat length, slots in the seat locating bolts for even further adjustment, extra slots in the seat for more vertical travel, plus extra height adjustment in the main rail bolts. And the integrated headrests are infinitely adjustable.

Carpeting is comfortable — but a little tatty in appearance. Odd item storage runs to two document bins — the centre console, plus the glovebox. Rear seat room is in the occasional quick-across-town-to-a-party two-plus-two category. A fold-down backrest with adequate padding does a good job and supplies great additional luggage stowage space when laid flat — aided by special straps to stop it floating round the cockpit.

Detail touches include a dippable interior mirror, interior light that has a remote master switch but also acts by tipping the glass itself, and easy-to-reach fuses under the dash.

For the safety bugs, a well-padded impact-absorbing steering column is built on the split-universal principle, but window wipers which virtually have to be operated with the opposite hand reaching across the body need transferring to a sensible location down near the front lower-corner of the door. However they open windows that provide breeze and buffet-free motoring at speed.

The boot is above average for a compact sports coupe — it carries reasonable gear, has a big (covered) spare on the floor and contains jack and adequate tool kit.

The handbook carries a terse warning to owners on driving with the boot lid partially open — and this serves as good advice for owners of many cars with through-flow ventilation. Since extraction of cockpit air is through the boot, induction of CO emission is easy in reverse via the same route — if you have an overloaded and slightly open boot drive with all windows closed, and the through-flow on full-blast (including fan).

The mechanicals are not vastly reworked. The engine is the B20 development of the B18 four cylinder water-cooled four. It has no fancy tricks like overhead camshafts or hemi-heads, and in standard form is not capable of pushing a sports coupe to today's market demands. Built of solid cast iron with liners machined in the block, it is a tough, durable motor, easily capable of carrying the demands imposed by a sophisticated four-port computerised fuel-injection system developed by Bosch (B20E engine).

For those who understand, the electronic injection has triggering contacts or sensors in the distributor timing (spark), coolant (actual engine temperature), induced air temperature (to cylinders), and engine pressure (actual engine load). By computing the information from these areas and controlling the data by impulses through a throttle switch, precise fuel delivery is guaranteed — four solenoids control the injectors. It is dramatically efficient — with a hefty boot, the car can be persuaded to optimum performance without dragging excess reserves from the tank, and gentle use pushes the fuel economy way up. Over 28 mpg is possible with gentle running, and full-bore work shouldn't ever push the car below 20 mpg. Added to that, efficient burning means reduced emissions. And the overdrive helps.

The transmission is not new — and Volvo has mated it to the overdrive unit proved over many years. Getting it all to ground is a live rear axle locating by coils, support arms, torque rods and a lateral track rod. It's so efficient the car won't spin it's back wheels if you drop the clutch at 6000 rpm — unless you get a well-worn surface such as the start-line on Calder's dragway.

There is no tramp with power-on in the dirt and hard cornering doesn't introduce snarky rear wheel angles that give changeable handling characteristics.

The front end is pretty conventional — wishbones and coils with an anti-roll bar, but it is well engineered to keep the loaded wheel upright under cornering, and positive location in a strong boxframe gives isolation from road shock and great durability.

Steering is cam and roller, the shock absorbers are telescopic and the differential is optioned for limited slip — not yet available here. A two-piece prop-shaft cuts transmission vibration and mechanical noise — apart from the engine which isn't adequately soundproofed from the interior.

Brakes are comforting discs, built on dual circuit to Volvo's unusual triangle system — in case of failure the two front discs and one rear brake always work, and though the distributed effort is normally 50 percent each system, this can rise to 80 percent for a single system in an emergency. There is a pressure limiting valve for normal braking.

The whole product is exceptionally durable and can take the worst punishment our roads can hand out — unlike most imported sports cars. Volvo still offers a completely free first (1500 mile) comprehensive service, and other services at about 6000 mile intervals are reasonable for a luxury car.

The Volvo's compromises are few. Most of the observations of this road test are ultra-critical — they wouldn't be noticed by the average Volvo owner. And the line-up of potential owners is great. There's already a queue at your friendly Volvo dealer.

Millionaires in Volvo terminology are owners who've wound the numbers right off the clock. The odometer — not the speedometer.—END.

GORDON CHITTENDEN PHOTOS

VOLVO 1800 E

The model enters its 11th year, and greatly improved
performance fails to keep it competitive with newer designs

THE VOLVO 1800 coupe was first shown as a prototype in January 1960, so it qualifies nicely for Volvo's slogan "The 11-year car." Though running changes—particularly those in this new E version—have kept its performance and handling up with the times, its body is hopelessly outdated in both style and function, having never been particularly good in the first place.

E stands for *einspritzer,* we guess—for the 1800E has the Bosch electronic fuel-injection system that is being adopted by so many European manufacturers as a way to get more power, meet the American emission limits and still get clean running (see p. 21). "Brain" of the system is a box full of solid-state electronic components that lives under the dash;

ram-length intake pipes and "wilder" valve timing take advantage of the injection's precise metering to get 12 more bhp and 7 more lb-ft torque than the carbureted 2-liter Volvo engine at no increase in engine speed. Other changes for the E include jazzy styling touches headed by some cast alloy spoked wheels, flow-through ventilation system with outlets in the rear flanks and a nicer instrument panel, the beefier gearbox of the 164 and 4-wheel disc brakes as used on other Volvos. Overdrive continues to be standard equipment, and a heated rear window now is too.

Two liters and injection make the E a much stronger car than the last 1.8-liter 1800S we tested. The engine, noted for its durability rather than refinement—it's neither mechanically smooth nor quiet in the coupe—has good low-speed torque as well as the ability to pull nicely all the way to its 6500-rpm redline, and in overdrive the car will now do an honest 115 mph. The 0-60 mph and ¼-mile times are quite respectable too, putting the 1800E into the same class with such as the Alfa 1750, BMW 2500 or Mercedes 280SL. Furthermore, the engine runs cleanly without any trace of emission-control leanness symptoms and uses very little more fuel than the earlier test car.

The hefty lever on the new gearbox gives one an impression of unbreakability that is borne out by the gearbox itself; we manhandled the box unmercifully in the acceleration tests and▶ **42**

ROAD TEST
VOLVO 1800 E

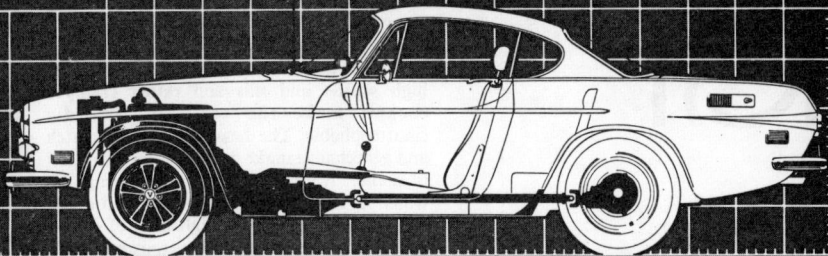

SCALE: 10" DIVISIONS

PRICE

List price, east coast....... $4555
List price, west coast...... $4655
Price as tested............ $4655

IMPORTER

Volvo Inc.,
Rockleigh, N.J. 07647

ENGINE

Type............4 cyl inline, ohv
Bore x stroke, mm.....89.0 x 80.0
  Equivalent in.......3.50 x 3.15
Displacement, cc/cu in...1986/121
Compression ratio..........10.5:1
Bhp @ rpm.........130 @ 6000
  Equivalent mph...........133
Torque @ rpm.........130 @ 3500
  Equivalent mph...........77
Fuel injection.....Bosch electronic
Type fuel required.......premium
Emission control.....fuel injection

CHASSIS & BODY

Body/frame............unit steel
Brake type: 10.6-in. disc front,
  11.6-in. disc rear, vacuum as-
  sisted.
  Swept area, sq in. 400
Wheels....cast aluminum, 15 x 5J
Tires.......Michelin XAS 165-15
Steering type......worm & roller
  Overall ratio............15.5:1
  Turns, lock-to-lock.......3.25
  Turning circle, ft. 29.9
Front suspension: unequal-length
  A-arms, coil springs, tube shocks,
  anti-roll bar
Rear suspension: live axle on trail-
  ing arms with Panhard rod, coil
  springs, tube shocks

DRIVE TRAIN

Transmission.....4-speed manual
                 plus overdrive
Gear ratios: o'drive (0.797)..3.42:1
  4th (1.00)...........4.30:1
  3rd (1.34)...........5.76:1
  2nd (1.97)...........8.47:1
  1st (3.14)...........14.50:1
Final drive ratio..........4.30:1

ACCOMMODATION

Seating capacity, persons....2+1
Seat width, front/rear.2 x 19.5/39.5
Head room, front/rear...38.0/28.0
Seat back adjustment, degrees..10
Driver comfort rating (scale of 100):
  Driver 69 in. tall............90
  Driver 72 in. tall............85
  Driver 75 in. tall............65

INSTRUMENTATION

Instruments: 120-mph speedometer, 7000-rpm tachometer, 999,-
999 odo, 999.9 trip odo, oil press,
oil temp, water temp, fuel level,
clock.
Warning lights: brake system, overdrive, generator, high beam,
directionals, hazard flasher.

MAINTENANCE

Service intervals, mi:
  Oil change...............6000
  Filter change...........6000
  Chassis lube...........6000
  Minor tuneup...........6000
  Major tuneup..........12,000
Warranty, mo/mi.....6/unlimited

GENERAL

Curb weight, lb............2535
Test weight...............2835
Weight distribution (with
  driver), front/rear, %....51/49
Wheelbase, in..............96.5
Track, front/rear.....51.6/51.6
Overall length..............171.3
  Width..................66.9
  Height.................50.4
Ground clearance............6.1
Overhang, front/rear....30.2/44.6
Usable trunk space, cu ft......8.1
Fuel tank capacity, U.S. gal...11.8

CALCULATED DATA

Lb/bhp (test weight)........21.8
Mph/1000 rpm (o'drive).....20.8
Engine revs/mi (60 mph)....2880
Engine speed @ 70 mph....3360
Piston travel, ft/mi......1510
Cu ft/ton mi (4th gear).....89.5
R&T wear index...........44
R&T steering index........0.97
Brake swept area sq in/ton....283

ROAD TEST RESULTS

ACCELERATION

Time to distance, sec:
  0-100 ft 3.4
  0-250 ft 6.2
  0-500 ft 9.6
  0-750 ft 12.3
  0-1000 ft 14.7
  0-1320 ft (¼ mi).......17.5
Speed at end of ¼ mi, mph....80
Time to speed, sec:
  0-30 mph..............3.5
  0-40 mph..............5.2
  0-50 mph..............7.1
  0-60 mph.............10.1
  0-70 mph.............13.1
  0-80 mph.............16.8
  0-100 mph............32.9
Passing exposure time, sec:
  To pass car going 50 mph...6.5

FUEL ECONOMY

Normal driving, mpg........20.9
Cruising range, mi..........245

SPEEDS IN GEARS

O'drive (5480 rpm)..........115
4th (6500) 108
3rd (6500) 80
2nd (6500) 56
1st (6500) 35

BRAKES

Panic stop from 80 mph:
  Deceleration rate, % g 81
  Stopping distance, ft......310
  Control............very good
Fade test: percent increase in pedal
  effort to maintain 50%-g deceler-
  ation rate in 6 stops from 60
  mph....................25
Parking: Hold 30% grade?.....yes
Overall brake rating.....very good

SPEEDOMETER ERROR

30 mph indicated is actually...26.0
40 mph....................35.2
60 mph....................53.2
70 mph....................62.3
80 mph....................71.0
100 mph...................88.0
Odometer, 10.0 mi...........9.46

ACCELERATION & COASTING

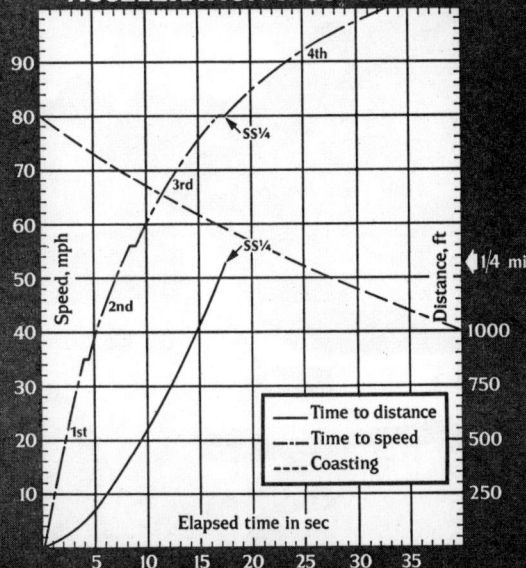

Time to distance
Time to speed
Coasting

Elapsed time in sec

ROAD TEST

VOLVO 1800ES

Twelve years ago, when the P1800 was first shown in public (at the 1960 Brussels Show) Volvo pledged that its dateless styling would allow a very long production run. Well, they kept their pledge even though the high-waisted semi-finned body dated a lot more quickly than Volvo perhaps anticipated. Ultimately one suspects the car sold — albeit in dwindling numbers — despite its appearance rather than, as originally planned, because of it.

Mindful of the astronomical cost of retooling for something quite different, Volvo have remained faithful to the original theme by cleverly grafting on a new tail, Reliant GTE style, to produce the 1800ES. With the new shape — highly distinctive if

hardly beautiful — comes a welcome new versatility since the luggage accommodation has been significantly increased and the enormous rimless glass tailgate, the car's most striking visual feature, allows estate car access to it.

But clever though the grafting may be, it doesn't in any way camouflage the car's ancestry: in many respects the 1800ES feels as long in the tooth as it is. For instance, the high scuttle and sills and rather cramped cockpit make the car feel decidedly claustrophobic. The heavy long-travel clutch and gearchange make driving in traffic rather tiresome, while long-distance touring — which is what the 1800ES is really all about — is marred by a very high level of engine and wind noise, an almost uncontrollable heater and virtually non-existent ventilation.

Certain weaknesses in the suspension and chassis departments — like roll oversteer and rather vague steering — perhaps also betray the car's age, though we must hastily add that the ride is good, the cornering powers are high and the handling on the whole very sound, entirely in keeping with the car's sporting pretensions. In fact it is these qualities, together with an excellent performance from the 2-litre fuel-injected engine — better even (on acceleration) than that of the cheaper 3-litre Scimitar GTE — that are the 1800ES's most endearing features.

Volvo owners tend to be fanatically partisan, a loyalty largely induced by the marque's almost legendary reputation for reliability and longevity. We certainly hope that these qualities are strongly evident in the 1800ES for it is a car, we feel, that must rely heavily on such things, not only to justify its very high price but also to compensate for its many dated features.

PERFORMANCE AND ECONOMY

Eight years ago Volvo raised the capacity of their engine from 1780 cc. to 1985 cc. With Bosch electronic injection the unit now

develops a healthy 124 bhp at 6000 rpm and a useful 123 lb. ft. of torque at 3500 rpm. Owing to the design of the injection sensors (which work off engine speed, cooling water temperature, inlet temperature and manifold vacuum) a few seconds' churning is needed when starting from cold. This is followed by a short period of uneven running after which the engine — a bit rough and noisy at low speeds — warms up quickly. It then smooths out up to its rev limit of 6500 rpm, although the sheer noise — a deep roar — is sufficient to deter many owners from making full use of the available performance.

We achieved a maximum speed of 110.5 mph round MIRA's banked circuit — corresponding to maximum revs in direct top gear. Overdrive top gave a more relaxed 107.1 mph at 5050 rpm although this would probably build up to a higher speed on a flat road. For a 2-litre car of some 23 cwt. this is a respectable speed, as is the acceleration with 60 mph coming up in 9.7 sec. and 100 mph in 33.1 sec.

The low speed flexibility of this version of Volvo's B20 unit (not a feature of the 1800E that we tested two years ago) is largely attributable to the vice-free Bosch electronic

injection; the car pulled happily from 20 mph in top gear and took just 8.1 sec. to accelerate from 30–50 mph.

A 10-gallon fuel tank gives the ES a touring range of only 200 miles at our overall consumption of 20.6 mpg, as usual the product of hard driving. Doubtless continued motorway cruising in overdrive would produce considerably better figures. Due to the fuel injection we were unable to measure the steady speed (and hence the touring) consumption accurately. Despite the relatively high compression ratio of 10.5:1 the engine runs happily on 4-star petrol and at no time did we detect any pinking.

TRANSMISSION

In an age of featherlight clutches and finger-tip gearchanges, the rather agricultural feel of the Volvo's transmission is a bit of a shock; fast changes are possible although they certainly demand a fair amount of effort. Some of our testers disliked the fat gear knob that literally fills your hand, but it probably facilitates the operation of what is on the whole a rather awkward change with easily beatable synchromesh.

The clutch is in keeping with the gearbox; it not only has a very long travel (every bit of which was required to make a gearchange) but it is also very heavy to push. The clutch of our 1800E suffered from much the same maladies, which at the time we put down to lack of suitable adjustment on the operating cable. Now we're not so sure. The ratios, however, are well chosen and there are certainly no awkward gaps. 35 mph is available in first gear — which coped easily with the 1-in-3 test hill; 55 mph is on tap in second and a useful 81 mph in third for overtaking.

The ES has a J-type Laycock overdrive, operating on top gear only, controlled by a stalk on the steering column. It is particularly smooth in engagement on both up and down changes and a warning light on the dash indicates when the unit is engaged.

There was no detectable noise from either gearbox or the live axle.

HANDLING AND BRAKES

Perhaps because the 1800ES has a steering box rather than the more common rack and pinion set-up, the steering has a rather slack feel in the straight ahead position; but it is good on lock, inspiring confidence at high speed with a ratio of 3½ turns from lock to lock, the steering is reasonably direct. Parking requires rather more effort, as the steering becomes heavy at low speed. However, the car is very manoeuvrable with a turning circle of under 30 ft. A certain amount of bump steering causes the car to wander over undulating surfaces. Although this can be a little disconcerting it requires little correction.

The handling of the ES is good and quite fun to exploit, and the car can certainly be thrown about with confidence. The initial understeer is followed by a controllable amount of roll oversteer, whereupon the car tends to dig in at the rear. Thus hard cornering is sometimes terminated with the inside front wheel off the ground. Despite this and fairly prominent body roll the ES remains quite controllable, even though there is not a tremendous amount of feel, either through the steering or the seat of your pants.

The front suspension is by double wishbones and coil springs, together with a substantial anti-roll bar. At the rear, the live axle is located by trailing arms, lateral positioning being taken care of by a Panhard rod. The roadholding on the fat Goodyear

Above: The famed Volvo lumbar support is wound in and out by this knurled knob. Left: We found the leather seats, with built in head restraints to be lacking in lateral support. Below: Strictly a +2

Grand Prix radials is pretty good even on a wet surface, and the car made short work of long journeys, taking both long and tight corners in its stride. Our test car was affected by side-winds, but not to any alarming degree.

The servo-assisted all-disc brakes certainly passed our tests without any trouble: 1g maximum retardation, no fade and virtual immunity to a soaking in the watersplash. Yet despite this good performance — not to mention the hidden asset of diagonally split circuits which, should one fail, still leaves braking on two front wheels and one back one — we did not like the feel of the brakes at all. As the figures show, a panic stop requires a very hard push: worse still, the brakes did not release as progressively as they came on so that it was difficult to "feather" them smoothly when coming to rest. The handbrake, a particularly powerful device, easily locked the wheels at 30 mph to give a good deceleration figure of 0.43g. It certainly had no trouble in holding the car on the 1-in-3 test hill.

COMFORT AND CONTROLS

The ride of the ES is unexpectedly good and the car soaks up bumps without fuss, thumping or undue jarring. Since our test of the 1800E, though, Volvo appear to have changed the seats — most of our test staff found the new ones a bit hard and lacking in lateral support. For a few, the fully adjustable lumbar support – a unique feature — proved ideal and they were able to obtain a really restful position; for most of us, however, the backrest was too hard even with the lumbar support fully retracted. There's plenty of fore and aft adjustment and the squabs almost fully recline (almost, because they come to rest against the rear seat arms before reaching the horizontal).

The rear seats are very much of the occasional variety, with a particularly hard backrest and very little leg or elbow room. A reasonably comfortable compromise can be obtained for one person by sitting side-saddle. Headroom in the back is tolerable for people of average height.

The driving position feels rather old fashioned and restricted, with the high scuttle and window sills and thick pillars pressing in. Your hands rest on a large, relatively upright steering wheel and your feet on large, heavy pedals. In this respect the 1800ES compares more with sports cars of the 'fifties than with saloons of today.

The range of push/pull switches on the leading edge of the dash includes an effective wiper/wash control and the light switch. Two column stalks control the overdrive, indicators, headlamp dip and flash. Other controls include the heater boost and the hazard warning light switch.

Visibility is not a strong point: the side windows mist up very easily as well as suffering from a build-up of dirt on the outside. Add to this thick pillars and a low driving position and you'll understand why vision is rather poor on a wet night. The heated rear tailgate keeps surprisingly clean, but there is no wiper (as on the Volvo estate). The lights are not outstanding, being only 45/40 watt filament units, but the two-speed wipers and electric washers are particularly effective.

Noise is the worst fault in the ES; it seems

Motor Road Test No 12/72 Volvo 1800 ES

Maximum speed mph

		100	105	110	115	120	125	130
Datsun 240Z	£2389							
Lotus Elan + 2S 130	£2650							
Triumph Stag	£2176							
Reliant Scimitar GTE	£2379							
Volvo ES	£2651							
BMW 2000 Touring	£2248							

Acceleration sec

	0	2	4	6	8	10	12
Lotus Elan + 2S 130	0 - 50 / 30 - 50 in top						
Datsun 240Z							
Volvo ES							
BMW 2000 Touring							
Triumph Stag							
Reliant Scimitar GTE							

Fuel consumption mpg

	5	10	15	20	25	30	35
Datsun 240Z	Overall / Touring						
BMW 2000 Touring							
Lotus Elan + 2S 130							
Triumph Stag							
Volvo ES							
Reliant Scimitar GTE							

Make: Volvo
Model: 1800 ES
Makers: Aktiebolaget Volvo, Goteborg, Sweden
Concessionaires: Volvo Concessionaires Ltd, Raeburn Road, Ipswich, Suffolk
Price: £2119.00 plus £531.62 purchase tax equals £2651

Performance tests carried out by Motor's staff at the Motor Industry Research Association proving ground, Lindley.
Test Data: World copyright reserved; no unauthorised reproduction in whole or in part.

Conditions
Weather: Dry and sunny; Wind S.W. changing to S.E., 0-10 mph.
Temperature: 40-43°F.
Barometer: 29 in. Hg.
Surface: Damp initially.
Fuel: 98 octane (RM) 4 Star rating.

Maximum Speeds
	mph	kph
Mean lap banked circuit	110.5	177.8
Best one-way ¼-mile	112.4	180.8
3rd gear at	81	130
2nd gear } 6500	55	88
1st gear } rpm	35	56

"Maximile" speed: (Timed quarter mile after 1 mile accelerating from rest)
Mean 105.9
Best 107.2

Acceleration Times
mph	sec
0- 30	3.3
0- 40	4.8
0- 50	7.0
0- 60	9.7

		13.0
0- 70		13.0
0- 80		16.7
0- 90		23.8
0-100		33.1
Standing quarter-mile		17.1
Standing Kilometre		32.0

	O/d		
	Top	Top	3rd
mph	sec	sec	sec
10- 30	—	—	6.3
20- 40	12.4	8.0	5.7
30- 50	12.0	8.1	5.6
40- 60	12.5	8.1	5.6
50- 70	12.8	8.7	5.9
60- 80	14.7	9.7	7.1
70- 90	19.0	11.3	—
80-100	—	15.8	—

Fuel Consumption
Overall 20.6 mpg (=13.7 litres/100km)
Fuel tank capacity .... 10 gals
Total test distance .... 1330 miles

Brakes
Pedal pressure, deceleration and equivalent stopping distance from 30 mph
lb	g	ft
25	0.27	111
50	0.50	60
75	0.73	41
100	0.88	34
150	1.00	30
Handbrake	0.43	70

Fade test
20 stops at ½g decleration at 1 min intervals from a speed midway between 40 mph and maximum speed (=75 mph)
	lb
Pedal force at beginning	37
Pedal force at 10th stop	33
Pedal force at 20th stop	32

Steering
Turning circle between kerbs: ft.
Left 30
Right 28¾
Turns of steering wheel from lock to lock 3.6
Steering wheel deflection for 50 ft. diameter circle 1.0 turns

Clutch
Free pedal movement .... 2 in.
Additional movement to disengage clutch completely 3¼ in.
Maximum pedal load .... 47 lb.

Speedometer
Indicated	20	30	40	50	60	70
True	21	31	41	50	58	69
Indicated	80	90	100			
True	77	86.5	97			
Distance recorder 3% fast

Weight
Kerb weight (unladen with fuel for approximately 50 miles) . 23.1 cwt.
Front/rear distribution .. 51/49
Weight laden as tested .. 26.8 cwt.

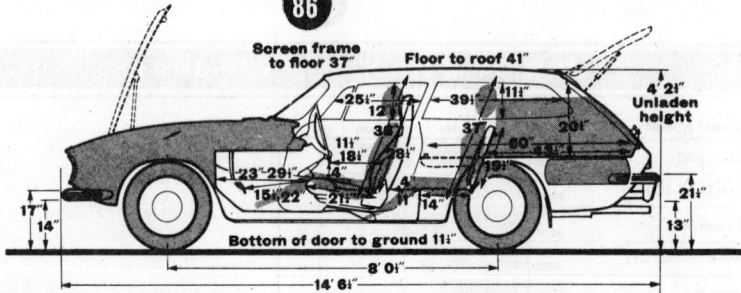

Screen frame to floor 37"
Floor to roof 41"
Unladen height 4' 2½"
25½" 12¼" 39¾" 11¾" 20¼"
34¾" 37"
11¾" 40" 31"
18¼"
23-29½" 4"
15½-22 21½" 4"
14"
21½"
17"
14"
Bottom of door to ground 11½"
13"
8' 0½"
14' 6½"

Engine

Block material	Cast iron
Head material	Cast iron
Cylinders	4 in line
Cooling system	Water; sealed
Bore and stroke	88.9mm (3.50 in.) 80mm (3.15 in.)
Cubic capacity	1985cc. (121 cu. in.)
Main bearings	5
Valves	ohv
Compression ratio	10.5:1
Induction	Bosch electronic fuel injection
Fuel pump	Electric
Oil Filter	Full flow
Max. power (net)	124 bhp at 6000 rpm
Max. torque (net)	123 lb.ft. at 3500 rpm

Transmission

Clutch	8½ in. dia., sdp, diaphragm
Internal gear box ratios	
Top gear	1.0
3rd gear	1.36
2nd gear	1.99
1st gear	3.13
Reverse	3.13
Overdrive top	0.797
Synchromesh	On all forward gears
Overdrive type	Laycock J type
Final drive Hypoid bevel	4.30:1
Mph at 1000 rpm in:—	
o/d top gear	21.3
top gear	17.0
third gear	12.5
second gear	8.5
first gear	5.4

Chassis and body

Construction . . . Unitary, all steel

Brakes

Type	Split circuit servo assisted discs all round. Drums for handbrake
Dimensions	Front 10.59 in. dia. rear 11.6 in. dia.

Suspension and steering

Front   Coil springs, wishbones with anti-roll bar

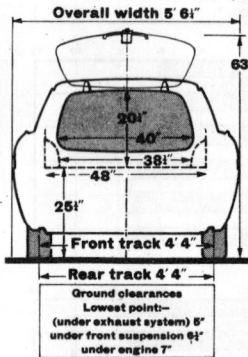

Overall width 5' 6½"
63"
20¼"
40"
39½"
48"
25½"
Front track 4' 4"
Rear track 4' 4"

Ground clearances
Lowest point:—
(under exhaust system) 5"
under front suspension 6½"
under engine 7"

Rear	Coil springs, live axle located by four radius arms and a Panhard rod.
Shock absorbers	
Front and rear	Double acting telescopic
Steering type	Cam and roller
Tyres	Goodyear G800 Grand Prix 185/70 HR-15
Wheels	Pressed steel with cast aluminium hub caps
Rim size	5½ J

Coachwork and equipment

Starting handle	No
Tool kit contents	Box spanner for plugs and wheel nuts; tommy bar; adjustable spanner; pliers; plain blade and crosshead screwdrivers
Jack	Scissor type
Jacking points	4
Battery	12 volt negative earth 60 amp hrs capacity
Number of electrical fuses	12

Headlamps	45/40W
Indicators	self cancelling flashers
Reversing lamp	yes; operated automatically by gear lever
Screen wipers	Two-speed electric
Screen washers	Electric
Sun visors	Two
Locks:	
With ignition key	steering lock
With other keys	a. doors and boot b. central lidded console
Interior heater	Fresh air type with booster fan
Upholstery	Leather
Floor covering	Carpet
Alternative body styles	None
Maximum load	484 lb.
Major extras available	Automatic transmission

Maintenance

Fuel tank capacity	10 galls
Sump	6.6 pints SAE 20/50
Gearbox	2.46 pints SAE 20/50
Rear axle	2.3 pints SAE 90 EP
Steering gear	0.44 pints SAE 90 EP
Coolant	1.87 gals (1 drain tap)
Chassis lubrication	None
Maximum service interval	6000 miles
Ignition timing 10 deg btdc at 700-800 rpm, vacuum pipe disconnected	
Contact breaker gap	0.016-0.020 in.
Sparking plug gap	0.028-0.032 in.
Sparking plug type	Bosch W225T35
Tappet clearance	Inlet 0.016 in. Exhaust 0.016 in. (hot or cold)
Valve timing:	
inlet opens	29°btdc
inlet closes	71°abdc
exhaust opens	71°bbdc
exhaust closes	29°atdc
Rear wheel toe-in	0-.16in.
Front wheel toe-in	0-.16in.
Camber angle	0-+1°
Castor angle	0-+1°
King pin inclination 8° with no camber	
Tyre pressures:	
Front	25 psi
Rear	27 psi

1 cigar lighter; 2 clock; 3 oil pressure gauge; 4 wiper/washer switch; 5 fuel gauge; 6 overdrive tell-tale; 7 seat-belt warning light; 8 tachometer; 9 oil temperature gauge; 10 water temperature gauge; 11 speedometer; 12 tripmeter; 13 odometer; 14 handbrake and brake system warning light; 15 ashtray; 16 and 17 heater distribution controls; 18 heater temperature control; 19 heater boost switch; 20 indicator/headlamp dip and flash stalk; 21 hazard warning lights; 22 trip zero; 23 horn press; 24 panel light rheostat; 25 bonnet catch; 26 steering/lock/ignition/starter; 27 overdrive stalk; 28 light switch; 29 rear window heater switch

to come from everywhere. To start with the engine has a loud induction roar, which is joined at various times by harsh tappet noise and other mechanical mutterings. There are no particular vibration periods and the transmission is inaudible, the chief source of noise other than the engine is the leading edge of the doors, the windscreen pillars and quarter-lights which promote tremendous wind noise. Talking becomes strained at 70 mph, and the particularly good radio fitted to our test car was inaudible at 100 mph, even in overdrive.

There is no proper through-flow ventilation on the ES, just some fresh air vents, operated by ram pressure, below the dashboard and some extraction vents in the rear wings. There is no face-level ventilation. The heating is controlled by means of three sliding knobs — two for distribution, one for temperature — which are not very clearly marked. Moreover, the latter is so sensitive that it's difficult to maintain the desired temperature in the car without continuously altering the lever. The two-speed heater blower is very powerful when full on, although very noisy in operation. The car was leakproof, but there were some draughts around the leading edge of the doors which may account for some of the wind noise.

FITTINGS AND FURNITURE

Instrumentation on the ES is comprehensive. Through the steering wheel, the driver views the water and oil temperature gauges together with the symmetrically mounted speedometer and rev-counter. The oil pressure gauge, fuel gauge and clock are laid out in a line to his left. We found them to be well positioned and easy to read, although there seems little point in having all the noughts on the rev-counter calibrations. The rather bright overdrive and main beam warning lights can be dimmed by means of a switch under the driver's side of the dash. The corresponding switch on the passenger side operates a map light; automatic courtesy lights are fitted in the passenger compartment and inside the tailgate. Safety has obviously featured high on the list in the design of this car and some of the standard fittings include head restraints, laminated windscreen, heated rear screen, mud flaps all round, and an anti-glare mirror.

The facia is quite tastefully laid out, although the simulated wood instrument background could never be confused with the genuine article. The seats are trimmed in quality leather and the main floor and rear compartment are neatly tailored with carpet. There are plenty of cubby holes; with map pockets in the doors, an oddments tray and locker on the end of the console — neatly built into the rear floor — a couple of deep wells for extra tools and other more bulky oddments. The safety belts, which are factory fitted, are of the inertia reel lap-and-diagonal type. Fixed clips are mounted on the transmission tunnel, and the seat belt warning light is only extinguished when the driver's belt is locked into place. Automatic reversing lights are standard.

SERVICE AND ACCESSIBILITY

The lockable bonnet is self-supporting, and is released and secured by means of an

over-centre catch under the facia. Most items are fairly accessible except for the dipstick, which has a tiny handle and no extension tube. Reaching for it usually means an oily sleeve. There is a labelled fusebox mounted on the nearside bulkhead of the cockpit, above the passenger's legs.

There are now over 300 Volvo dealers and distributors in the country and the ES needs their attention every 6000 miles after the first 3000. There are no greasing points. Tow hooks are built into the front and rear. The spare wheel, jack and tools are under the rear floor, concealed by a trap door. ■

Top: The B20E engine with Bosch electronic fuel injection. Access to the major service areas is fair, but the miniscule dipstick is completely hidden. Above: The rear seats fold down to expose a nicely tailored floor. The rimless glass tailgate is supported by two gas filled struts. Right: The rear floor lifts to expose the spare wheel and tools, and two reasonable sized storage spaces. Below: the car rolls fairly heavily, but the handling and roadholding are good

VOLVO 1800ES

*A successful conversion from dated GT
to genuine sportswagon*

WHO'D HAVE THOUGHT the Volvo people would turn the 1800E into a sports wagon? It certainly never occurred to us until the car appeared. The 1800 coupe, now in its 13th year, seemed a candidate for discontinuance but not much else. After all, it was heavy, ugly, cramped, noisy and overpriced. Frank insiders at Volvo didn't equivocate about it: they weren't sure two years ago whether they'd continue the 1800 a while longer, replace it with an up-to-date car, or simply get out of the sporty car business altogether. That business certainly isn't a major part of their activity, although the 1800's design is a good reason it isn't.

But lo and behold, they've had a clever spell, spent a little money on the old coupe and turned it into a sports wagon. And, we must grudgingly admit, the result is amazingly successful. Whoever is responsible for Volvo's station wagon rear sections does nice work indeed, having proved his mettle earlier with the large rear window of the 145 wagon. On the 1800ES he went further with a window that takes up two-thirds of the rear end's height, has hinges and locking handle attached directly to it, and is the entire tailgate. It's futuristic and handsome.

Extension of the roofline straight back put more head-

room over what are jokingly called rear seats in the coupe, and in profile view the wagon roof and the well done rear side window give the car such a different profile that many people approached us to ask what the car was, as we toured car-knowing Southern California in it. The whole front end, which was the most acceptable portion of the coupe anyway, is unchanged. The windshield and side glass remain narrow slits, the beltline high and the sides bloated in a most antique way. There's still that corny upsweep in the door that leads to the equally corny chrome-topped fins, but we can't deny that given what they had to work with the designers did a nice job of the transformation.

Sports wagons are by no means a new idea. The MGB, a borderline case because it's so small, has been around since 1966, Chevrolet's first Nomad was based on the Corvette, Reliant builds its Scimitar GTE in England, and there was a handsome Pininfarina one on the Peugeot 504 sports platform last fall. We cannot help being a little parochial, though, and so we note that Volvo's sports wagon, nearly 20 inches longer, roomier, and more wagon-like than the MGB, is the one that's going to put sports wagons on the U.S. map. If the reactions we got from people "on the street" and the fact that Volvo's western U.S. branch is or- ⟫⟫⟫

LARRY GRIFFIN PHOTOS

ROAD & TRACK
R&T
ROAD TEST

VOLVO 1800ES

dering all its 1800s for 1972 in the wagon body are any indication, it's going to be successful in spite of its dated characteristics and stiff price.

So much for styling critique and market prognostications. What's the car like? Well, as one might have guessed, pretty much like the last 1800 we tested, the first fuel-injection 1800E two years ago. The engine is still two liters, not 1.8—it mystifies us why Volvo doesn't go ahead and rename the car 2000—but it's one of those that suffered a power cut at the hands of no-lead fuel this year. The rating used to be 124 bhp net with 10.5:1 compression ratio; 10.5 is mighty high and Volvo had to lop off 1.8 points to make the engine run on 91-octane blend, so the power is down to 112 bhp. This shows in two ways. First, the performance is off as expected, with this 1800ES taking 1.2 sec longer to reach 60 mph and 0.7 sec longer to cover the standing quarter-mile than the older car which was 100 lb lighter at test weight. Second, the engine is slightly smoother and quieter than before, a natural consequence of a lower compression ratio. It's still a relatively noisy unit, its pushrod-operated valves clicking classically. It sounds just like the vintage engine it is, but vintage or no it's sturdy and produces good power for its size. Another of our many plugs for electronic fuel injection: it helps this engine to start well from cold, warm up gracefully and run cleanly at all times, its only problem being hard starting when hot.

The 1800's gearbox, inherited from the big Volvo 164, reinforces the engine's sturdy character with its big, heavy shift lever and knob and is a most satisfactory unit. Behind it is the old Laycock-de Normanville overdrive, which engages or disengages hydraulically at the flick of a steering-column stalk and works on 4th gear only. A modern 5-speed box would be better because after slowing down and downshifting the driver has to do two separate operations or skip a gear on the way back up; but at least the OD provides mechanically relaxed, if not quiet, cruising. A lot of wind noise keeps the car from being quiet at speed.

Seating for the 1800 driver is classic too, with a near-vertical steering wheel, tight dimensions for the shoulders and a "buried" feeling resulting from the relatively high window sills and cowl. The seats are very good, offering not only a backrest angle adjustment but Volvo's unique lumbar-support adjustment. One-operation inertia belts are standard

and this was our first test car to have the federally required belt warning: a light on the dash shines until the driver has plugged the belt into its center receptacle between the seats, which is supposed to be lighted but wasn't on the test car. We found no provision for warning the front passenger about his belt.

The rear area encompasses 10.8 cu ft when loaded up to the side window sills; if the jump seats (which are still good only for small kids) are folded down this goes to 14.8 cu ft. And if one is willing to sacrifice rear vision he can stuff nearly 28 cu ft of things into the back end. So the ES is a very capacious 2-seater for long trips, and for local hacking the rear area will be handy too. It always takes a key to get the tailgate open, which is a bother in this sort of use.

Vision outward is far better in the ES than in the coupe because of the large rear glass areas; the super-window at the rear makes it one of the easiest cars imaginable to parallel-park. Up front the slit-like windshield is a problem, however, when the sun visor is needed; it takes up half the windshield's height when it's down! The visor is contoured to conform to the roof shape and its bent-back edge makes it impossible to pivot it down close to the windshield itself—Volvo would do well to adopt a floppy-edged visor.

The ES is a good-riding car over a wide variety of road surfaces and despite having a live rear axle has good suspension travel for large bumps and dips. In fact the car is a little on the soft side and there's a lot of body roll in hard cornering. Combine this with the new and larger Goodyear 70-section tires (same as on the Capri V-6 but in a 15-in. size) and you've got a car that handles well in ordinary-to-brisk driving but gets tippy and squishy at the limit. Thus the benefits of the wider wheels and tires now standard on both the coupe and wagon aren't so significant, at least in comparison with the smaller Michelin tires on our last coupe; the ES has little more cornering power than an average sedan. The steering is precise and reassuring but heavy in parking maneuvers; our test car had a slight steering shimmy at about 50 mph.

The 1800ES is one of those cars that leaves a road-test staff a bit frustrated. Here Volvo has done a nice transformation, produced the first sports wagon big enough to really serve as one that we can buy in America, and done such a nice job with the esthetics that the car is a real head-turner. But they did it on a car that should have been replaced, not reworked. It's a good, solid car but a crude and old-fashioned one; still it's one-of-a-kind and if you must have a sports wagon this is the one you have to choose. We don't think Volvo will have any trouble selling it.

ROAD TEST
VOLVO 1800ES

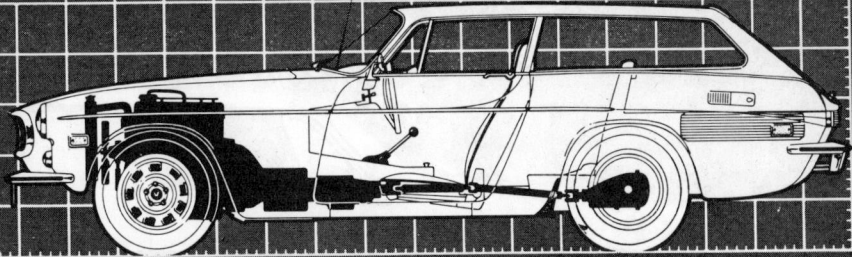

SCALE: 16" DIVISIONS

PRICE

List price, west coast......$5032
Price as tested, west coast...$5340
Price as tested includes standard equipment (overdrive, radial tires, leather upholstery, rear window defroster), AM-FM stereo radio ($212), dealer prep ($95)

IMPORTER

Volvo, Inc.
Rockleigh, N.J. 07647

ENGINE

Type............. ohv inline 4
Bore x stroke, mm.. . 89.0 x 80.0
 Equivalent in.... . 3.50 x 3.15
Displacement, cc/cu in.. 1986/121
Compression ratio..........8.7:1
Bhp @ rpm, net. . . 112 @ 6000
 Equivalent mph............124
Torque @ rpm, lb-ft...115 @ 3500
 Equivalent mph............74
Fuel injection.... Bosch electronic
Fuel requirement.. regular, 91-oct
Emissions, gram/mile:
 Hydrocarbons...............1.5
 Carbon Monoxide...........28
 Nitrogen Oxides...........2.3

DRIVE TRAIN

Transmission: 4-speed manual plus overdrive
Gear ratios: OD (0.797)....3.43:1
 4th (1.00).............4.30:1
 3rd (1.36).............5.85:1
 2nd (1.99).............8.56:1
 1st (3.13)............13.45:1
Final drive ratio..........4.30:1

CHASSIS & BODY

Layout.....front engine/rear drive
Body/frame............unit/steel
Brake system: 10.6-in. disc front, 11.6-in. disc rear; vacuum assisted
 Swept area, sq in.........400
Wheels.....styled steel, 15 x 5½ J
Tires............Goodyear G800
 185/70 HR-15
Steering type........cam & roller
 Overall ratio..........15.5:1
 Turns, lock-to-lock.........3.2
 Turning circle, ft.........31.5
Front suspension: unequal-length A-arms, coil springs, tube shocks, anti-roll bar

Rear suspension: live axle on upper & lower trailing arms with Panhard rod; coil springs, tube shocks

ACCOMMODATION

Seating capacity, persons.....2+2
Seat width, front/rear.2 x 19.0/41.0
Head room, front/rear.. 35.5/35.5
Seat back adjustment, degrees..40

INSTRUMENTATION

Instruments: 120-mph speedometer, 7000-rpm tach, 99,999 odometer, 999.9 trip odo, oil press, oil temp, coolant temp, fuel level, clock
Warning lights: ammeter, high beam, directionals, hazard flasher, handbrake, overdrive, seatbelt

MAINTENANCE

Service intervals, mi:
 Oil change...............6000
 Filter change.............6000
 Chassis lube.............6000
 Minor tuneup............6000
 Major tuneup..........12,000
 Warranty, mo/mi.....6/unlimited

GENERAL

Curb weight, lb............2570
Test weight................2935
Weight distribution (with driver), front/rear, %....50/50
Wheelbase, in./.........96.5
Track, front/rear.....51.6/51.6
Length.................172.6
Width...................66.9
Height..................50.4
Ground clearance..........6.1
Overhang, front/rear....30.2/45.9
Usable trunk space, cu ft....10.8
Fuel capacity, U.S. gal......11.9

CALCULATED DATA

Lb/bhp (test weight).........26.2
Mph/1000 rpm (o'drive).....21.4
Engine revs/mi
 (60 mph o'drive).........2800
Piston travel, ft/mi........1470
R&T steering index.......1.02
Brake swept area, sq in/ton...272

RELIABILITY

From R&T Owner Surveys the average number of trouble areas for all models surveyed is 11. As owners of earlier-model Volvos reported 10 trouble areas, we expect the reliability of the Volvo 1800ES to be average.

ROAD TEST RESULTS

ACCELERATION

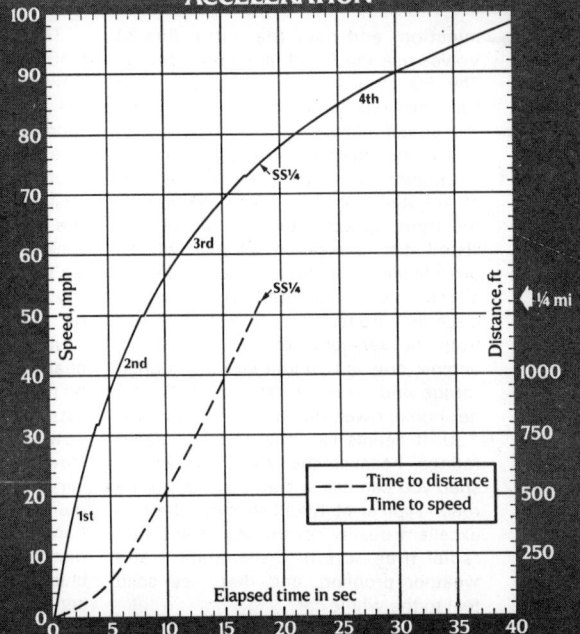

Time to distance, sec:
 0–100 ft................4.0
 0–500 ft................9.9
 0–1320 ft (¼ mi).... . .18.2
Speed at end of ¼-mi, mph....74
Time to speed, sec:
 0–30 mph...............3.7
 0–40 mph...............5.6
 0–50 mph...............8.0
 0–60 mph..............11.3
 0–70 mph..............15.5
 0–80 mph..............21.4
 0–90 mph..............30.1

SPEEDS IN GEARS

O'drive (5600 rpm)...........116
4th (6500)................108
3rd (6500).................80
2nd (6500).................56
1st (6500) 36

SPEEDOMETER ERROR

30 mph indicated is actually...28.5
50 mph....................47.5
60 mph....................57.0
70 mph....................66.5
80 mph....................75.0
Odometer, 10.0 mi...........9.9

BRAKES

Minimum stopping distances, ft:
 From 60 mph..............178
 From 80 mph.............299
Control in panic stop........good
Pedal effort for 0.5g stop, lb...20
Fade: percent increase in pedal effort to maintain 0.5g deceleration in 6 stops from 60 mph......50
Parking: hold 30% grade?....yes
Overall brake rating.... . good

HANDLING

Speed on 100-ft radius, mph. 31.5
Lateral acceleration, g.......0.660

FUEL ECONOMY

Normal driving, mpg........22.5
Cruising range, mi (1-gal res.).245

INTERIOR NOISE

All noise readings in dbA:
Idle in neutral...............57
Maximum, 1st gear.......84
Constant 30 mph........ . 65
 50 mph..................75
 70 mph.................77
 90 mph.................82

ACCELERATION

Time to distance
Time to speed

Speed, mph — Distance, ft — ¼ mi — Elapsed time in sec

The handsome dash is full of instruments, softly illuminated and easy to read. Interior is very well done and the seats are super comfortable.

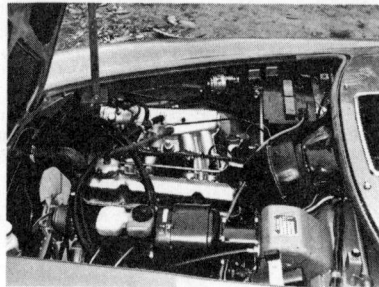

Two liter, four cylinder engine is fed by Bosch fuel injection, a good way to beat the emission standards and retain smooth running in heavy traffic situations.

The 1800ES is a station wagon built on a sports car chassis, the roof rack is a U.S. add on, flow through ventilation works very well, and visibility is excellent all around.

injection, and now the entire line of Volvos use the Bosch electronic device. The ES comes with a choice of two transmissions with no extra cost. The four speed manual gearbox is fitted with an electric overdrive on fourth gear that is triggered by a little stalk on the right of the steering wheel. Also available is the three speed automatic. Power assisted disc brakes on all four wheels provide plenty of stopping power, in fact all the Volvos sold here have four wheel discs that are really super. Power comes from the venerable four cylinder B20F engine; now in two liter size it has good torque and power is rated at 112 SAE net horsepower, down from the original 130. It seems like one of those paper ratings, because the Volvo has all the snap you can use in traffic or out on the road. Typical of Swedish cars, there is excellent quality control inside and out, radial tires, lots of undercoating and weather proofing, and that nice solid feel to the whole car.

There are a few new touches on the 1800ES for 1973. The front bumper is now mounted on special shock absorbers, attached to steel bracing and extended a bit further from the body. It is a relatively attractive solution to the 5 mph impact requirement. New windshield wipers sweep 10 percent more of the glass, and the dash panel has new rocker switches on the controls. There isn't much else that looks different on the Volvo, nor was any change expected on the year old model. Volvo seldom changes anything for the sake of change, and we expect the 1800ES will be much the same next year too. The car lists out for over five thousand dollars, putting it in the affluent buyer class. However, it is one sports car that can serve as a family wagon. It is ideal for a dual purpose machine for it has all the handling of a sports car, and all the background of the Volvo sedans including the much publicized longevity of service. ●

1800ES
Data in Brief

DIMENSIONS
Wheelbase . . . . 96.5 in.
Overall length . . . . 176.6 in.
Height . . . . 50.4 in.
Width . . . . 67.0 in.
Tread — front/rear . . . . 51.6/51.6 in.
Steering type & ratio . . . . cam & roller, 15.5 to 1
Fuel capacity . . . . 11.9 U.S. gals
Luggage capacity . . . . 35 cu ft
Design pass. load . . . . 2 + 2
Turning diameter . . . . 30 ft
Curb weight . . . . 2646 lbs

ENGINE — Standard
Type . . . . 4 cylinder, in line, OHV
Horsepower . . . . 112 (SAE net) at 6000 rpm
Displacement . . . . 1986 cc/121 cu in.
Torque . . . . 115 lb/ft (net) at 3500 rpm

DRIVELINE
Transmission . . . . 4-speed, all synchro, with electric overdrive or 3-speed automatic
Drive axle ratio . . . . 4.3 to 1
(3.91 to 1 automatic)

BRAKES
Front . . . . 10.7 in. disc, power assist
Rear . . . . 11.6 in. disc, power assist

SUSPENSION
Front . . . . independent, unequal length A arms, coil springs, telescopic shocks, anti-sway bar
Rear . . . . live axle, trailing arms on panhard rod, coil springs, telescopic shocks

WHEELS & TIRES
Wheels, type & size . . . . steel, 5½ J x 15 in.
Tires, type & size . . . . . 185/70 HR x 15 radial

NA — Data not available
DNA — Data not applicable

ROAD track&traffic TEST

A bold expression of the sportswagon theme

photos by John Plow

VOLVO 1800/ES

THIS month, we're combining two Volvos of distinctly different pretensions. Recently, the venerable 1800 series was updated with an astute bit of coachwork magic. The Swedes took this twelve-year-old design and gave it a totally new personality by stretching out the roofline, adding a huge window-hatch at the rear and named it the 1800ES (actually that 1800 is now largely erroneous . . . the engine displacement has long since been bumped up to two liters). As a basic concept, the sports-wagon idea as applied to the 1800ES is clever. You'll never be able to carry the same kind of loads as a "normal" station wagon, but the available space is still impressive. We were able to carry a fully

assembled bicycle with room to spare. If you're a golfer, two full-sized bags and their carts will fit in the rear with no trouble, too. As far as baggage is concerned, the space will take two passengers' luggage with ease. There is a rear seat of sorts in the ES, but it's best suited to the use of small children or medium-sized dogs. It's just too small for an adult, and we found that most times we left it folded down, allowing for full use of the 60-inch-long load bed. The feature that received most comment was the generously-sized rear window. It's so large that the handle has been installed right in the glass, and an added safety feature is that you cannot open this without the key. From the driver's spot you

can literally see the road right behind the car . . . in fact, the road less than *six feet* behind. This may not be wholly useful, but it inspires a lot of confidence. Of course, 70% of the window area is covered with electric defroster wires, assuring a clear view at all times.

The 1800 series first hit the road in 1960, and since that time the car has not been changed in any radical way. The engine has been enlarged, and a couple of years ago, fuel injection was added, along with minor body changes and some trim alterations. But the basic car is still very much as it was then: rather weighty with narrow windows and fairly limited visibility. In fact, the car has needed a new body design for the last three years. There are reasons

Up front the Volvo 1800 retains the basic appearance of the P1800 introduced in 1960

why Volvo hasn't seen fit to make any startling changes over the years, and this latest modification is the biggest since the car was introduced. The coupe version is still being offered alongside the ES at about $400 less, by the way, but given a choice, we'd opt for the ES ... it just makes more sense from an appearance and practicality standpoint.

Our test ES was equipped with the optional Borg-Warner three-speed automatic transmission, and while we had preferred the manual version with overdrive, it was difficult for Volvo Canada to find one for us. The automatic works well, but soaks up some of the car's potential performance through the speed ranges. On a long drive, we noticed a few vagaries that were not annoying, just there, and in need of attention. At cruising speeds in the area of 60 to 70 mph, the ES tended to show a little "wander," particularly

in the side winds. Overall noise level was high for a car in the ES's $6,000 price bracket. This could be traced to the old, reliable B20 engine, working away at around 4,000 rpm, and a goodly part of this noise emanated from the overhead valves. The heating system was, as with all Volvos up to the task, but the ventilation left a little to be desired. Once the weather warmed up we found that the cockpit area became very hot, and the ventilation system couldn't keep up to the heat wave from the engine room.

Volvo is known for spending engineering time on good seats, and the buckets in the ES were no exception to this rule. They feel just right (though we found the black leather a trifle hot, preferring cloth-covered seats for all-year use) and for added comfort, you can set a lumbar control for lower back support. The ES can't be faulted

for the way it's put together. The interior has the "bank-vault" feeling, and the instrumentation is laid out so that you can see everything at a glance. In addition to the speedometer (120 mph) and matching tachometer (7000 rpm), there are neat white-on-black gauges for oil temperature, water temperature, fuel and clock. Warning lamps are included to tell you about alternator charge, handbrake, high beams, flashers and seatbelts. The steering wheel, as in other Volvos, seems over-large, with an outside diameter of over 16 inches. If a smaller, leather-rimmed wheel were substituted, we're sure the steering effort wouldn't be measurably increased.

Many manufacturers should study Volvo's inertia reel seat belts. They're easy to adjust, simple to snap on, and allow lots of movement. If all belts were as well designed as these, you'd

Simple, but amazingly successful

Huge steering wheel dominates

see many more people harnessed up while driving.

We didn't expect to set up any shattering times with the ES at Cayuga's Dragway Park because of a lag in the fuel metering system. Several times, the car would bog on the line, losing about 5/10 of a second. After much practice, we were almost able to cure this, and some of the times reflect the problem. Our best 0-60 time was 12.7 seconds with the worst 14.3. Through the quarter mile, we averaged 18.9 seconds, or 73 mph. Braking was the ES's long suit. We managed 171 feet from 75 mph and an impressive 124 from 60, and at no time did we feel any loss of pedal pressure or braking force. As tested, the ES weighed in at 2800

pounds (1410 pounds front, 1390 rear) which all adds up to almost neutral distribution, about 51/49%. We're certain that the ES automatic could easily make the 60 mark in under 12 seconds, given a fuel metering system in top-notch operating order.

The ES exhibits a tendency to lean heavily in tight bends, but the light positive steering, 185/70 radial ply tires, and almost 50/50 weight distribution go a long way to assisting enthusiastic driving.

There is another problem with noise level in the ES (we also noted it in the 145E, but to lesser extent). The fuel pump, mounted at the rear near the fuel tank, gives off a middle-pitched

hum that you cannot ignore at idle and low speeds. It does tend to vanish at higher speeds, wiped out, so to speak, by other operating sounds.

Price of the 1800ES is set at a base of $5800, so if you do buy one you'll see little change from $6000, and if you order a radio, automatic box and special styled wheels, the tag will be considerably over six grand. The ES falls into a category all its own, really, but looking at the car objectively, it's frankly a little dated. Judging by the attention we received from the general public while driving it, this will make little difference to potential buyers. In most every case, questioners thought it was an all-new car. Score another one for the Swedes.

Considerable understeer is evident

Bosch fuel injection helps engine pump out 125 hp.

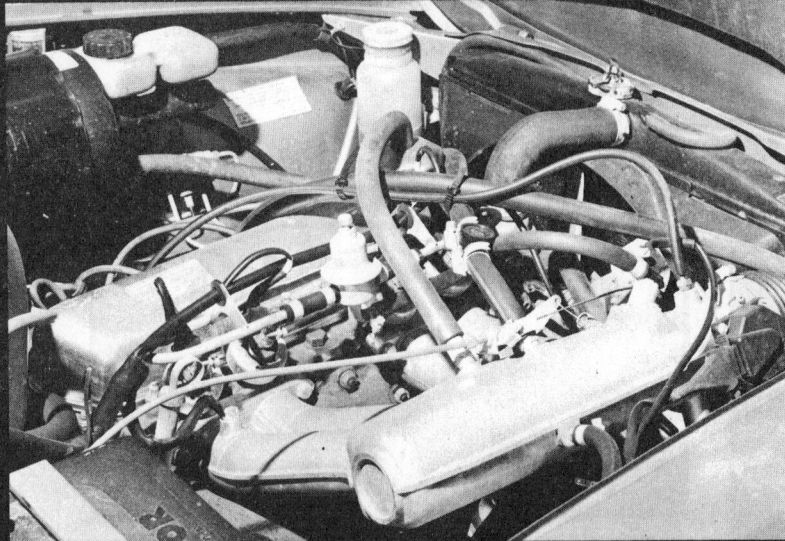

ROAD track&traffic TEST technical data

VOLVO 1800 ES

SPECIFICATIONS

ENGINE
Location	front
No. of cylinders	four in line
Valve operation	pushrod operated overhead
Compression ratio	8.7:1
Carburetion	electronic fuel injection, computer under dash
Bore/Stroke	3.50 ins./3.15 ins.
Displacement	121 cu. ins. (1986 ccs)
Power	125 hp @ 6000 rpm

TRANSMISSION
No. of forward speeds	three, BW automatic
Gear ratios	1st—2.39; 2nd—1.45; 3rd—1.00; Rev.—2.09
Final drive	3.91:1

BRAKES
Front	discs 10.7 in. dia. power
Rear	discs 11.6 in. dia. power
Lining area, swept	38.8 sq. ins.

DIMENSIONS
Wheelbase	96.5 ins.
Track	front — 51.6 ins.
	rear — 51.6 ins.
Width	66.9 ins.
Height	50.4 ins.
Weight, as tested	2800 lbs. (51% front, 49% rear)
Fuel capacity	10 gals.
Tires	185/70 HR radial ply Goodyear

STEERING
Type	Cam and roller
Turning circle	31 ft. — 6 ins.

SUSPENSION
Front	Independent, wishbones, ball joints, rubber mounted control arms, Anti-sway bar, coil springs, telescopic shocks.
Rear	Solid axle, longitudinal rubber mounted arms, torque rods. Rubber mounted transverse track rod.

CALCULATED DATA

Braking distances in feet: average of 3 stops

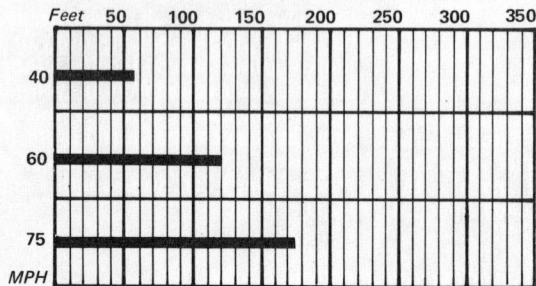

Feet 50 100 150 200 250 300 350

40
60
75
MPH

Acceleration in seconds

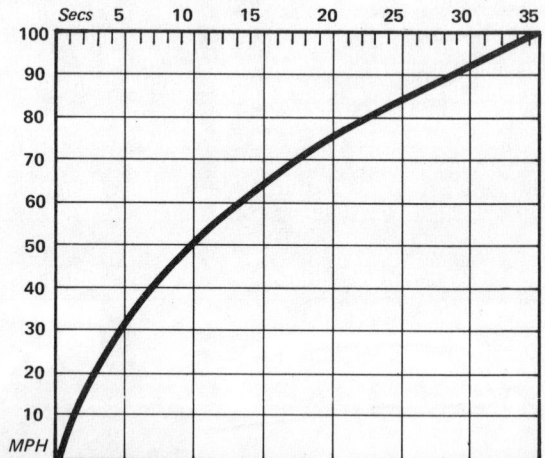

Secs 5 10 15 20 25 30 35

100 90 80 70 60 50 40 30 20 10 MPH

BRAKING
75-0	176 feet
60-0	120 feet
40-0	57 feet
Fuel consumption	22.3 mpg
Quarter mile	18.0 secs./74 mph.

ACCELERATION
0-40	7.0 secs.
0-60	13.5 secs.
0-80	22.8 secs.

SUGGESTED RETAIL PRICE

$6,185.00*
(manual trans. version $6,125.00)*

*Standard equipment includes inertia reel seat belts, rear window demister, lockable console, map light.

VOLVO

Volvo 1800ES shows its heritage from the P 1800 in the front. New impact bumper is an attractive addition, and big windshield wipers are very effective in foul weather.

Volvo's sports car for 1973 is a grand touring station wagon!

Well over a decade ago Volvo brought out their first modern sports model, the P 1800 with all the tough durability that Volvo sedans were noted for. The somewhat heavy coupe had unique styling for its day, and it remained much the same in general aspect throughout its life span. Last season Volvo introduced the companion 1800 ES sport station wagon, and for 1973 the two plus two coupe has been dropped from the line, leaving the ES as Volvo's lone entry in the sports car game.

The Volvo 1800ES is basically the P 1800 with the roof line extended and a keen glass tailgate style rear door. It is the only station wagon we can bring to mind that grew on a sports car chassis

and body. The practical Swedes have developed a true Grand Touring machine with all the luggage space one could desire for the grandest of tours. Usually a GT car has minimal luggage room, and some we can think of won't even carry a weekend's worth of needs. The 1800ES has two rear bucket style seats, but they are positioned in traditional sports car fashion with leg room suitable for midgets. The seats are completely upholstered though and fitted with seat belts; they pop forward easily to form an extensive carpeted rear platform that will contain a ton of baggage or anything else one could cram into a regular station wagon. Loading is accomplished through the frameless glass rear window that rises up well beyond head level to make loading simple. The lack of a metal surround and the electric rear window defroster wires, call for a careful hand when closing the rear

door/window, if it is to remain intact.

In the cockpit are a pair of handsome and comfortable bucket seats, designed by orthopedic surgeons to fit any size body, and the seats do that quite well. Adjustment is infinite for these armchairs go forward and aft, up and down, and the seat backs recline to a full sleeping position. The good looking wood grained dash panel is stuffed with instrumentation that includes all the usual stuff and an oil temperature gauge right in front of the driver; that instrument is seldom seen on a liquid cooled engine, but there must be a good reason for it. There are good sized door pockets on each front door, and a small but handy locking glove box on the console. Everything in the decor is rich looking and very continental.

There have been no mechanical changes on the 1800 ES since it arrived here last year. The E stands for fuel ➤ 92

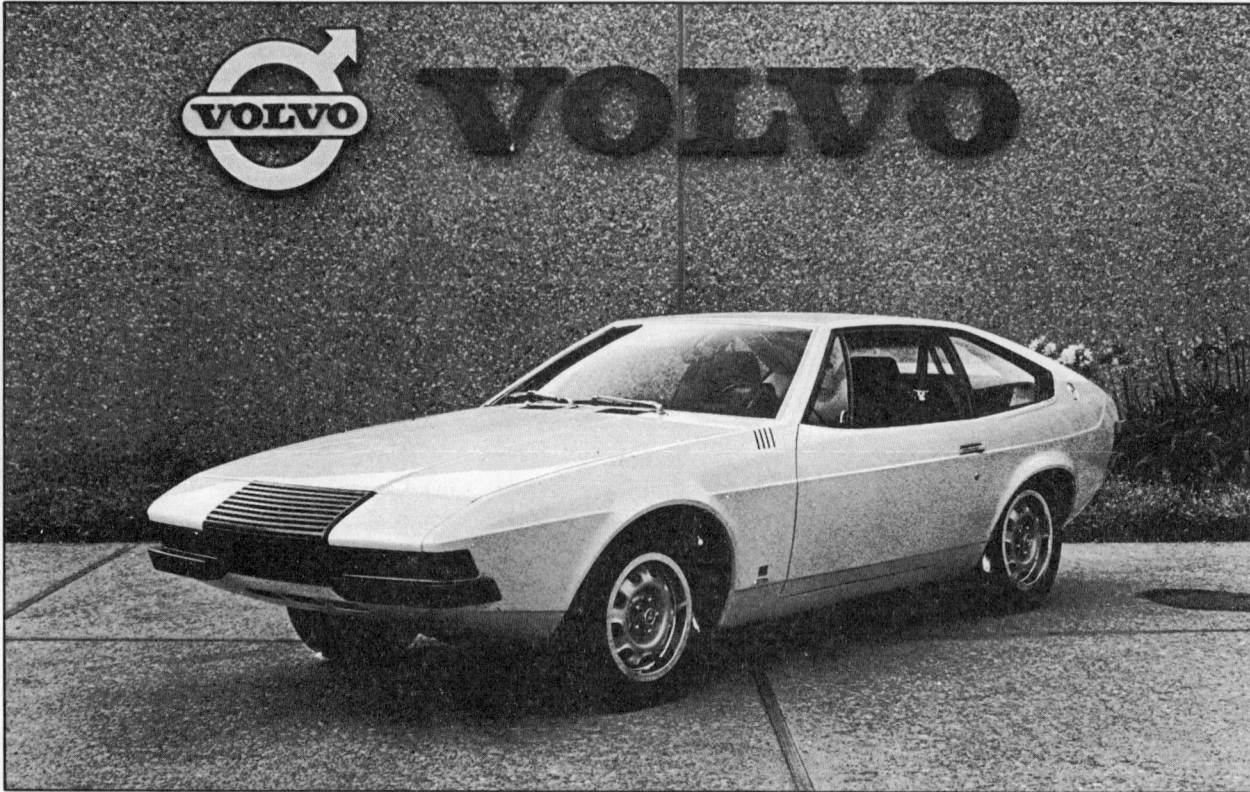

New from Sweden & Italy:
COGGIOLA VOLVO 1800ESC

This practical but exciting design by a little-known Italian designer is a logical way for Volvo's sports model to go

BY RON WAKEFIELD

PHOTOS BY JOE RUSZ

W HEN VOLVO brought out the 1800ES sportswagon version of their venerable 1800 late last year we relaxed back into our editorial chairs, sighed and resigned ourselves to another several years of the sturdy but old-fashioned series. The coupe was barely stylish when it was introduced in 1960, and though Volvo had mechanically updated it many times with more displacement here, more disc brakes there, and electronic fuel injection, there remained the cramped, poorly laid-out body. True, the wagon version was a big improvement but it didn't quite succeed in converting the sow's ear.

A few show cars on the 1800 chassis—still, curiously, called 1800 by Volvo even though the engine was increased to two liters some time ago—have appeared from time to time. Zagato showed a bland-looking one at Geneva last year, for instance. But this year's Paris show brought a new one—this time one commissioned and paid for by Volvo itself, which can only mean that something's up in Göteborg. Are those nice people at Volvo finally thinking of a fresh new body for this fine old chassis? Of course we hope so, and the new show car shows eve   sign of being a serious study of the possibilities. When

it came to Los Angeles to be shown at L.A.'s finest motor show, Auto Expo, we took a close look at it and liked what we saw.

The builder, Sergio Coggiola, is a former Ghia designer now on his own. He's actually been running his own design firm since 1966 and has done projects for car companies in Europe and Japan, but this is the first complete car we've seen from him.

First let us emphasize that the Coggiola 1800ESC, as it is called, is no far-out show car. No, it is a practical car, an exercise not in gimmickry but in getting more useful space out of essentially the same package size as today's 1800E *and* giving it a modern look. Mind you, the name ESC implies a relation to the 1800ES—the wagon—and that's what Volvo people like to refer to when they're comparing it to the present model. But the ESC is clearly a coupe, not a sportswagon, and for this reason we prefer to compare it to the production coupe.

The Coggiola body resides on the 1800 chassis—wheelbase, track, suspension pieces, engine, drivetrain, floor platform and all. But all the sheet metal and the body layout are as new as using the existing chassis would allow. Coggiola has kept exactly the same overall height as the production car—which

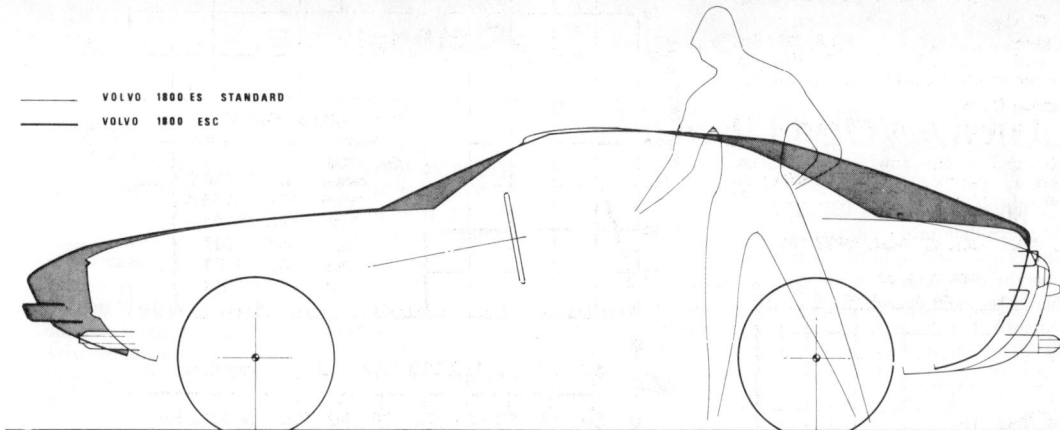

VOLVO 1800 ES STANDARD
VOLVO 1800 ESC

STYLE AUTO DRAWING

is plenty low—but has gone five inches longer while reversing the balance of front to rear overhang. Thus the nose is long and the tail short, following both current styling trends and the direction future safety requirements dictate. The roof drops off less abruptly than that of the current coupe, thus carrying full headroom a bit farther back over the passenger compartment, but the rear seating is still occasional in the fullest sense of the word.

The lines are handsome if not especially original—there's a strong flavor of recent Bertone and Giugiaro themes and the car is even reminiscent of that earlier Zagato effort. A strange, but functional, gray-painted grille wraps up into the long, sloping hood and is flanked by matching semi-bumpers (hardly practical in view of U.S. bumper regulations coming up) and hiding headlights that are raised by hydraulic units responding to a pedal inside the car. The light units come straight up and Coggiola perhaps declined a bit of corny cuteness by not finishing off their exposed edges airfoil-style.

Body sides are very much in the Giugiaro idiom of a year or so ago, with the upper body structure blended smoothly into the lower, the window ledge dropping well down into the lower body, and a crease originating across the front carrying itself all the way to the rear with only an interruption at the front wheel arch, finally kicking up to repeat the quarter-window motif. The cowl is high, almost as if to remind us that this is an 1800 Volvo; the pushrod, vertically mounted engine is fairly high but it seems that only Coggiola's determination to make a virtually straight slope from nose to windshield has necessitated its being as high as it is.

The standard 185/70-15 tires aren't overly emphasized in the design and are mounted on regular 1800 wheels. Repeating the quarter-window lines are ventilation flow-through outlets behind the windows, and at the rear the bumpers are doubled up but still impractically close to the bodywork. Nearly everything on the tail is clean too, but Coggiola succumbed to

temptation here with what we might call simulated louvers under the rear window. These are part of a conventional decklid that ends beneath the window rather than including it.

Inside, the low window ledge is much appreciated even though the high cowl (here again) reminds one of the old 1800. All the instruments are straight from the production car (and are nice), set into a clean, contemporary panel with a full-width brushed aluminum band that's matched by the central console. The 1800's large, traditionally vertical steering wheel obscures one or two of the gauges, depending upon driver position. Switches for non-driving functions are laid out within easy reach of the driver above radio, heater and what would be air-conditioning controls if the car actually had it (the innards are missing), and the steering column presents three stalks for more critical driving functions. Surprisingly, there are no face-level air vents.

The two front seats are roomier in feel and in fact than the production car's—extra headroom and, even more so, shoulder room are noticeable. The +2 seats behind, though, almost might

DIMENSIONS

	Production 1800E	Coggiola 1800ESC
All dimensions in inches:		
Wheelbase	96.5	96.5
Track, front/rear	51.6/51.6	51.6/51.6
Length	171.3	176.3
Overhang, front/rear	30.2/44.6	40.8/39.0
Width	66.9	68.2
Height	50.6	50.6

COGGIOLA VOLVO 1800ESC

as well be left out, just as in the current model—there's less headroom there than in the current sportswagon though more than in the coupe. Seat upholstery is much overdone and the armrests on the doors carry out the same silly theme, but door panels themselves and everything else are simple and elegant.

The gearshift is far away, as are the pedals, and the steering wheel too close—more evidence of the old 1800 mechanical arrangement and surely something that would be changed if the car were put into production. In fact, every mechanical control is right where it is in today's car, including the odd outboard handbrake lever.

The rear seats are flanked by wheelwells, and forward of these are large cubby boxes that could be useful storage. Inertia-reel seatbelts feed out of the interior panels nearby. At the

aft end is a carpeted floor under which the spare tire lives, not encompassing a lot of luggage space, but things can be set upon or stuffed into the occasional seats. The live rear axle doesn't cost a lot of room here; it requires a full-width rise across the front of the luggage area but this is only a few inches lengthwise.

The pictures tell their own esthetic story. We like the Coggiola Volvo very much and consider it a perfectly logical basis for a new production 1800—let's go ahead and call it a 2000—coupe. Sure, it needs a few changes: driver position is one, the bumpers another. And since new tooling would inevitably drive the price even higher than the present $5000, Volvo might well question using a pushrod inline 4-cyl engine and consider a compact V-6 to reduce height and give more refined running. This could use the four's pistons, rods, valvegear and so forth, give an attractive 3-liter capacity and do away with the need for overdrive.

How about it, Volvo?

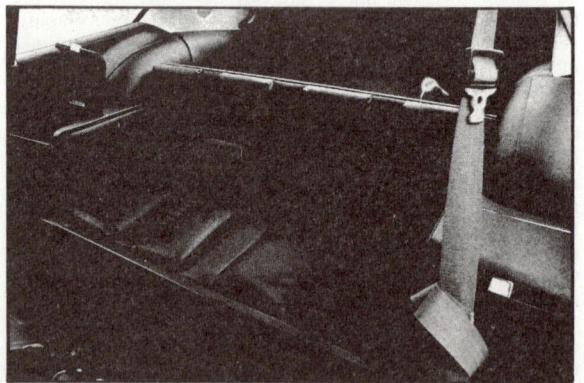

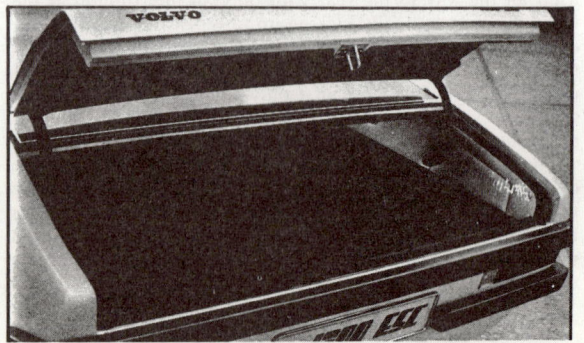

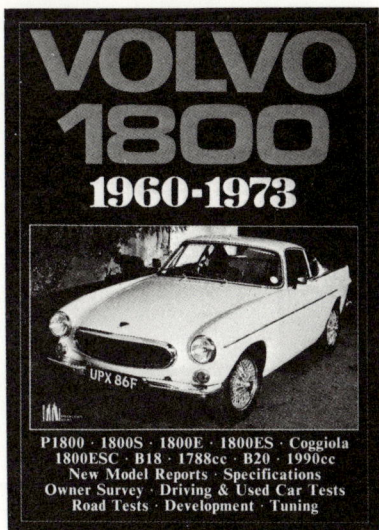

VOLVO 1800 1960-1973
The Volvo 1800 Story is told through 27 articles of which some 17 are road tests. There is also a U.S. owner survey and a used car test. All models are covered including the British and Swedish assembled cars plus the 1800E, the 1800ES and the Coggiola 1800ESC. Both the B18 and B20 engined cars are reported on in detail.
　　100 Large Pages

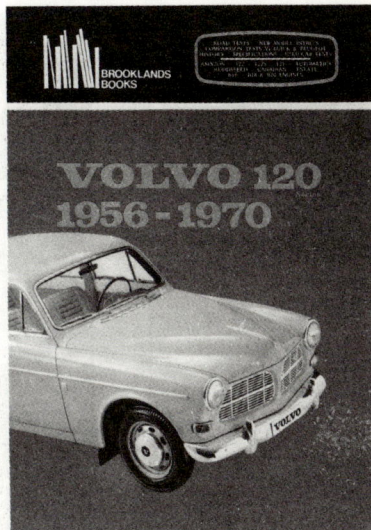

VOLVO 120 SERIES 1956-1970
The 31 articles in this book are drawn from five countries on three continents and cover the 121, 122, 122S, the automatic versions and estate cars, plus the Ruddspeed conversion and the Canadian built car. Engines reported on are the B16, B18 and B20. There are 16 road tests, plus comparison tests vs. the Buick Special and the Peugeot 404 also a used car test.
　　100 Large Pages

These soft-bound volumes in the 'Brooklands Books' series consist of reprints of original road test reports and other stories that appeared in leading motoring journals during the periods concerned. Fully illustrated with photographs and cut-away drawings, the articles contain road impressions, performance figures, specifications, etc. NONE OF THE ARTICLES APPEARS IN MORE THAN ONE BOOK. Sources include Autocar, Autosport, Car, Cars & Car Conversions, Car & Driver, Car Craft, Classic & Sportscar, Modern Motor, Motor, Motor Manual, Motor Racing, Motor Sport, Practical Classics, Road Test, Road & Track, Sports Car Graphic, Sports Car World and Wheels.

From specialist booksellers or, in case of difficulty, direct from the distributors:
BROOKLANDS BOOK DISTRIBUTION, 'HOLMERISE', SEVEN HILLS ROAD,
COBHAM, SURREY KT11 1ES, ENGLAND. Telephone: Cobham (09326) 5051
MOTORBOOKS INTERNATIONAL, OSCEOLA, WISCONSIN 54020, USA.
Telephone: 715 294 3345 & 800 826 6600

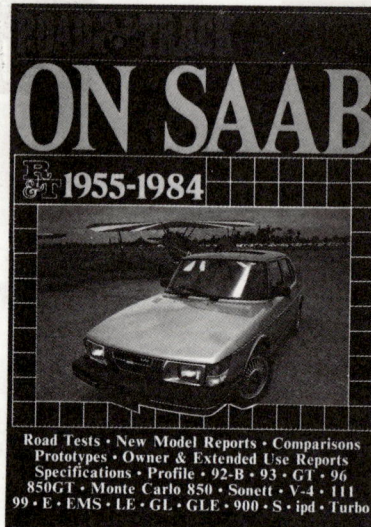

ROAD & TRACK ON SAAB 1955-1984

Some 37 stories take us from the modest 1955 SAAB 92Bs up to the modern 99 and 900 Turbos. There are 14 road tests, 2 up-dates, a brief test and a comparison against 3 other family sedans. Also included are owner and extended use reports, a profile of Erik Carlsson plus full specifications. Models covered are the 92B, 93, 96, the Monte Carlo 850 & GT, the V-4 Sonett and the Mk.III plus the 99, 99E, 99EMS, the LE Wagonback and the Turbo.   The more recent 900 series is dealt with in detail with articles on the S & ipd Turbo in both Sedan and 5 door configuration.

100 Large Pages.

These soft-bound volumes in the 'Brooklands Books' Road & Track series consist of articles drawn from this important US journal. Fully illustrated with photographs and drawings, the articles contain road tests, driving impressions, performance figures and full specifications etc. Fascinating to read the books form an important reference source for owners, restorers, and other enthusiasts.

Some of the articles in the above books appear in the regular Brooklands Books reference series.

From specialist booksellers or, in case of difficulty, direct from the distributors:
BROOKLANDS BOOK DISTRIBUTION, 'HOLMERISE', SEVEN HILLS ROAD,
COBHAM, SURREY KT11 1ES, ENGLAND. Telephone: Cobham (09326) 5051
MOTORBOOKS INTERNATIONAL, OSCEOLA, WISCONSIN 54020, USA.
Telephone: 715 294 3345 & 800 826 6600

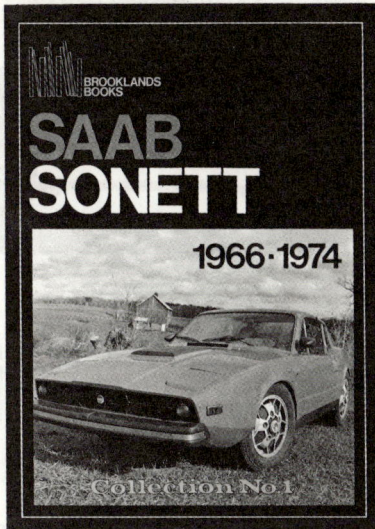

SAAB SONETT COLLECTION No. 1 (1966-1974)

The development of the Sonett is revealed in the twenty stories that lead us through its 8 year life span. Works are drawn from the US, Britain and Australia and deal with all models including a piece on the rare Series 1. Articles cover road testing (9), a visit to Sweden, new model reports, specifications plus a comparison test vs. the Opel GT, Porsche 914 and the VW Karmann Ghia.
70 Large Pages.

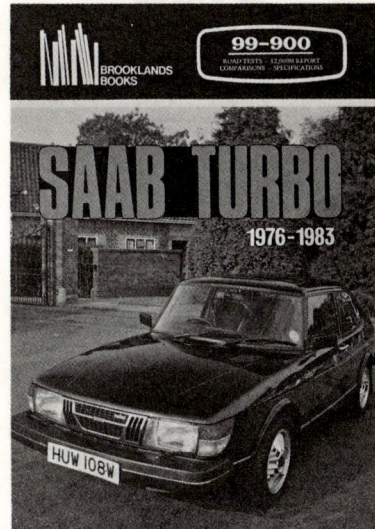

SAAB TURBO 1976-1983

Reports from 4 continents make up the 27 stories that cover the first seven years of the SAAB Turbos. Models covered are the 99, 900 and 900 APC. Included are 13 road tests, 4 comparison tests, a 12,000 m. report, plus articles on development and the introduction of new models.
100 Large Pages.

These soft-bound volumes in the 'Brooklands Books' series consist of reprints of original road test reports and other stories that appeared in leading motoring journals during the periods concerned. Fully illustrated with photographs and cut-away drawings, the articles contain road impressions, performance figures, specifications, etc. NONE OF THE ARTICLES APPEARS IN MORE THAN ONE BOOK. Sources include Autocar, Autosport, Car, Cars & Car Conversions, Car & Driver, Car Craft, Classic & Sportscar, Modern Motor, Motor, Motor Manual, Motor Racing, Motor Sport, Practical Classics, Road Test, Road & Track, Sports Car Graphic, Sports Car World and Wheels.

From specialist booksellers or, in case of difficulty, direct from the distributors: BROOKLANDS BOOK DISTRIBUTION, 'HOLMERISE', SEVEN HILLS ROAD, COBHAM, SURREY KT11 1ES, ENGLAND. Telephone: Cobham (09326) 5051 MOTORBOOKS INTERNATIONAL, OSCEOLA, WISCONSIN 54020, USA. Telephone: 715 294 3345 & 800 826 6600